Psychotherapy as
Positive Psychology

Dedication

This book is dedicated to all those people who stand or work next to me in serving all those others in so many countries and in so many languages who find my work useful. These are the camera people, the interpreters, the translators, the producers, the assistants, the directors, the helpers, the runners, the tea-makers, the cleaners, the moral supporters, the interviewers, the copy-editors – all those who facilitate this work in these often rather invisible but invaluable ways. I am grateful to you.

Psychotherapy as Positive Psychology

PETRŪSKA CLARKSON

D LITT ET PHIL, PHD, FBPS, FBACP, CPSYCHOL

W

WHURR PUBLISHERS

LONDON AND PHILADELPHIA

© 2005 Whurr Publishers Ltd

First published 2005
Whurr Publishers Ltd
19b Compton Terrace, London N1 2UN, England and
325 Chestnut Street, Philadelphia PA19106, USA

British Library Cataloguing in Publication Data

A catalogue record for this book is available from the
British Library.

ISBN 1 86156 342 6

Printed and bound in the UK by Athenaeum Press Limited,
Gateshead, Tyne & Wear.

Contents

Preface

This collection of well-loved unpublished and published papers is offered in response to popular demand. All of them are essentially in the spirit of what Seligman (2002) has baptized 'positive psychology' – a fundamental ideal of my life's work. According to Seligman, psychology since World War II has been sidetracked by an overemphasis on mental illness from its other two important missions – making the lives of all people more fulfilling and identifying and nurturing high talent. These are the themes that have always concerned me.

Inevitably, this emphasis requires us as psychotherapists to rethink and re-evaluate many notions, assumptions and ingrained habits that have perhaps too unquestioningly been accepted, taught and promulgated in our disciplines. One of these is the ideologically based notion of 'schoolism' in Eurocentric psychotherapy. Schoolism is defined as 'the result of passionately held convictions of being right which fly in the face of the facts' (Clarkson, 1997).

As I wrote in *On Psychotherapy 2* (Clarkson, 2002a) each psychotherapy school, of course, has its own bibles, its own sales talk and its own special language, which usually defines who's 'in' and who's 'out'. When such psycholanguages are used to exclude, devalue or negate other *psycholanguages* and disregard the established scientific findings about what actually makes psychotherapy effective – *the therapeutic relationship* that is found in all forms of healing across history and all over our planet – they too become forms of oppression instead of liberation.

According to Frank and Frank's (1993) masterly survey, the necessary ingredients for all healing practices globally and eternally are: (1) the therapeutic relationship; (2) a dedicated space (e.g. a consulting room, a circle drawn in the sand, an appointment in cyberspace); (3) a prescription for some action (e.g. 'free associate', 'take these pills', 'keep a mood diary'); and, finally, (4) a culturally congruent narrative. Most simply the last means: 'Speaking the client's language.'

The domain 6 narratives of psychotherapy theory are located in a *different universe of discourse* from the domain 5 factual findings emerging from our research. Surely it behoves psychotherapy to avoid the simplistic category errors that Ryle (1960) pointed out decades ago in his philosophy classes at Oxford (see also Clarkson, 1975, 2002b).

Theories are the stories that we tell about the facts, explanations about how we understand the phenomena, about how the observer perceives and co-creates the field of research and practice. Each well-developed theory, as each well-developed question, has its own language, grammar, rhetoric, classics and poetry. Psycholanguages can live like English, die like Latin or be deliberately created like Esperanto. At the very least theories can be as essential, beautiful, and useful as their tools are to the artist and the craftsman.

'Theory' can be likened to the grammar of a psychotherapy 'approach'. Each, of course, also has its own technical 'vocabulary' – its own domain 3 nominative 'dictionary' which delineates a particular linguistic community from others. Yet, whatever different *words* we use, we are all referring to *the same phenomena in our shared world.* And yes, if a language doesn't have a word for something, it is possible that that something may be made invisible by the absence of a naming word for it – or we may have to create new words.

Personally I believe that the more languages we can speak, the more of the world we can see. The more we can understand each other's languages, the more we can *together* contribute to the alleviation of human suffering and the development of human potential. Therefore, this collection is also an example of practising *psycholinguistic multilingualism*. In different chapters I speak about transactional analysis (TA), psychoanalysis, Jungian, gestalt, transpersonal and, of course, the integrative language of the therapeutic relationship in its five modes.

As usual, there is a range of concerns from philosophical practice to researching supervisory competencies, from providing useful tools for clinicians to deeply theoretical investigations, from poetry to developing human potential, and from the individual client to the philosophical foundations of the profession.

Chapter 1 is based on a paper that was nominated for the Eric Berne award for contribution to theory. The early Greeks conceptualized physis as the generalized creative force of nature that eternally 'strives to make things grow and to make growing things more perfect' (Berne, 1968, p. 89). This paper highlights this unique, and most neglected contribution of Berne's – a truly positive psychology approach – which I originally exhumed and have hopefully enlivened in TA practice. It also contrasts physis with the two other major drives in human motivation – eros and thanatos – while considering some implications for psychotherapy generally.

Chapter 2 is concerned with alternatives to traditional psychiatric diagnoses. It presents a *first nature typology* that is intrinsically non-pathologizing and potentially liberating.

The notion of inborn temperamental differences is explored using the metaphor of individual kinds of life rhythms – like different kinds of music. This is illustrated with 12 temperamental vignettes of different types and clinical considerations.

Chapter 3 is actually a study of excellence or genius contributing an apparently original approach to Jungian typology. Jung's typological differentiations (the feeling, thinking, intuitive and sensation functions, whether introverted or extraverted in attitude) are dynamic structures that are said to contain the seeds of their opposites.

Contrary to the more usual counsel of concentrating on the development of the inferior function, this chapter suggests a reversal (or alternative) of attitude that in turn suggests that, if the superior function is developed to its fullest extent, it will tend to an *enantiodromia* – a turning into its opposite.

This means that there can come into being a natural and even superior manifestation of the inferior function that is more of the hallmark of gift or genius or extraordinary talent than the prescription for the linear and incremental development patterns more usually associated with the development of the inferior function itself. Clinical and historical examples are included for the purposes of illustration, discussion and application.

Chapter 4 extends the generally very negative view of TA 'drivers' such as 'hurry up', 'try harder', 'please me', 'be strong' and 'be perfect' by focusing on the *positive ideals* inherent in such human desires to improve and develop.

Chapters 5 and 6, looking at the 'reclamation of the Child', review TA as a *phenomenological* psychology according to Berne's stated intention, and recapitulates understandings of ego and ego states, emphasizing the subjective reality of ego states.

Phenomenology is discussed, as well as the central role of time in psychic life, supplemented by understandings from modern physics. Definitions of structural (or phenomenological) Child ego states are then retrieved from Berne as well as other major TA theorists, and it is shown from both literature and subjective experience that there are at least two varieties of such Child ego states – fixated and accessible. Differentiating between these in clinical practice and in life has substantial implications for clinical practice, but even more profoundly for the understanding and encouragement of human creativity – wherever it is encountered.

Chapter 7 is an example of a paper showing how my five relational modes can be found, practised and taught from an exclusively gestalt perspective. It is also historically important because the first conference presentation of this material was at a Gestalt conference in 1989 – 2 years before the psychodynamically oriented version of the five relationships was published in the *British Journal of Psychotherapy*.

Chapter 8 is another take on identifying and using the positives in a person's life experience – specifically in terms of providing the reparative or developmentally needed therapeutic relationship in psychotherapy. It presents a clinical, training and supervisory tool (or 'aid') that facilitates the clinician and patient to put positive experiences alongside the negative experiences in a person's life. This is illustrated by an analysis of Freud's 'Rat Man' case in these terms and includes a blank form that you can use with your own clients or trainees.

Chapter 9, written with Dr Marie Angelo, provides a content analysis of published literature on supervision competencies and examines the balance between different aspects of the therapeutic relationship emphasized in the design and assessment of supervisor training. In parallel, supervisees were asked to reflect and comment on the supervision competencies that they look for, via a set of open-ended questions completed in confidence. Thematic analysis of each set of competencies revealed markedly different areas of focus. Supervision training competencies were strongly weighted towards the working alliance, whereas supervisees themselves tended to place emphasis on a much wider range of relationships, including the person to person and the transpersonal.

Chapter 10 is included as a rather exuberant keynote speech delivered at the World Gestalt Conference in 1996 held in Cambridge, Massachusetts, celebrating the awesome grand arch that I find over pre-Socratic Heraclitus, gestalt psychology and the twenty-first century sciences such as complexity and quantum physics.

My sincerest thanks go to all the usual suspects who have encouraged and helped me to bring this work to its completion. I wish this book's readers joy of it.

Be with those who help your being.
Don't sit with indifferent people, whose breath
Comes cold out of their mouths.
Not these visible forms, your work is deeper.

A chunk of earth thrown in the air breaks to pieces.
If you don't try to fly,
And so break yourself apart,
You will be broken open by death,
When it's too late for all you could become.

Ode 15 from Rumi – *These Branching Moments*

References

Berne, E. (1968) A Layman's Guide to Psychiatry and Psychoanalysis, 3rd edn. New York: Simon & Schuster (first published 1947, revised 1957).

Clarkson, P. (1975) Quantitative research in clinical psychology, PhD thesis, Rand Afrikaans University, South Africa.

Clarkson, P. (1997) The therapeutic relationship beyond schoolism. Post-conference seminar: Psychotherapy in Perspective, 29 June 1997, at the Seventh Annual Congress of the European Association for Psychotherapy, Rome.

Clarkson, P. (2002a) On Psychotherapy 2: Including the 7-level model. London: Whurr.

Clarkson, P. (2002b) The Clarkson seven-level model – developing epistemological consciousness about psychotherapy. On Psychotherapy 2: Including the 7-level model. London: Whurr, pp. 146–172.

Frank, J.D. and Frank, J. B. (1993) Persuasion and Healing: A comparative study of psychotherapy. Baltimore, MD: Johns Hopkins University Press.

Ryle, G. (1960) Dilemmas: The Tarner lectures. Cambridge: Cambridge University Press.

Seligman, M.E.P. (2002) Positive psychology, positive prevention and positive therapy. In: Snyder, C.R. and Lopez, S.J. (eds), Handbook of Positive Psychology. Oxford: Oxford University Press, pp. 3–9.

Acknowledgements

I am grateful to the editors of the following books and journals for publication of material that forms portions of this book:

Clarkson, P. (1992) Physis in transactional analysis. *Transactional Analysis Journal* **22**: 202–209. This was a version of Chapter 1 in this book. It is included here with the permission of the International Transactional Analysis Association.

Clarkson, P. (1996) Discovering your true self – On the trail of first nature. *ITA News* **42**: 32–35. This was a version of Chapter 2 in this book.

Clarkson, P. (1997) Conditions for excellence: the *coincidentia oppositorum* of the inferior function. In: Clarkson, P. (ed.), *On the Sublime: Psychoanalysis, archetypal psychology and psychotherapy*. London: Whurr, pp. 219–243. This is Chapter 3 in this book.

Clarkson, P. (1992) In praise of speed, experimentation, agreeableness, endurance and excellence: counterscript drivers and aspiration. *Transactional Analysis Journal* **22**: 16–20. This is Chapter 4 in this book. It is included here with the permission of the International Transactional Analysis Association.

Clarkson, P. (1997) Variations on I and thou. *Gestalt Review* **1**(1): 56–70. This is Chapter 7 in this book.

Clarkson, P. and Angelo, M. (2000) In search of supervision's soul: a research report on competencies for integrative supervision in action. *Transpersonal Psychology Review* **4**(2): 29–34. This was a version of Chapter 9 of this book. This was based on a paper, 'In search of supervision's soul: perceptions of competencies via the five relationship model', delivered at the British Association for Counselling's Fourth Annual Counselling Research Conference, 20 March 1998, Birmingham.

Clarkson, P. (1997) The beginning of Gestalt. *Gestalt Journal* **XX**(2): 23–42. This is Chapter 10 in this book.

Chapter 1
Physis in Transactional Analysis

The early Greeks conceptualized physis as the generalized creative force of nature that eternally 'strives to make things grow and to make growing things more perfect' (Berne, 1968, p. 89). This chapter highlights this unique, and most neglected, contribution of Berne's and its further developments in transactional analysis (TA) in my work. It also contrasts physis with the two other major drives in human motivation – eros and thanatos – while considering some implications for TA psychotherapy.

This chapter reviews the definitions and uses of the concept of the growth force physis in TA from Berne to Clarkson – the only two transactional analysts who have theoretically acknowledged this drive to date of writing. It briefly differentiates the two major different meanings in the lexicon of the pre-Socratics – change as flux itself and change as curative and creative evolution. Berne used it in the latter sense only. The chapter also contributes a theoretical comparison contrasting physis with eros and thanatos as major drives in human motivation, and considers some applications in TA psychotherapy.

Berne referred to physis (sometimes spelled phusis [Berne, 1947/1968, p. 91]) in his first major work, *A Layman's Guide to Psychiatry and Psychoanalysis*, as follows:

> The growth force, or Physis, which we see evidence of in the individual and society, if properly nourished in infancy, works along with the Superego, so that the individual has an urge to grow and to behave 'better' – that is, in accordance with the principles of the adult stage of sexual development which takes the happiness of others into consideration. Both Superego and Physis, if normal, oppose crude or brutal expressions of Id wishes. They start the individual off in not soiling his diapers, and end up in the ideals of the United Nations.
>
> Berne (1968, p. 129)

Berne also wrote about physis in *The Structure and Dynamics of Organizations and Groups* (Berne, 1963), as well as in *What Do You Say*

After You Say Hello? (Berne, 1972). The biological force of physis is thus one of his most enduring and unchanging core concepts accompanying all the developments of his theory and practice in TA.

Berne (1947/1968) first defined physis in the word list as an entity, of a similar order to the death instinct. In the reprinted edition of this book (Berne, 1957/1968), it also appeared in the word list, of a similar order to the child ego state. In his book, Chapter 9, written by Dusay, is of course a whole chapter on TA, incorporated into the third edition of this book, which was published in 1968. Berne (1968) wrote that 'an extensive revision was undertaken' (p. 11), so we may conclude that he decided to keep the 10 listed references to physis in this work.

> As we shall see later, a neurosis has many advantages for the individual. If he is better off in many respects with his neurosis, what is the force which makes him 'want' to get better? What is the curative force of nature which makes sick bodies and sick minds strive to become healthy again so that they can continue to grow? What makes an embryo develop? Why doesn't it just stay an embryo? Growing is hard work and uses up a lot of energy. What made some jellyfish evolve into men? Why didn't they just stay jellyfish forever? Evolving is also hard work.
>
> Berne (1968, p. 88)

Berne (1968) accepted the importance of the two major Freudian (and Federnian – Federn, 1977) drives, destrudo or mortido (the energy of the death instinct) and libido (the energy of the sexual instinct). Throughout his life, he never minimized the destructive potential of people as individuals and nations but he also adhered to his belief in the person's inner drive to health and growth. He used the notion of physis to encapsulate this conviction that healing and change are possible. For this reason, Berne (1972) trusted people to heal themselves. He differentiated four powerful forces working within each human life.

> The forces of human destiny are foursome and fearsome: demonic parental programming, abetted by the inner voice the ancients called the *Daemon*; constructive parental programming, aided by the thrust of life called *Physis* long ago; external forces, still called Fate; and independent aspirations, for which the ancients had no human name, since for them such were the privileges mainly of gods and kings. And as a resultant of these forces there are four kinds of life courses, which may be mixed, and lead to one or another kind of final destiny: scripty, counterscripty, forced and independent.
>
> Berne (1972, p. 56)

So, contrary to some conceptualizations, in addition to the forces of deterministic limitation (the daemon and fate), Berne acknowledged the forces of growth and evolution – the thrust of the life force physis and individuals' independent aspirations.

Definitions

Physis as a verb means 'to grow', or 'to be' – 'what things really are' (Edwards, 1967, p. 100). To Aristotle (1933, pp. 219–221), physis meant 'that imminent thing from which a growing thing first begins to grow. . . . The source from which the primary notion in every natural object is induced in that object as such'. The concept, developed by the pre-Socratic Heraclitus, originally meant 'change or growth which comes from the spirit within the person' (Guerriere, 1980, p. 100).

Heraclitus held that the nature of life and existence is perpetual change itself. 'All things and the universe as a whole are in constant, ceaseless flux; nothing is, only change is real, all is a continuous passing away' (Runes, 1962, p. 124). Physis, then, is the workings or mechanism of that change. Change is spontaneous or at the very least originates internally within that which has changed. There must be the capability and proclivity for change in that which changes. The Stoics saw all existence as part of the flux whose nature is change; we are born from and re-enter it upon death. Change as physis comes spontaneously from within as part of a greater and general *fire* (the metaphor, along with its associated *flame*, most aptly connected with physis).

Change must occur because change is life. Physis is the all-powerful force for both physical growing and ageing, and mental/emotional change, which is characterized as that which gives us life (our spirit, so to speak). For Heraclitus, physis has no *telos* (there is nothing normative about the concept); it is simply change as flux or a state of being. The nature of the change that occurs is determined by outside circumstances and by ourselves. The Stoics identified physis with the gods and the active principle, whereas the Epicureans saw it as consisting of atoms and the void (Edwards, 1967). The pre-Socratics, including Zeno (Guerriere, 1980), conceived of physis as the healing factor in illness, the energetic motive for evolution and creativity in the individual and collective psyche. For the pre-Socratics, it is conceived as more biological than psychical because it represents the evolutionary impulse inherent in every cell. It is also viewed as more spiritual because it implies that it is in the nature of the person and the planet to evolve creatively.

Physis and evolution

There are thus two ancient conceptualizations of physis – change as flux itself without source or goal and change as cure, growth or creative evolution. It is in this latter sense that Berne took it on as the major motivating force of cure, individual aspiration and collective evolution. Berne (1968) formulated his view of physis from his sources as follows: 'The growth force of nature, which makes organisms evolve into higher forms, embryos develop into adults, sick people get better, and healthy people strive to attain their ideals' (pp. 369-370).

This view of physis, as used by Berne (1968) (who attributed it to Zeno), was taken from Murray (1955, p. 215):

> But in the rest of the world, we can see a moving Purpose. It is Physis, the word which the Romans unfortunately translated as 'Nature', but which means 'growing', or 'the way things grow' - almost what we call Evolution . . .

Berne was indeed concerned, if not preoccupied, throughout his life with the destructive aspects of human existence as his awareness of *thanatos*, the *little fascist*, in each one of us, and the roles of the *four horsemen of the Apocalypse* in human lives repeatedly testify. However, in keeping with the optimistic climate and atmosphere of the times he maintained that, even if there were no hope for the human race, individual members retained the human capacity to change and evolve (Berne, 1968, p. 88):

> But there is something beyond all this - some force which drives people to grow, progress and do better. We may regard this as a fourth force of personality besides the Ego, the Superego and the Id. Psychiatrists and psychologists know little or nothing about this fourth part. Religious people might say it was the soul. Scientists have no answer at present . . . . But it helps to suppose that there is a system of tensions which normally pushes living things continually in the direction of 'progress'. We may suppose the existence of such a system in order to explain why people grow and why the human race tries to get 'better', and why animals gradually become more venturesome through evolution, and why a creative love of beauty is added to the mind as that energy system becomes more complicated from the jellyfish up through the frogs and monkeys to man. We can forget the question of whose 'benefit' this is for and still suppose that there is a force within us which keeps us striving to go 'onward and upward'.

It is precisely this emphatic insistence on cure, progress and evolution that differentiates TA from its psychoanalytic cousins. It is the concept of physis and aspiration in script formation and script transformation that invokes respect and appreciation for Berne. He can be seen as the original integrator of the psychodynamic tradition with a perspective of human capacity to make princes and princesses out of frogs (Berne, 1966) by their own decision, and in spite of whatever else life had meted out to them. This is the major departure point of TA, which must be preserved if it is not to become 'collapsed into a psychodynamic framework' (Cornell, 1988, p. 281) and appear deterministic, reductionistic and neglectful of developmental concerns that emphasize and celebrate the child's (and the adult's) capacity for mastery and individuation.

Physis, mortido and libido

Berne (1968) noted that Freud (1920/1973) expressed his doubt about the existence of a general creative force of evolution (such as physis), terming it 'a pleasing illusion'. Freud was none too sure at one time, however, that something like physis did not assist Ananke (necessity) as the motive force in evolution. 'This appreciation of the necessities of life need not, incidentally, weigh against the importance of "internal developmental trends" if such can be shown to be present' (Freud, 1916-1917/1973, p. 400). He seemed to have much more conviction about the death instinct, and later he gave equal weight to eros and thanatos – metaphoric personifications of the sexual and death instincts (Rycroft, 1968, pp. 45-46 and 165). Libido and mortido (or 'destrudo' in Weiss, 1950, pp. 33 and 111), respectively, are thought to be the associated psychic energies.

In this psychoanalytic process of emphasizing the human drives towards sexuality and death, a person's unconscious drive towards health, wholeness and creative evolution was ignored, denied or neglected. Berne, along with Jung and several of the humanistic psychotherapists, had a larger vision, which took account of the healing and creative instincts that can transform both the sex and the death drive. Berne (1968) thought that physis, as the evolutionary healing growth force of nature, was 'only one aspect of inwardly directed libido, *but it may be a more basic force than libido itself*' (p. 370, italics added). In this respect I agree with him and conceptualize physis as onto- and phylogenetically before the other drives.

Berne (1968) therefore added physis to the other two great, unconscious forces (energies) – eros and thanatos – in human life, and he saw all three as the background of psychological life. Physis is not a derivative of libido or mortido energies, although aspects of each can be used to understand it. Physis is larger and more impersonal, infusing eros and thanatos (and their more individual needs) in its creative, healing and evolutionary quest. Physis is at least an equal and probably a much more fundamental and basic force than the other two in individual and collective evolution (Table 1.1).

Physis and aspiration

The importance of physis as a generalized creative drive towards health in TA is equalled only by its neglect in the theoretical literature since Berne. Perhaps unwittingly (and certainly without due acknowledgement, because it has not been referenced by any other TA author I have been able to trace to date of writing), Berne used this mythical notion, comparable to eros and thanatos in evocative power. It could be the unifying symbol for the whole of

Table 1.1 Characteristics of thanatos, eros and physis

Thanatos	Eros	Physis
Death	Survival	Life
Death instinct	Life or sexual instinct	Life instinct
Destruction	Procreation	Creation/creativity
Self-destruction	Self-preservation	Self-transformation
Mortido (inwardly directed)	Libido (outwardly directed)	Libido (inwardly directed) Mortido (outwardly directed)
Seeks freedom from striving	Seeks pleasure/gratification	Seeks fulfilment/realization
Ending	Beginning	Evolving
Expiration	Inspiration	Aspiration

'third-force psychology' (Maslow, 1963, p. iii). However, if physis subsumes the other two forces, it may be more accurately conceptualized as the first force coming from the *basis* of human motivation.

To the pre-Socratics, physis was *nature* itself, conceived of as coming from the deepest biological roots of the human being and striving towards its greatest realization. Berne (1972), indeed, had the idea that the autonomous aspiration of a human being rises from the depths of the somatic child (oldest, most archaic or undifferentiated ego state), and upwardly transcends the limit-inducing downward pressures of the script, which is shaped by the matrix of love (affection) and death (destruction) in our earliest relationships.

It is not surprising to me that TA has been described as over-emphasizing deterministic forces in script formation (Cornell, 1988) if the teachers and practitioners of TA have ignored or overlooked this most crucial central contribution. It *is* surprising to me that its philosophical thrust is so *present* in the humanistic impetus of TA practice, celebrating potential for development and autonomy but so *invisible* in all subsequent literature, even though it merited inclusion by Berne in a major seminal diagram in the TA canon. As Clarkson (1992b) noted, he concretized his conception of the role of aspiration in the script-matrix diagram in Berne (1972) (Figure 1.1).

The script-matrix diagram (see Figure 1) showing the aspiration arrow has been, as far as the author is aware, omitted (excluded?) from the standardised international introduction to Transactional Analysis (also called the 101) and is nowhere listed as essential teaching, nor has it ever yet been referenced. Yet it contains in schematic form the exact symbolic juxtaposition of predetermining forces predicated by attachment (parental love) and despair (parental and

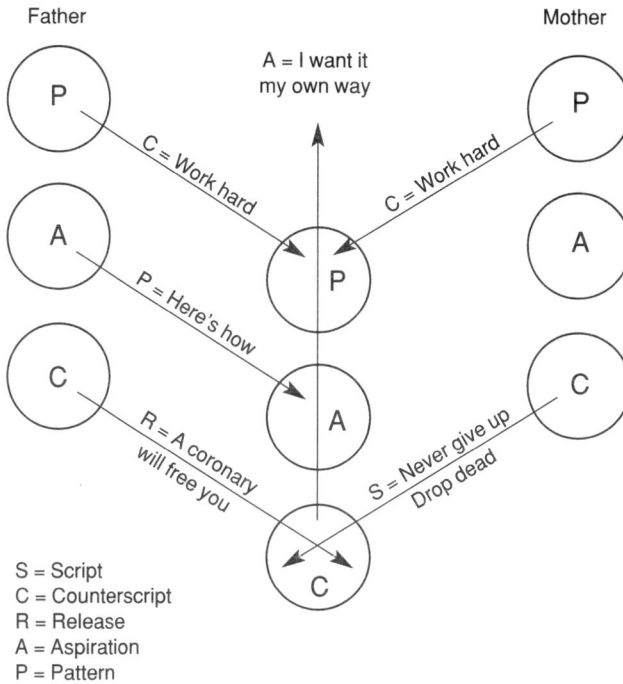

Figure 1.1 Script matrix showing aspiration arrow (Berne, 1972, p. 128).

existential restriction), counterbalanced by the primary, deeper (and higher) force for change and individual transformation as a natural process of human aspiration.

Berne (1972, pp. 11–12)

. . . Berne's script diagram which includes the aspiration arrow, represents one of the most powerful images in TA literature of the potential of human beings to liberate themselves from the deterministic constraints of their scripts. Neglect of this script diagram may lead psychotherapists and clients alike to overvalue the gravity force of scripting at the cost of the concept of transcendence. It encapsulates the spirit of transactional analysis as a humanistic, existential approach to psychotherapy which is based in the psychodynamic knowledge of eros and destrudo as well as recognition of physis.

Clarkson (1988a, p.12)

Aspiration may be the strongest determinant in personal, social or global change after all. Berne (1972) represented the individual's aspiration as an arrow rising from the ground of the child ego states, moving through the Adult and through the Parent, and emerging well above the script matrix with the head of the arrow pointing ever upward (Berne, 1972).

The object of script analysis is to free Jeder and Zoe so that they can open the garden of their aspirations to the world. It does that by cutting through the Babel in their heads until the Child can say: 'But this is what I want to do, and I would rather do it my own way'.

Berne (1972, p. 131)

Implications for TA psychotherapy

A crucial implication of the rediscovery and re-instatement of physis as a major concept in TA psychotherapy is that the concept of physis *provides a drive theoretical base* for the Bernian belief and TA practice founded on the conviction that human beings can free themselves from the shackles of their script and become autonomous and self-actualizing.

Taking on board such a generalized creative force which is also evolutionary in nature – and therefore essentially *developmental* – goes a long way towards dealing with the criticisms of script theory articulated so well by Cornell (1988, p. 281): 'Script analysis as it has evolved over the years is overly psychoanalytic in attitude and overly reductionistic in what it communicates to people about human development'.

If physis as a drive towards creativity (tested under sometimes adverse conditions) and an evolutionary developmental impetus for individuals and the collective is re-instated as an essential part of the conceptual matrix from which we forge TA, the possibility for flexibility, resilience and remarkable creativity that we encounter in psychotherapy can be accounted for theoretically and *philosophically*.

In 1988 Cornell stated that 'Transactional analysts need to either significantly challenge and broaden the current conceptualization of script or to introduce a second parallel term – such as psychological life plan – to describe healthy, functional aspects of "meaning-making" in the ongoing psychological construction of reality' (p. 281). In the same year I (Clarkson, 1988a) reintroduced the concept of physis into the TA literature and made the connection of the generalized creative force of physis as exemplified in script terms with Berne's concept of *aspiration*. A recent find was the following quotation from a book on the work and life of Bergson (which we know Berne had read):

The directive stimulus of joy and the *aspiration* [italics added] of our moral nature are not contradictory of any science, even the most abstract or the most exact. Intellect and intuition are not opposed, except when the one refuses to adopt precision through contact with facts that have been scientifically questioned and arraigned, or the other, instead of keeping within the limits set to it by science, makes for itself, more or less unawares, a metaphysic falsely pretending to be based on science.

Bergson (1914, p. 241)

I showed how the diagrammatic representation of the *aspiration arrow* in Berne's (1972) script diagram corresponds pictorially with the philosophical conceptualization of physis (Clarkson, 1988a). I applied this to crisis theory, referring to the well-known phenomenon (in crisis theory and in life) that *times of crisis may precipitate enhanced opportunities* for the recognition and manifestation of physis – individuals and nations responding out of script with enhanced creativity, resilience, serendipity and spontaneity to life's vicissitudes. In these times of crisis, people often seem to have greater opportunities to break free from their scripts than at other times because the habitual, script-bound patterns are disrupted and the psychic equilibrium already de-stabilized. Thus opportunities are opened for massive reorganization along lines that are developmentally healthier and creatively more productive. According to Bergson (1914, p. 241): 'for every man there lies open one unfailing source of joy, the creation of himself by himself, the enriching of his personality by new elements not procured from without but drawn or driven upward from his own depths.' One look at the upward thrust of the aspiration arrow and the philosophical and attitudinal correspondences between the core of Bergson's view of human nature and that of Berne and TA becomes clear – people are deeply influenced by external forces, but ultimately each one is responsible for his or her self-creation.

Next I differentiated the concept of *metanoia* which could be seen as a non-linear evolutionary change (Clarkson, 1988b). Change can usually be seen in one of two major forms – as a result either of physical healing or evolution or of a second-order change or metanoia (turning). This conceptualization recognizes that evolutionary developments (the path of physis) do not always proceed in linear progressive ways, but sometimes by discontinuous leaps or turns which are sometimes unpredictable, often disruptive, and usually creative, rather than in easy incremental and anticipated planned ways (Corballis, 1991). However, the *possibility of creative and evolutionary change* is characteristic of the TA approach to psychotherapy, organizations and life.

This knowledge that *change is possible* (which has been honed on personal and collective experiences of oppression, poverty and injustice) is encapsulated in the name metanoia, which means to change or to turn around, or a transformation of mind or character. Metanoia is derived from the Greek verb *metanoeo* which also suggests 'to change one's mind on reflection' (Liddell, 1963, p. 439). Metanoia is elsewhere defined as 'a change of the inner man' and a 'turning about' (Burchfield, 1976, p. 911). Keen (1985, p. 224), an existential psychotherapist, sees metanoia as the opposite of 'paranoia' and akin to repentance, a 're-owning of the shadow and a turning around away from the persona toward the Self' (Clarkson,

1989; now Chapter 4 of this book). The change that is referred to in a metanoia is for all practical purposes a permanently transformed state of being, whether it is a spiritual or psychological transformation: 'Something more active and fruitful, the setting up of an immense new inward movement for obtaining the rule of life' (Burchfield, 1976, p. 911).

In 1989 I reviewed the contribution of Kahler (1975) and Kahler and Capers (1974), showing how the counterscript drivers ('hurry up', 'try hard', 'be strong', 'please me', 'be perfect') need to be differentiated from the human aspirations to be fast, energetically experimental, pleasing, enduringly strong and excellent (Clarkson, 1989). The counterscript drivers are still under the influence of script (thus thanatos and eros) whereas the correlated script-free aspirations are under the influence of *physis*.

As students of history, human nature and statistics we are well aware of the apparently overwhelming presence of determinism as it affects the individual and the group. Based on similar observations we have also participated in and witnessed individuals, groups and societies making profound and lasting changes in directions that few, if any, observers would have predicted (Clarkson, 1990). So, although we value insight, analysis and understanding, we see these as in service of the processes of *individual transformation* and *collective evolution* (Clarkson and Lapworth, 1991). In considering large-scale changes in countries such as the former Soviet Union, South Africa and Germany, we can also see physis at work. Despite the inevitable disappointments, their regressions and failures, there is also always present:

> . . . the removal of limitation and the burgeoning of horizons and the resurrection of the questing, insurgent, indomitable force for hope and health and human aspiration which Berne referred to as Physis.
>
> Clarkson (1990, p. 8)

In 1990 I wrote with Gilbert (Clarkson and Gilbert, 1990) that TA recognizes the constraints of heredity, specifically the relationship of temperament or basic limitations of intellect and physique to psychological health in the person (James, 1981, pp. 24–27), but considers that the drive towards psychological health in the person can modify, adapt to or overcome many apparent limitations. In this way individuals create the manifestations of *the 'conceivable self' as a product of Physis* (Clarkson and Gilbert, 1990, pp. 201–202):

> In psychotherapy we discover over and over again that as clients get closer and closer to their true self or 'First Nature' (which always involves a sense of somatic and organismic integrity), they connect more profoundly with an inner healing and actualising drive. In this way, they discover Physis working within themselves at the most basic levels. At the same time, this psychophysiological evolution is usually

accompanied by a growing awareness and appreciation of universal meanings –
striving towards connectedness with spiritual, religious or transcendental values . . .
the core self can be conceptualised as the organising principle of physis.

Clarkson (1992a, p. 197)

Finally, the rediscovery of physis in TA psychotherapy (as well as organizational and educational implications) brings an added dimension and emphasis to our work – that of an *enhanced awareness of the spiritual, transpersonal or transcendent dimension* of our endeavours. (James [1977] is already outstanding in her contribution.) It does not really matter what names we attach to such awareness, but it does matter that we develop an attitude in psychotherapy that can allow mystery, healing and the unexpected to challenge our diagnoses, our treatment planning and our countertransference analyses.

In Heraclitus (Guerriere, 1980, p. 96) physis equals Zeus equals God. It can be seen to assist the struggle for a definition of God as a constantly evolving process. The transpersonal relationship is potentially present in all healing encounters in individual psychotherapy. It is characterized by its timelessness and a sense of numinousness. In Jungian thought (Guggenbühl-Craig, 1971) this aspect of psychotherapy is conceived of as the relationship between the unconscious of the analyst and the unconscious of the patient.

Berne showed his awareness of *the transpersonal relationship* in TA psychotherapy when he quoted the following: 'Je le pensay, et Dieu le guarit . . . we treat them, but it is God who cures them' (Agnew in Berne, 1966, p. 63). By acknowledging physis in its incarnation as a name to indicate some of the transpersonal, inexpressible and graceful aspects of the mysterious process of healing in psychotherapy, this awareness of the transpersonal relationship can be brought back into TA. It is hoped that, in this way, technique, theory and cleverness will take their necessary backseats to the therapist's humility, which is the proper ambience for clients' self-discovery of physis inside themselves.

Conclusion

Physis could be the name people, including philosophers such as Bergson (1965) and psychologists such as Maslow (1963) and Rogers (1980), have been looking for in describing the life force in the western tradition. I am increasingly convinced that this is the most important force to which to pay attention in psychotherapy. Berne's unique contribution lies in naming it in our time. What is needed over the next few years is to reintroduce physis – the life force – of which we are the servants in psychotherapy. The task of psychotherapists and educators is to allow people to get back in touch with that life force within each individual in order to facilitate healing and self-realization. The task of the psychotherapist is to rekindle the self-healing flame in the person – the spark of physis. For people to change, they first need to feel well and OK – or in touch with their life force. To kindle this is perhaps the most central and important of our therapeutic activities. Without this there is not the energy, the belief or the capacity to even *use* help. So this is the first requirement in psychotherapy, and perhaps the last.

To see a person change, to see that flame sputter into life, to see hope rise where once there was despair, to see the laughter at absurdity bubbling over from confusion and self-deception, to see a new child born from an adult who never was one – this is the excitement and this is what makes our work worthwhile. Every day I understand that we are given this small handful of life energy for this day – this day's quota of sand in the endless timer of life measured on the grand chronologies of eternity. I walk every day into life with this my treasure to waste, to spend, to reduce to ashes, to squander on worthless activity and toxic people, soluble or insoluble problems, my destiny and my freedom; to suppress in some petty way, to free with tender nurturing – this is my life energy, the precious *élan vital* that Bergson (1965) wrote about. Every day I have my share, and every day it is mine to spend and there is no way I can save it up to use another day. I am repeating these things over and over again because I can only now begin to understand it – life is an everyday affair. The energy that I save today (in resting, in squandering, in suppression) will not be available tomorrow. I must have to do it today, now, to take my energy as it rises, every moment. Every single moment because it cannot and will not come again, I cannot bank energy, life's energy, to be available to me at another time; just this portion, this little bit, is mine today. Everyone else also has only their day's allotment to spend on love and care and creation and celebration – this is only this handful of mine today against the dawning of mortality. [This paragraph was the last paragraph of this paper which the then TAJ editorial board *required* to be deleted from the paper on physis by Clarkson, 1992b.]

References

Aristotle (1933) In: Goold, G.P. (ed.), Metaphysics: Books I–IX, XVII (H. Tredennick, trans.). Cambridge, MA: Harvard University Press.
Bergson, H. (1914) An Account of His Life and Philosophy. London: Macmillan.
Bergson, H. (1965) Creative Evolution. London: Collier-Macmillan.
Berne, E. (1963) The Structure and Dynamics of Organizations and Groups. New York: Grove Press.
Berne, E. (1966) Principles of Group Treatment. New York: Grove Press.
Berne, E. (1968) A Layman's Guide to Psychiatry and Psychoanalysis, 3rd edn. New York: Simon & Schuster (first published 1947, revised 1957).
Berne, E. (1972) What Do You Say After You Say Hello? New York: Bantam Books.

Burchfield, R.W. (ed.) (1976) A Supplement to the Oxford English Dictionary, Vols 1-4. Oxford: Oxford University Press.

Clarkson, P. (1988a) Crisis and aspiration. ITA News 9: 12.

Clarkson, P. (1988b) Metanoia: A process of transformation. Transactional Analysis Journal 19: 224-234.

Clarkson, P. (1989) In praise of speed, experimentation, agreeableness, endurance and excellence. ITA News 25: 6-11.

Clarkson, P. (1990) What was your contribution to bringing down the Berlin Wall? ITA News 26: 6-8.

Clarkson, P. (1992a) Transactional Analysis Psychotherapy: An integrated approach. London: Routledge.

Clarkson, P. (1992b) Physis in transactional analysis. Transactional Analysis Journal 22: 202-209.

Clarkson, P. and Gilbert, M. (1990) Transactional analysis. In: Dryden, W. (ed.), Handbook of Individual Therapy in Britain. Milton Keynes: Open University Press, pp. 226-251.

Clarkson, P. and Lapworth, P. (1991) Profile - metanoia: Core philosophy. Self and Society, 19(2): 16-23.

Corballis, M.C. (1991) The Lopsided Ape. New York: Oxford University Press.

Cornell, W.F. (1988) Life script theory: A critical review from a developmental perspective. Transactional Analysis Journal 18: 270-282.

Edwards, P. (ed. in chief) (1967) Encyclopedia of Philosophy. New York: Macmillan.

Federn, P. (1977) Ego Psychology and the Psychoses. London: Maresfield Reprints (first published 1953).

Freud, S. (1973) Beyond the pleasure principle. In: Richards, A. (ed.), On Metapsychology: The theory of psychoanalysis (J. Strachey, trans.). Pelican Freud Library, Vol. 11. Harmondsworth, Middx: Penguin, pp. 275-338. (Original work published 1920.)

Freud, S. (1973) Some thoughts on development and regression - aetiology. In: Richards, A. (ed.), Introductory Lectures on Psychoanalysis (J. Strachey, trans.). Pelican Freud library, Vol. 1. Harmondsworth, Middlesex: Penguin, pp. 383-403. (Original work published 1916-1917.)

Guerriere, D. (1980) Physis, Sophia, Psyche. In: Sallis, J. and Maly, K. (eds), Heraclitean Fragments: A companion volume to the Heidegger/Fink seminar on Heraclitus. Alabama: University of Alabama Press.

Guggenbühl-Craig, C.A. (1971) Power in the Helping Professions. Dallas, TX: Spring.

James, M. (1977) Techniques in Transactional Analysis. Reading, MA: Addison-Wesley.

James, M. (1981) Breaking Free: Self-reparenting for a new life. Reading, MA: Addison-Wesley.

Kahler, T. (1975) Drivers: The key to the process of scripts. Transactional Analysis Journal 5: 280-284.

Kahler, T. and Capers, H. (1974) The miniscript. Transactional Analysis Journal 4: 26-42.

Keen, S. (1985) The Passionate Life. London: Gateway.

Liddell, H.G. (ed.) (1963) A Lexicon Abridged from Liddell and Scott's Greek-English Lexicon. Oxford: Oxford University Press.

Maslow, A. H. (1963) Toward a Psychology of Being. Princeton, NJ: D. Van Nostrand.

Murray, G. (1955) Five Stages of Greek Religion. Garden City, NY: Doubleday Anchor Books.

Rogers, C. R. (1980) A Way of Being. Boston, MA: Houghton Mifflin.

Runes, D. D. (ed.) (1962) Dictionary of Philosophy. Totowa, NJ: Littlefields, Adams.

Rycroft, C. (1968) A Critical Dictionary of Psychoanalysis. London: Thomas Nelson.

Weiss, E. (1950) Principles of Psychodynamics. New York: Grune & Stratton.

Chapter 2
Nurturing First Nature in Psychotherapy and Life

It is unethical to call someone borderline because they are having more fun than you.

Ellenbogen (1987)

Some of the most painful distress in human experience is caused by learning to adapt to ways of living or values that are hurtful or limiting to the self. Many children make decisions to hold back, twist or amputate parts of themselves in order to get love, approval or even plain safety from harm. Here are some examples. My mother is very slow and phlegmatic, so I learn to hold my excitement as tension in my tummy. My father gets angry a lot, so I decide never to explore my own anger in case it hurts others, like his anger hurt my brother. My teachers called me 'know-it-all', so I decided to give up my curiosity and my desire to excel. I hold back or demonstrate the opposite 'acceptable behaviour' at tremendous cost to my own organismic integrity. The somatic child, the child in the Child, can lose touch with itself – its own sense, its own rhythms, its own beat.

'Second nature'

We adapt to the parents in the home, the teachers at school and the social pressures of our schoolmates or colleagues, the collective pressures of advertising, the films and books – even the fashion images and histories of our times. Sometimes these adaptations are so profound and so ingrained that it begins to feel like you were never any different.

This is often what is meant by a 'type three impasse' (Goulding and Goulding, 1979). That is when a person says: 'It's become second nature to me – I cannot remember ever being different.' Of course the story is already clear at the *ulterior* level – if we listen carefully to this metaphor. It may indicate the gravestone of where I 'buried' my *first nature*.

14

This is the sense of who I really am or really truly felt myself to be before I learnt some behaviour, some adaptation so well that it has become habitual. Before it got wired into a conditioned reflex that sits on my first nature like armour, like a shield – protective in some ways but stultifying and smothering the very unique and special human being attempting to grow underneath. 'Thus psychotherapy can be seen in many ways as a process of helping people back to their first natures – the original, spontaneous, creative and natural Child self' (Clarkson, 1992, p. 197).

> Cline (Mr C) had struggled most of his life with intense [very real] feelings of depression. He often felt like staying in and reading philosophy rather than socialising with people. He found past-timing [small-talk] painful. He was highly valued in his work as a lecturer and had good relationships with two special friends, but never the inclination to marry. In therapy we spent some months doing 'archaeology': for example, trying to relate this to a residue from his early evacuation experiences in World War II. Frustrated by not reaching a resolution in this area, we finally agreed to accept the 'melancholic' essence of his inner self. This did not 'cure' his feelings but helped him to handle a life where he could take his own and the world's suffering seriously. He felt more authentically in relation to his life – his existential reality. As far as *he* was concerned, he was 'cured' – he had made peace with his 'first nature'.

What is first nature?

As people grow and change as a result of counselling, therapy, education, love or crises in their lives, they discover that they have sacrificed their first nature along the way – sometimes a very long time ago (Clarkson, 1989). This may happen as an infant at the breast of a depressed and sick mother, a boisterous child at the knee of an impatient father, a very creative, dreamy sibling growing up in a family of practically minded, down-to-earth children.

Finding one's true nature can be a difficult but exciting adventure. Potentially it is possible to discover the treasure of feeling 'comfortable in my own skin' – or, as a client once said, 'sitting comfortably in the middle of my self'. Sometimes, however, one's first nature may be divorced, estranged or so frozen that it can hardly be found, and some clues or special kinds of help and education may be needed to locate it.

Of course, many so-called first-nature features start showing when the restrictions, the injunctions and the numbness of painful past experiences begin to wear off. Then a woman may discover that she likes quiet cool colours such as black or navy and not the bright sunny florals that her mother liked her to wear. Then a man may discover that he needs only 4 hours' sleep – he is not the insomniac that his wife believed him to be, he is simply a person who does not need or enjoy sleeping as much as many other people. A young boy may discover that he likes doing things with his hands more than reading or listening to music – and this may have little to do with ability or competence, and everything to do with temperamental preference.

First nature is often about difference

It is easy to be made to feel ashamed or wrong or sick or bad if 'who you really are' is *different* from those around you. Any form of labelling concentrates on similarities to devalued others – whether or not patients. A little black boy in a white neighbourhood tried to wash his beautiful dark skin off until it bled, because he felt that others hated him for himself – his real, true colour. Black, like manic–depressive, meant 'less valuable than'.

A little girl who liked running about and jumping because that's the way she liked learning best grew quiet and ill because the teacher was always telling her to 'sit still and behave'. Psychologists know that sitting still is probably the antithesis of good learning for many people who temperamentally prefer to learn 'by doing', not listening. Many women are constantly irritable or anxious with hunger in trying to force their bodies to conform to shapes and metabolic processes that were never possible with their particular genetic heritage (Wolf, 1990).

In any given culture, certain behaviours will be labelled diagnostic of mental disorders, and others – sometimes equally crippling – as models of mental health and good adjustment. Women are often diagnosed as mentally ill more frequently than men (Howell and Bayes, 1981), and people from immigrant stock more often than accultured Europeans (Van Dijk, 1987). What we label as bad, mad or desirable is often affected more by cultural factors than intrinsic respect for difference, uniqueness and delight in exceptions to the rule, e.g. accepting western European models of child development can have enormous detrimental consequences for justice, equality and, particularly, the practice of psychotherapy (Cornell, 1988; Samuels, 1993). Are there other ways? Yes – many.

A particularly pernicious form of pathologizing difference has in some training institutes now become the norm or the culture. Yesterday a trainee cried in supervision because her trainer had many years ago labelled her as 'passive–aggressive'. The implication she took from this was that there was little hope for her. Her *reliving* of the experience of being shamed in front of her fellow students was as traumatic and profound as if it had happened the day before. Certainly her learning and self-confidence became impaired as she used her life energy – her physis (Clarkson, 1996) – to live down such a damaging label. I vividly remember the physical shock that I felt when a gestalt therapist matter-of-factly told me in supervision that 'I just cannot think of myself outside of my diagnostic label' (this was 'borderline'). And this from a tradition that so valiantly fought against 'boxing' people in terms of psychiatric psychopathology?

Frequently, I hear colleagues pathologize each other (perhaps because they envy the other for some reason or other), calling so-and-so histrionic, paranoid, dependent or even psychotic – anything that can strip the other of their humanity and have them act as a container for the unacceptable in themselves. This mechanism has been called *projection*. Its transactional counterpart – when 'the dog lives up to his bad name' – is called *projective identification*. In this way, genuine engagement, empathy and relationship are avoided.

The labelling of others by pejorative labels or abbreviation is of course common practice in familial or organizational abuse, torture and war. The first step is to dehumanize the perceived enemy by calling them 'wogs', 'Argies', 'uppity bitches'. It's easier then to drop atom bombs, kill prisoners and rape women when 'the other' has first – by the selective use of language – been de*human*ized. 'They are not PLU' (people like us).

What has happened?

As a result of a growing emphasis on psychiatric nomenclature for reimbursement by medical insurance companies and the need to communicate with our psychiatric colleagues, as well as negotiate the conventional psychiatric system (e.g. mental hospitals), it has become necessary for psychotherapists to learn the 'language' of psychiatry and the underlying medical model.

Use of psychiatric labels can appear to make a certain kind of cross-comparison research on large numbers seem easier, but it is fraught with contradictions in practice. The existence of two major modes of classifying mental and emotional disorders (*Diagnostic and Statistical Manual of Mental Disorders* or DSM and *International Classification of Disease* or ICD) also confuses the issues between different countries and even between different hospitals and different specialists in any one country. A common misconception is that a classification of mental disorders classifies individuals, when actually what are being classified are the disorders that individuals suffer from, so the DSM recommends the more accurate and admittedly more worthy 'an individual with schizophrenia' or 'an individual with cocaine dependence'.

Changing 'fashions' in discovering or labelling different kinds of disorders (nineteenth century 'hysteria', mid-twentieth century 'narcissistic person-ality disorders', late twentieth century 'disassociative disorders') have also affected the industry.

Another very important value of learning such psychiatric nomenclature is that it opens up the wisdom of our predecessors or contemporaries so that we can learn from their teaching and writings how they responded to and handled certain types of problems. However, for myself, I have rarely found that any one of my clients in psychotherapy 'fitted neatly' into any box. They seem to insist on being themselves. And when they do seem to fit the box or the textbook, I have learned that I probably need some more psychotherapy or competent supervision because I have lost sight of this individual person in this unique, unrepeatable relationship with myself.

Too often, black people are diagnosed as 'non-treatable' by the 'talking therapies', 'addicts' are seen as hopeless cases or we say something like 'but so-and-so lacks the "ego strength" to make use of a long-term therapeutic relationship'. The *person* becomes identified with their *problem* and then we get ward staff referring to 'schizos', therapists sniggering about 'borderlines' and community psychiatric nurses talking about 'alkies' (alcoholics). Of course I am not suggesting that this is true about all practitioners in all places at all times.

I remember the consultant psychiatrist Dr Hart of Tara Hospital, to whom I owe all my diagnostic skills, confronting us professionals on a hospital ward round one day. We, as his junior staff, had all just concluded that a particular patient was 'character disordered', i.e. a psychopath. Dr Hart said, 'When we use that label, all we are stating is our own inadequacy. We don't know how to treat them, so we blame them by labelling *them* inadequate to our current ways of curing people. It is actually *our problem*'. However, the incident occurred about 30 years ago, so I may have gotten only some of his actual words. His lesson comes to me whenever I feel that I cannot really help a client and it constantly acts as inspiration to keep me searching and researching and researching again. That is how I have come to believe, to paraphrase Socrates, that 'the unexamined practice is not worth doing'. And writing is one of the major ways of doing such examination (see Clarkson, 1998).

So, pro or con diagnosis?

This is not a question that should be answered without substantial reflection, some of which I have done elsewhere:

> The very process of the debate is, however, an interesting and worthwhile exercise. Psychotherapy trainees are encouraged to build their ability and evidence in order to argue equally passionately and intelligently on either side and to add to the considerations. . . . Obviously there are individual preferences but perhaps a metaperspective is a realisation that this may be a false polarity, a paradox and a non-question.
>
> Clarkson (1992, p. 63)

It now seems necessary to emphasize that 'diagnosis' is defined in the *Shorter Oxford English Dictionary* as 'Determination of the nature of a diseased condition; identification of a disease by investigation of its symptoms and history' (Onions, 1973, p. 538), i.e. diagnosis is a word and an activity that is applied to *disease* or a *diseased condition*.

Disease has been de-constructed to mean dis-ease, i.e. a lack of ease, inconvenience, disturbance, but colloquially it is usually understood by most people as 'a condition of the body [or mind] in which its functions are disturbed or deranged' (Onions, 1973, p. 565). So diagnosis is properly applied when someone's functioning is disturbed or deranged, i.e. he or she is ill.

In my opinion it is improperly (and possibly unethically) applied to someone who is not ill. Too frequently, diagnosis is being used to pathologize difference rather than for its true purpose – to help those who come to us for psychotherapy because their functioning in life is disturbed or deranged. But, of course, many people come to psychotherapy to improve their lives and their functioning, not to be treated as diseased minds or sick people. Many psychotherapists rarely see such very ill patients in private practice. Indeed the requirement for psychiatric placements in many training programmes was instituted in recognition of this fact. Are psychotherapists perhaps becoming collectively engaged in a potentially destructive game of 'psychiatry'? Berne (1967) recalls that Ambroise Paré said, 'I treat them, but God cures them'. In *Games People Play*, Berne (1967, pp. 135–136) writes:

> Every medical student learns about this dictum, along with others such as *primum non nocere* [not to cause damage] and phrases such as *vis medicatrix naturae* [it is Nature, physis, that cures]. Non-medical therapists however, are not so like to be exposed to these ancient cautions. The position 'I am a healer because it says here [on the diploma] that I am a healer' is likely to be an impairment, and may be replaced to advantage with something like: 'I will apply what therapeutic procedures I have learned in the hope that they will be of some benefit.' This avoids the possibility of games based on: 'Since I am a healer, if you don't get better it's your fault'.

Many kinds of difference

There is substantial evidence that temperamental difference can be identified in infants at birth, i.e. before much external experience or behavioural conditioning could have taken place (Chess and Thomas, 1986). The psychoanalyst Bollas (1989) also refers to an individual's 'personality idiom' whereby 'infants, at birth, are in possession of a personality potential that is in part genetically sponsored and that this true self, over the course of a lifetime, seeks to express and elaborate this potential through formations in being and relating' (p. 11).

Whether our individual rhythms are fast or slow, strong or gentle (Clarkson, 2003a), introverted or extraverted or focused on sensation, intuition, feeling or thinking as in Jung's (1971) typology, visual, auditory or kinaesthetic learning styles as, for example, in neurolinguistic programming (NLP) – all these and many more – can help individuals find their way back to their true selves. These are some of the non-pathologizing and thus non-*iatrogenic* typologies, emphasizing individual differences rather than boxing comparatively healthy people engaging with life's challenges in psychiatric diagnoses.

There is a major benefit of using typologies to highlight uniqueness and to find difference to understand and appreciate each other better. Such differences can then be used not as dehumanizing and de-individualizing 'boxes' but as routes for self-exploration and self-discovery. This is different from descriptions that are based in value judgements about what is wrong and what is socially acceptable. What I am saying is that difference in itself may be pathologized by society, by psychotherapists, by ourselves. I'm against that.

A therapeutic approach to the *healing relationship* that relies on uniqueness and the appreciation of difference and idiosyncrasy is possible without an implication or pathology, with no trace of psychiatrically articulated diagnosis and an absence of collectively formed value judgements. An anti-example concerns the psychoanalyst Professor Socarides' (1995) late twentieth century psychiatric pronouncements on the pathological 'genital immaturity' of men and women who are making homosexual love choices (his son is gay). Positive examples abound in the literature accumulating around the concept of 'positive psychology' (Snyder and Lopez, 2002).

Although the vital and important challenges of Szasz (1961), Laing (1965) and his collaborators, and the Radical Psychiatry Movement (e.g. Steiner, 1974) seem to have faded in the collective consciousness of psychotherapy, there are fortunately still pockets of resistance. After a teaching session when comparatively healthy adult psychotherapists had been practising 'diagnosing' each other, one trainee retorted to her trainer who was pathologizing her as 'histrionic': 'At least I'm easier to cure than you!' (an obsessive–compulsive).

This incident reminds me of what the £200 000 per year model Heather Mills (now Mrs Paul McCartney) said to the counsellor who was helping her 'adapt' to the amputation of her right leg. The counsellor, no doubt trying to help her mourning process, reportedly said, 'You must accept that men will not be attracted to you'. Heather replied, 'Listen darling, if all my arms and legs were missing, I'd still be a lot more attractive than you' (Bracchi and Hewett, 2000, p. 6).

I consider this kind of practice as *iatrogenic* – the medicine is causing disease (Illich, 1975). Sometimes I think that shaming shamers in powerful positions is a valid interruption to a potentially devastating psychological game pay-off (Clarkson, 2003a).

'Treatment' considerations

Although it is a valuable improvement, particularly when the pejorative labels are omitted, I am not that comfortable with the notion of 'adaptation' to box human beings either. Surely if they are 'cured' those categories could never fit again. Living for the rest of your life with a pathologizing label is not cure. Furthermore, it imports the notion that children are 'adapting' to their life circumstances rather than actively co-creating them. Modern research on infants and children (Draghi-Lorenz et al., 2001) shows them *in relationship*, not necessarily adapting. Anyway, an adaptation is not spontaneous and is hardly likely to enhance autonomy or intimacy.

It is a learning theory truism to acknowledge that 'what you stroke you get'. Therefore, by stroking (or reinforcing) pathologizing or self-pathologizing labels, it is entirely predictable that people will produce more of the pathological behaviours that will in turn reinforce the problem. This is of course based on substantial and uncontroversial, psychologically proven facts about reinforcement in learning. So, if I can only pass my exams by such behaviours, these are the behaviours that I will produce. If we want to encourage creativity, choice, freedom, uniqueness and particularity, perhaps we could change our lenses to appreciate the inherent unique aspirational *physis* of each individual person and concentrate on that.

Ethical considerations

I have frequently heard colleagues ask students: 'How would you diagnose this client?' It is not then surprising to hear supervisees say: 'I have diagnosed this client as . . . [psychiatric label].' It is a fundamental, professional, ethical principle *not* to work outside the area of one's competence. Counsellors and psychotherapists are not usually competent to make such diagnoses. Psychiatrists are.

Aetiology

Sometimes people may attempt to minimize the deleterious effects of diagnoses by concentrating on the aetiology – or causes. Drug companies favour chemical imbalances that fit with their products. Psychotherapists may favour clients who fit their preferred client profile – usually those most similar to themselves, i.e. educated, white and middle-class. An attempt to deal with differences in terms of diagnostic categories is made when different adaptations, traits or disorders are explained in terms of what happened to people as children. This is a popular, but only a Eurocentric and only a historically recent (100 years), theory. Yet emotional distress and healing do occur *all over the world*, and have been *recorded all through history* – without this narrative (story). So it does *not* appear to be essential for psychological understanding or healing (compare Frank and Frank, 1993).

Furthermore, there appears to be almost no scientifically accepted *evidence* for the theory that childhood experiences cause adult disorders – apart from gross injury, neglect or malnutrition. And yet, there are many exceptions to this as well. It is always possible to link some aspect of today with some aspect of one's history. Often that helps some people, providing what Frank and Frank (1993) identified as a *culturally congruent narrative*. This is one of the four factors that they found from their extensive research to be necessary for any psychological healing to happen. (The other three are the relationship, the space and a prescription for action.) Developmental theory seems to have great retrospective explanatory power, but virtually no reliable predictive power. It can help us make sense of what *has* happened, but cannot reliably say what *will* happen. (Free will at it again?)

A theory is not a fact. A fact becomes a fact only when it is proved (and until other facts are proved) (Clarkson, 2003b). It needs only one apple to float in order to disprove the law of gravity. There are many possible and potentially useful ways of explaining adult personality patterns and life experiences. There are destiny and astrology, archetypal collective patterns of human beings and karma, to name but a few. A good example of the *teleological* narrative (claiming that our *future* determines our *past*) is very well and vividly described in Hillman (1996).

Temperament

It is a fact that certain psychophysiological patterns (sometimes called temperament) can be identified within minutes of birth. Such neurological patterns have been studied for many decades. This means that people are differently 'hard-wired' – the baby born with cortical excitation and behavioural inhibition will *never* be able to change the fact that he or she responds to or seeks out stimuli of a certain kind – unless he or she is actually brain damaged later.

This experience of different temperaments (or neurological difference) is *empirically* corroborated by most mothers (from their experience). Even the Walton sextuplets, born at the same time and growing up in the same house, have vividly different temperaments and personalities (Hardy, 2000).

Yet I hope no mother or clinician would 'label' a newly born infant as having a depressive personality disorder or borderline traits!

So, imagine twelve very young healthy children growing up with at least two 'good-enough' parents.

1. Henrietta seems to need her mother all the time. She is most cuddly and blissful when at the breast and gets very, very angry when her mother is not there, screaming until she returns. Her face shows remarkable contrast between her happy moods and her cross moods, which change very quickly. Her parents can't always find out what she's upset about. They are exhausted.

2. Ari goes to strangers without much trouble and sticks everything he finds in his mouth. He hates being bored and likes noise. He has trouble falling asleep. He doesn't scream, he bellows loudly and long – even when he's just been changed or fed. His parents need to keep a careful watch on him because he wriggles himself to the end of the bed or constantly tries to get out of his cot.

3. Persi is a sensitive and rather fearful baby. She is rather quiet, doesn't cry a lot, but also needs her mother there all the time. When she wakes up at night she doesn't really cry; she mostly kind of whimpers. She doesn't sleep well and can't tolerate sleeping alone. Compared with the other two, she is on the passive side, rather letting people play with her until she feels that she can trust them before she engages. Her parents often worry about her health.

4. Neptus, on the other hand, doesn't cry too much, but also wakes up with night terrors. It's a bit uncanny, but he appears to sense his parents' moods, being quiet and watchful when they are tired and happy when they are happy. He is fearful of strangers and sudden changes in the home atmosphere, such as a party or many visitors.

5. Dite is a cry-baby. She cries about anything; sometimes it looks as if it is for the sake of crying. She needs a lot of attention. However, she's also a very responsive baby, loving, cuddly and adorable with her big eyes and little fingers. She often gets sick. She tires her parents out with worry, but they just love her.

6. Heptus is a much quieter child. He loves hanging on to his mother no matter what she is doing. He is forever pulling her hair to bring her face near or pulling at her necklace. He gets despondent when she's not there and sometimes, like the cat in the house, won't engage with her till some time after she has made some effort with him on coming home.

7. Atty is the archetypal good baby. She sleeps well and eats moderately. She plays with a fair amount of enthusiasm. She likes to follow a routine

and gets upset when things are not done in the right order for her. (First this, then that, then the story.) Changes in the pattern of the household really upset her and she does not like going in the car. She sometimes goes on with an activity too long for her parents.

8. Zade is the curious one - clearly a bright child. His eyes appear to focus on faces; he likes playing hand games, often initiating them. It almost looks as if he is studying the pictures on the wall. He doesn't sleep much, but sleeps well when he does. He is very eager to try out sounds and gestures and learned to speak very early. A confident, outgoing baby, he knows how to make his parents smile.

9. Metir needs her mother with her at all times to feel safe. If mother is out of her sight, she gets miserable and often ill. She's the clingy one. Otherwise she's a model baby, sleeping well, responding to play without being so demanding that she tires her parents out like Henrietta or Dite or Ari.

10. Brad is a rather serious, perhaps even sad, baby. It is difficult to make him laugh. He appears to spend a lot of the time thinking, not playing. Often it appears as if he just doesn't know what he wants - a bottle, a toy, what? His nursing patterns vary: sometimes it seems he just can't get enough; other times he just falls asleep at the breast.

11. Hermi is a rather puzzling child to his parents. They don't quite understand him like their other children when they were infants. Often they feel they are doing something wrong, but it's difficult to put a finger on what it is. Although he is a little unpredictable in terms of eating and sleeping, at least he is not demanding like some of the others.

12. Hesti is also a 'good baby'. She goes to sleep easily and soon sleeps all night. She doesn't appear to mind if her mother leaves her alone. Sometimes when she's supposed to be asleep, her parents discover her with her eyes wide open, but deeply peaceful. She feeds easily and well. Sometimes her mother worries that she's 'too good to be true', but her parents count their blessings from the angels on having such an 'easy child'.

How would you 'diagnose' these youngsters?

Are they 'abnormal' so as to deserve a psychiatrically based classification? Did they contract to be diagnosed by you? If you say no, it could be pointed out that colleagues and acquaintances are not our patients either. Therefore all diagnostic descriptions are non-contractual, offensive and unethical in terms of our obligations to each other as colleagues, to our profession and to our contractual patients - where such attention may be needed. However:

Is Henrietta a borderline, Ari an anti-social, Persi an avoidant, Neptus a paranoid, Dite a histrionic, Heptus a passive-aggressive, Atty an obsessive-compulsive,

Zade a narcissist, Metir a dependent, Brad a depressive, Hermi a schizotypal and Hesti a schizoid personality disorder?

Or do they already have these 'personality adaptations'? And if so, why? Why if, like the Waltons, they all were born to the same parents, born on the same day and grew up in the same household, did they not all 'adapt' in similar ways?

Berne (1972) asked each of six adults why three of them ended up as psychiatrists and three ended up as mental patients? Each one answered: 'My parents were crazy.' Berne located the source of variety and difference in the uniquely creative script decisions individual children make – given their respective genetic endowments and social circumstances.

A first nature typology

Different writers use different classifications to attach meaning to these patterns of differences. I researched this theme already in my first PhD thesis (Clarkson, 1975). To simplify this vastly, we can say that there are distinctions between the extremes of speed (fast or slow) and between the volumes (strong or gentle). Thus we get four major temperamental types (with infinite variations in between): fast and strong; slow and strong; fast and gentle; slow and gentle. It often helps to *imagine* that it describes the relative strength and speed with which data (sensations, information, perceptions) are transmitted at our synaptic neurons.

If we imagine this as the basic rhythm and volume (or amplitude) of a person's life-force pulsing – their temperamental beat – we could imagine it in vibrational or musical terms. Visually I think a waveform represents it best (Figure 2.1).

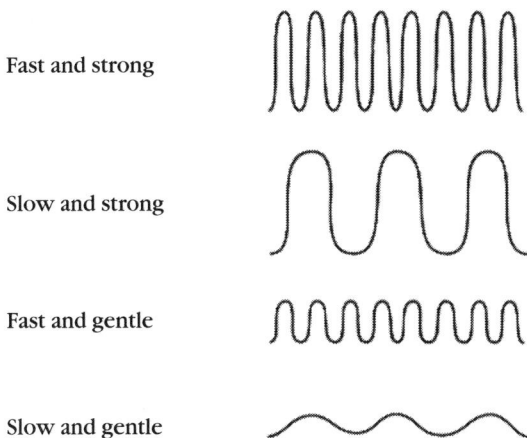

Fast and strong

Slow and strong

Fast and gentle

Slow and gentle

Figure 2.1 The four temperaments in waveform: (a) fast and strong; (b) slow and strong; (c) fast and gentle; and (d) slow and gentle.

Perhaps we could also then experiment with, for example, using musical terms to describe different kinds of adults by temperament, rather than by diagnosis. Perhaps we have different individual rhythms (as with our fingerprints). Then the task of the skilled psychotherapist, like that of the skilled musician, is to be able to play with, create dances or duets with, different kinds of volume and different kinds of tempo. This is another way of understanding *attunement*.

Any categorization reduces complexity and could also be abused by losing sight of the infinite variety of individual uniqueness. However, if some typology could be useful at some times, we could imagine 12 different kinds of individuals, knowing that each one can expand their range to their own aspirations (Table 2.1). It is possible that each one will be able to do that best if they attune themselves more, rather than less, to the cyclic rhythms of physis in their individual lives. After all, *the only thing in the world we can ever be perfect at is being ourselves*.

Imagine that these people are engaged with work and love in ways that are individually meaningful to them, that they have made some meaning to their lives, and that they can tolerate and learn from the happy and unhappy experiences that existence brings to us all. Note that contrary to appearances, these typologies are not gender specific.

Conclusion

This is of course just another story, another way of looking at people, *listening* to their physis, attuning to who they could be in fulfilment of their individual, unique potentials. Perhaps you could experiment with using it for at least as long as you have been (if perhaps you even sometimes have been) adapting to the use of using psychiatrically based diagnostic categories. Let me know how you get on.

Valuing difference

In a society where all socially acceptable women have their feet broken, the one who resists is crazy. In a world where adjusting to a corrupt social order or an unjust democracy is normal, the questioning individual is held to be bad or mad. In a society where mental health is defined at the expense of difference, we stand to lose ourselves indeed.

But we could also lose much more – the requisite variety that can give our children, our students, our societies the vibrancy of life, all the colours and smells of the spectrum – the vitality of experiencing one's true self as in the marching to the beat of a different drum – one's own.

Table 2.1 Twelve different kinds of individuals

Forte Staccato	Passionate Henrietta	We are the vibrant, intense and vivid people whose emotions can suddenly change from one extreme to another	Marilyn Monroe
Forte Staccato	Brave Ari	We are the impulsive, courageous ones who take risks, who enjoy fighting and winning	Che Guevara
Forte Staccato Con sordino	Sensitive Persi	We have an extremely intense inner life which you may not notice	Marie Curie
Forte Allegro	Intuitive Neptus	We are the passionate seekers after truth, the understanding of the universe, of things and of people	Einstein
Forte Allegro	Romantic Dite	We are the intense, emotional people who thrive on the excitement of relationships	Princess Diana
Forte Allegro Con sordino	Loving Heptus	We are the steady, quiet, loyal ones who have great endurance and perseverance	Churchill
Piano Adagio	Conscientious Atty	We are the careful, determined and responsible people	Swiss bankers
Piano Adagio	Creative Zade	We are the shining people for whom following our creative daimon is most important	Van Gogh
Piano Adagio Con sordino	Devoted Metir	We are the people who need to devote our lives to others	Mother Teresa
Piano Lento	Idealistic Brad	We are the leaders, seeking and acting for justice and a better world	John F. Kennedy
Piano Lento	Inventive Hermi	We are the soul of the party, charming and very well-informed about the world	Fred Astaire
Piano Lento Con sordino	Spiritual Hesti	We are the compassionate people who are quietly engaged in meditation and reflection	St Theresa d'Avignon

References

Berne, E. (1967) Games People Play. Harmondsworth: Penguin.

Berne, E. (1972) What Do You Say After You Say Hello? New York: Grove Press.

Bollas, C. (1989) Forces of Destiny: Psychoanalysis and human idiom. London: Free Association Books.

Bracchi, P. and Hewett, R. (2000) Daily Mail, 17 March.

Chess, S. and Thomas, A. (1986) Temperament in Clinical Practice. New York: Guilford Press.

Clarkson, P. (1975) Quantitative research in clinical psychology, PhD thesis, Rand Afrikaans University, South Africa.

Clarkson, P. (1989) Metanoia: a process of transformation. Institute of Transactional Analysis News 23: 5-15 (also published in 1989 in Transactional Analysis Journal 19: 224-234).

Clarkson, P. (1992) Transactional Analysis Psychotherapy: An integrated approach. London: Routledge.

Clarkson, P. (1996) The archetype of physis: the soul of Nature – our nature. Harvest: Journal for Jungian Studies 42: 70-93.

Clarkson, P. (1998) Writing as research in counselling psychology and related disciplines. In: Clarkson, P. (ed.), Counselling Psychology: Integrating theory, research and supervised practice. London: Routledge, pp. 300-307.

Clarkson, P. (2003a) How to Overcome Your Secret Fear of Failure: Recognizing and beating your 'Achilles syndrome'. London: Vega (first published in 1994 as The Achilles Syndrome – The secret fear of failure, London: Element).

Clarkson, P. (2003b) Philosophy for psychology: Reality ain't what it used to be – perhaps it's evolved! Clinical Psychology Forum.

Cornell, W. (1988) Life script theory: A critical review from a developmental perspective. Transactional Analysis Journal 18: 270-282.

Draghi-Lorenz, R., Reddy, V. and Costall, A. (2001) Re-thinking the development of 'non-basic' emotions: a critical review of existing theories. Developmental Review 21: 263-304.

Ellenbogen, G.C. (ed.) (1987) Oral Sadism and the Vegetarian Personality: Readings from the Journal of Polymorphous Perversity. New York: Brunner/Mazel.

Frank, J.D. and Frank, J.B. (1993) Persuasion and Healing: A comparative study of psychotherapy, 3rd edn. Baltimore, MA: Johns Hopkins University Press.

Goulding, M.M. and Goulding R.L. (1979) Changing Lives Through Redecision Therapy. New York: Brunner/Mazel.

Hardy, F. (2000) 'Weekend' magazine: 'Oh Boy! The Waltons Hit Sweet 16'. Daily Mail, 18 March.

Hillman, H. (1996) The Soul's Code: In search of character and calling. New York: Random House.

Howell, E. and Bayes, M. (1981) Women and Mental Health. New York: Basic Books.

Illich, I. (1975) Medical Nemesis: The expropriation of health. London: Calder & Boyars.

Jung, C.G. (1971) Psychological Types, C.W. 6. London: Routledge & Kegan Paul.

Laing, R.D. (1965) The Divided Self. Harmondsworth: Penguin.

Onions, C.T. (1973) Shorter Oxford English Dictionary. Oxford: Oxford University Press.

Samuels, A. (1993) The Political Psyche. London: Routledge.

Snyder, C.R. and Lopez, S.J. (2002) Handbook of Positive Psychology. Oxford: Oxford University Press.

Socarides, C.W. (1995) A Freedom Too Far: Homosexuality. New York: Roberkai.

Steiner, C.M. (1974) The Radical Therapist. Harmondsworth: Penguin.

Szasz, T. (1961) The Myth of Mental Illness: Foundations of a theory of personal conduct. New York: Hoeber-Harper.

Van Dijk, T.A. (1987) Communicating Racism – Ethnic prejudice in thought and talk. London: Sage.

Wolf, N. (1990) The Beauty Myth. London: Chatto & Windus.

Chapter 3
Conditions for Excellence: the *coincidentia oppositorum* of the inferior function

Jung's typological differentiations (the feeling, thinking, intuitive and sensation functions whether introverted or extraverted in attitude) are dynamic structures which contain the seeds of their opposites. Contrary to the usual counsel of concentrating on the development of the inferior function, this chapter proposes a reversal (or alternative) of attitude which suggests that if the superior function is developed to its fullest extent, it will tend to an enantiodromia – a turning into its opposite. This means that there can come into being a natural and even superior manifestation of the inferior function which is more of the hallmark of gift or genius or extraordinary talent than the prescription for the linear and incremental development patterns more usually associated with the development of the inferior function itself.

This hypothesis is offered here with some indicative clinical and historical examples for discussion, exploration and testing by students and colleagues in terms of their own subjective life experiences, their experiences of personality fulfilment in therapy and analysis, and even perhaps empirical validation.

Simply stated, it allows for the cases where dominant function is not inhibited, but allowed to flourish in their extreme, that the so-called 'inferior function' may manifest at a higher order of complexity, functionality and excellence. Thus thinking function may manifest as feeling function *in excelsis* or in its apotheosis. Similarly, feeling function transforms into a higher order of thinking when fully unfolded. Sensation likewise yields in its extreme the development of intuitive or even psychic insights, and intuition finds its enantiodromic peak in sensation function outcomes of remarkable acuity and success.

'Dealing seriously' with the inferior function

The concept of 'dealing seriously' comes from von Franz (1971b, p. 59). Jung, in his 'masterpiece' *Psychological Types* (1944) defines the inferior function as the term

> used to denote the function that remains in arrear in the process of differentiation. . . . Very frequently, indeed as a general rule, a man identifies himself more or less completely with the most favoured, hence the most developed, function. It is this circumstance which gives rise to psychological types. But, as a consequence of such a one-sided process of development, one or more functions necessarily remain backward in development. Such functions, therefore, may be fittingly termed 'inferior' in the psychological, though not in the psycho-pathological, sense, since these retarded functions are in no way morbid but merely backward as compared with the more favoured function (pp. 563-564).

Von Franz (1971b) writes that 'Jung found that active imagination was practically the only means for dealing with the fourth function' (pp. 63-64).

> Jung says that the process [of individuation] seems not to tend toward perfection but towards completeness. This means, I think, that you cannot get the thing up to the upper level (of the diagram) [see von Franz, 1971b, p. 60] but *you* have to come *down*, and that means a relative lowering of the level of the personality. If you are in the middle, the one side is not as dark, and there is more a tendency to constitute a kind of completeness which is neither too light not [sic] too dark.
>
> von Franz (1971b, p. 67)

She says that 'going to it and staying with it, not just taking a quick bath in it, effects a tremendous change in the whole structure of the personality' (p. 59). 'For instance, remaining with the difficulty for a long time, giving up other occupations in order to have enough time and energy for this main problem, practicing a kind of asceticism' (p. 65). She goes on to liken this effort to the discipline and rigours of monastic life. Also, in conversation with many of my colleagues, the received wisdom is that the inferior function needs to be developed, paid specific and painstaking attention to, and nurtured. One of the images is to treat it as the 'learning disabled' brother in the fairy stories – 'the devil in the corner' (p. 66) of one's life.

> Of course, it is often just this despised, unfavoured, symbolic brother who finally discovers the secret or the treasure. Furthermore, the inferior function has the 'strange character of wholeness, the mystical aspect, which the inferior function often has. . . . [It] is connected with [the individual's] deepest and greatest concern'.
>
> von Franz (1971a, p. 36)

Its deep-rootedness in the unconscious and its reluctance to come into the 'order of the day', its sometimes dogged and always hermetic ways of hiding from the harsh light of analysis or being 'forced' like bulbs for Christmas, is a problem only if it is a psychotherapeutic imperative that 'where unconscious was, consciousness should be'. Under such a regime, this 'regressive' function must be made to go to school, sit still and concentrate and perhaps, against his natural inclination, even be made to learn how to write with his right hand. If, however, we see the unconscious not only as a storehouse of personal memories, painful conflicts and repressed contents, but also as a treasure-trove containing all the richness of all cultures, archaic repositories of wisdom well beyond our capacity to imagine, and the very taproot of the sublime, then the so-called inferior function contains the alchemical secret of magical, immediate and totally transformative processes which can not only turn around the direction of individual lives and collective history, but also birth the genius in each one of us, or in all of us together.

According to von Franz this transformative moment often has the character of 'suddenness [which] snaps into the opposite'.

> The inferior function cannot be assimilated within the structure of the conscious attitude; it is too deeply implicated and contaminated by the unconscious. . . . Touching the inferior function resembles an inner breakdown at a certain crucial point of one's life. It has the advantage, however, of overcoming the tyranny of the dominant function in the ego complex.
>
> von Franz (1971b, p. 59)

Von Franz (1971b) says 'the fourth door of your room is where the angels can come in, but also devils!' (p. 72). Jung, von Franz and others have written well about that aspect. 'The inferior function, located as it is within the shadow [the part of the psyche not in the light] will find its place where it will not remain subordinated as do all the vicissitudes of the positive aspect of the shadow; usually this is in a concrete (prosaic) fashion; for example an intuitive type may be a good gardener, or a feeling type may play bridge rather well. This is not to be confused with the dynamic of excellence in the repressed function which is outlined in this chapter' (Adams, 1996, personal communication). I want to concentrate for a minute on how the angels can suddenly come in.

Enantiodromia

It is likely that this form of discontinuous, non-linear, second-order change in the manifestation of inferior function can characterize the sudden emergence of great gifts in individuals and the collective. It is similar to notions such as the 'flip-over effect' in chaos and complexity theory and the concept of the enantiodromia of Heraclitus which Jung also used.

These ideas are born from some 25 years of work as a psychotherapist, educator and supervisor of psychotherapists with a particular interest in and experience of working with highly creative, successful or gifted individuals with whom I have engaged in the intrapsychic and interpersonal conflicts, limitations and agonies of their personality development and their particular role in our collective evolution. In this sense, what I have to say will apply only to a small percentage of the population and then only to a small number of psychotherapists.

On the other hand, if we look at the problems of the few through a prism which sees individual problems as the problems of the collective writ small, we can consider that the work of the few is also the work of the many, perhaps just in smaller or different scales. 'As above, so below' read in terms of 'as inside, so outside' or 'as for the one, so for the many' (or fractal images on the computer, or patterns in the heavens).

An enantiodromic perspective has implications for how clinicians and educators view their task. It may even alleviate some of the iatrogenic distress caused by these professionals as well as the familiar and collective disapproval which so often tries to normalize, pathologize or regulate those who are 'the torch-bearers, chosen for that high office by nature herself' (Jung, 1954, p. 145).

> Enantiodromia means a 'running counter to'. In the philosophy of Heraclitus this concept is used to designate the play of opposites in the course of events, namely, the view which maintains that everything that exists goes over into its opposite. . . . I [Jung] use the term enantiodromia to describe the emergence of the unconscious opposite, with particular relation to its chronological sequence. This characteristic phenomenon occurs almost universally wherever an extreme, onesided tendency dominates the conscious life; for this involves the gradual development of an equally strong, unconscious counterposition, which first becomes manifest in an inhibition of conscious activities, and subsequently leads to an interruption of conscious direction. A good example of enantiodromia is seen in the psychology of Saul of Tarsus and his conversion to Christianity; as also in the story of the conversion of Raymond Lully; . . . in the transformation of Swedenborg from scholar into seer.
>
> Jung (1944, pp. 541-542)

The 'archaic attributes of the inferior function would erupt when an *abaissement du niveau mental* (lowering of consciousness) occurs, whether it is due to stress fatigue, or illness'. Yet, it may be that it is through these moments of lowering of consciousness, the emptying out of ego, that the angels erupt.

I suppose all of this is arguable, but I would like to propose these ideas, grounding them conceptually in Jung's first work and the work of von Franz. I think they are quite simple ideas, but with some potential. Wholeness is not achievable. Yet we are always whole. Always a cycle, like alchemy. And where one leads, the inferior will follow; and where the inferior was the inferior, it can become the superior. He who is last shall be first, and he who is first shall be the last.

Not comprehensive, only an idea. Examples are not meant to be exact or comprehensive, just indicative or suggestive. But sometimes because it becomes possible to see something, or the language develops a word, it becomes possible to see things (or ideas) which have always been there right in front of our eyes and perhaps to use them in a new way.

I am not going to summarize or discuss in detail matters about the typologies which are familiar (perhaps almost too familiar) to people in our field. This knowledge of the literature will be assumed in the following overview, as too will be the experience of some of the limitations imposed by clinical practice and personal experience on the received view when dealing with exceptional situations or exceptional people. In the absence of having at least felt or identified these problems, this way of intuiting a solution of practical use may simply not make sense enough to be useful.

A dynamic typology

Thus Jung's typology is reconceived as a dynamic system akin to the Taoist concept of change where the extreme of passive becomes an active and the extreme of active becomes a passive. In the words of the *I Ching*, the old Yang becomes a young Yin and the old Yin becomes a young Yang.

Too often Jung's typology, as it is used in practice, describes a fixed mode where the direction for development is frequently indicated as the development of the inferior function and the restraint or moderation of the superior function. The desired goal of such a conception tends to be wholeness, or a kind of homoeostatic outcome - certainly 'consciousness'.

In several places in *Psychological Types* (e.g. as quoted above, Jung, 1944, pp. 563-564) Jung uses the term inferior function in a sense which stresses that it is in 'arrear', regressive, and also of course its relationship with the shadow. He prescribes bringing the inferior function to consciousness, thus providing it with a new possibility of development. Yet there are also places and times where he says:

> The individual cannot give his life point and meaning unless he puts his ego at the service of a spiritual authority superordinate to man. The need to do this arises

from the fact that the ego never constitutes the whole of a man, but only the conscious part of him. The unconscious part, of unlimited extent, alone can complete him and make his a real totality.

Jung (1954, p. 143)

Then the 'deviation' from the mean 'takes place [not only . . . in the heights and depths of the same individual' (Jung, 1954, pp. 143-144) but also in our world.

In this chapter the perceived goals will not be directed toward developing inferior functions painstakingly to greater and greater consciousness - although this is quite an acceptable and fruitful route at times for some people. The potentiality signified here is toward the nourishment of superior functions to a stage of development (or a moment) where they transform to their opposites at a higher level of complexity or wholeness. It is as if the grammar of the inferior function may be deficient at one level, but capable of great poetry at another - but we have to conceive of such a possibility.

Exploring the possibilities of this perspective on typology opens the way to understanding more about the psychodynamics of creativity and genius in historical personalities, as well as new directions and emphasis in the analysis and the enablement of patients of great gifts. Often very creative personalities feel that analysis restricts and contains them. (This is of course not always true and many benefit greatly.) It is possible that in such cases the principles outlined here were unconsciously followed. It is also probable that conscious choicefulness about these possibilities can increase the flowering of the unique process of individuation where excellence in particular endeavours is the criterion. Always, another perspective may hold even a seed for more profound depths of understanding and greater achievements. It is only by sharing these ideas tentatively and in preliminary form at this stage, that other minds can begin to weigh in on this matter and help to refine and purify them.

The modifying influence and effects of the attitudes, extravert or introvert, on the functions as they are here used will have to wait for discussion in another paper.

It is well recognised that Jung was concerned with the dynamic of extraversion and introversion and its impact on typological functioning; in this [present] chapter the focus is unhampered in this respect, since post-Jungian thought has revisioned this troublesome dichotomy. Even so, it is certainly worth emphasising that enantiodromia may be more prevalent in coincidence with introversion, since the dynamic of reversal depends on an empathic original repression of the inferior function; a probability in those cases where the dominant function is less modified by social exchange.

Adams (1996, personal communication)

Naturally these ideas will be further verified, modified, found wanting or developed theoretically, clinically, experientially in our professional community.

The enantiodromia of the dominant thinking function becoming superior feeling

Definition of thinking function

Jung (1944) wrote that 'thinking is that psychological function which, in accordance with its own laws, brings given presentations into conceptual connection' (p. 611). It tends to be associated with lawyers, with analytical, linear, causal, logical, sequential styles of problem solving and dealing with the challenges of life. Dominant thinking function is most often (according to Jung, always) paired with inferior feeling – an inferiority of the 'subjective process' (p. 544).

Typical professional examples

When I use 'typical professional examples' in this chapter as an illustrative device, I *obviously* do not mean that 'all lawyers, or all physicists, or all entrepreneurs, or all detectives are . . .' – I use these as imaginative bridges for readers to fish for their own more real, more true, and more individually unique examples.

The profession which commonly is considered one of the exemplary manifestations of thinking function – the legal profession – has its training characterized by rote learning, by memory of many cases, the enhancement of reasoning to exclude subjective factors, mental exercises of logical rigour sometimes more demanding and punishing or rewarding because of its currency of financial assets, lives, freedom than philosophers in academia. The stereotypical judge in our culture, the wise woman or elder of the tribe in other cultures, represents the very storehouse of all the knowledge of the law and the reasonable application of those laws.

The culmination of legal expertise, the apotheosis of the profession (whether this is always true in fact or not) is embodied in the position of the judge – the great interpreter of the law and the functionary in the society which judges the veracity of facts, the indisputability of evidence, the 'just' verdict based on all the empirically established reasoned arguments. Thinking function at its highest – or?

Are the great judgements of the great judges indeed made on fact, or are they required to be made at the very borders of facticity at the end of all proof, in the regions beyond which intellect can no longer stand on its own feet? Where the knowledge of law ends, when we no longer know 'what to think', where does it go? When Solomon dispenses justice, he considers all the facts, all the evidence, the stories of both mothers, but his judgement rests on feeling – a very superior, gifted, exceptional kind of feeling.

> And the other woman said, Nay, but the living is my son, and the dead is thy son.
> And this said, No; but the dead is thy son, and the living is my son.
> Thus they spake before the king.
> . . . And the king said, Divide the living child in two, and give half to the one and half to the other.
> Then spake the woman whose the living child was unto the king, for her bowels yearned upon her son, and she said, O my lord, give her the living child, and in no wise slay it. But the other said, let it be neither mine nor mine, but divide it.
> The king answered and said, Give her the living child, and in no wise slay it: she is the mother thereof.'
>
> 1 Kings (3, 22-27)

At the far frontiers of thinking and reasoning, feeling culminates, the epiphany comes in the idiom of the opposite. Thinking reaches enantio-dromia in feeling. Jung (1944, p. 544) says:

> Hence feeling is also a kind of judging, differing, however, from an intellectual judgement, in that it does not aim at establishing an intellectual connection but is solely concerned with the setting up of a subjective criterion of acceptance or rejection.

So let's listen to Dworkin (1986, pp. 52-53) on legal judgement:

> If the raw data do not discriminate between . . . competing interpretations, each interpreter's choice must reflect his view of which interpretation proposes the most value for the practice – which one shows it in the better light, all things considered.

(And *value* is what feeling does – as we are reminded in the definition below.)

> But the story is something more besides; it is also a story where the sublime, propriety, self-sufficiency, decency – that is, religion and law – are never fully grasped, and are always kept at a distance. . . . Texts, including narratives of space, but especially narratives of the spacing of the sublime, open out perception to the space of narrative and the spaces in between, the elements that signify what the unknown signifying intention cannot intend.
>
> Douzinas et al. (1993, p. 182)

It is possible that the truly great artists, of which Leonardo da Vinci is an outstanding example, were dominant thinking types in the first place. Of course we can never analyse historical figures – but we can imagine. It is not hard to countenance the idea I am postulating here, if we see Leonardo in the legacy of his work as a scientist, as an engineer, or as an early chaoticist studying water turbulence. But what he is most truly remembered for, where he found the culmination of his enormous gifts, was in the transcendent 'finality without any end' of the painting whose name is now so famous that we can hardly pronounce it without honouring the angel. The angel who, however much we analyse the radioactive substrata of the paint pigments and preliminary scratchings, has simply mesmerized generation upon generation of those whose feeling functions only rose through education or inclination by incremental developmental trajectories to emulation or criticism or utter awe.

Clinical example

To end this section, I will let a patient – a so-called dominant thinking type – speak: one who spent many fruitless (by his account) years in analysis.

> I felt I was constantly being harangued to have my feelings, to respond from my subjectivity about my life, my marriage, my work. If I had dreams, they remained boring meanderings around my office, my feeble attempts at active imaginations more embarrassing than helpful. All along I subtly sensed that my analyst agreed with my wife (who had also gone into training as a psychoanalyst) that somehow I was lacking, failing in some important way because I did not have the emotional sensitivity, the affective intelligence which allowed them to assess situations easily and quickly by their emotional tone.
>
> I somehow felt their disapproval of my pre-occupation with conceptual and intellectual processes, and felt vaguely sick and defensive when accused of 'talking shop' over the dinner table with my friends who were working in quantum physics and complexity theory. I loved these discussions and felt exhilarated and valued for days afterward – until her disapproval blemished and tarnished whatever joy they had given me and whatever feelings of self-esteem and pleasurable discourse I had derived from them. She felt we had to be telling jokes or stories about our holidays with our friends if we were 'mentally healthy'. I always felt wrong, deficient, diagnosed and rejected in those aspects of my life I valued most highly. Years of an Oxbridge education don't come cheaply or easily and I had loved the life of the mind – if I can say it in such a way – with all my heart. I simply felt impotent when my wife raged at me to 'show my feelings', to weep or rage, when all I wanted to do was understand what she wanted from me. When I shed a tear, she wanted me to weep, when I restrained myself from shouting at her or the children, she warned me about the likelihood of developing cancer. When I read about Klein and went to courses on psychoanalysis, my analyst interpreted that to me as wanting to control her through my mind from my envy of my mother's fecundity.
>
> I got better and better at anticipating my analyst's interpretations and more and more depressed. I felt my greatest virtues, my mind, my intellect, my excitements were devalued and worthless whereas I would never ever be able to achieve the states of being which seemed so natural to others such as my wife. I

was successful, but my life lacked meaning. Too often I would sit in a pub at 11 o'clock wondering what it was all about and calculating rates and times of suicide by various causes.

I had originally gone into psychotherapy for liberation, but become progressively more oppressed. Not only the sites of my old injuries hurt, but weekly I had to assimilate new ones. I tried and tried to stop thinking and start feeling, but every attempt left me more demoralised and less confident that I would ever succeed. Finally I worked with a therapist who was intellectually my equal or superior with what I felt was due respect for the arts and crafts of the intellect. She offered me the opportunity to discuss with her the outer reaches of my intellectual imagination as I wrestled with the beginning of time, the architectural reasoning of the starry skies, the imponderability of 'what happens in a coffee cup when the cream goes in'. She also happened to have trained in Zen and gave me koans until my mind was exhausted. It happened suddenly one day in the middle of a meeting, the world opened and my mind cracked open, not breaking down, but breaking through. Impossible to say what happened, but the light just simply went on. I adore my new wife. We laugh and cry together and when I think, she joins me; when my thinking crashes into its barriers, we switch on the computer with its library of fractal images. I still worry too much sometimes, but the big prize came to me within two years of fully feeling the edges of my mind in this way. I don't know if, after all this time, I understand the 'meaning of life' any clearer. I know that I feel the meaning of life in my work and in my love.

Of course, there are many many ways to use psychotherapy or psychoanalysis to imprison, oppress and standardize or normalize. This is only one man's (fictionalized) story:

> Zen does not attempt to be intelligible, that is to say, capable of being understood by the intellect. The method of Zen is to baffle, excite, puzzle and exhaust the intellect until it is realised that intellection is only thinking about; . . . and then it contrives, when the disciple has been brought to an intellectual and emotional impasse, to bridge the gap between second-hand, conceptual contact with reality, and first-hand experience.
>
> Watts (1960, p. 19)

Sometimes it happens just so. And miracles sometimes follow.

The enantiodromia of the dominant feeling function becoming superior thinking

Definition of feeling function

Jung's (1944, p. 543) definition of feeling is as follows:

> Feeling is primarily a process that takes place between the ego and a given content, a process, moreover, that imparts to the content a definite value in the

sense of acceptance or rejection ('like' or 'dislike'); but it can also appear, as it were, isolated in the form of 'mood', quite apart from the momentary contents of consciousness or momentary sensations.

And this concern with value is characteristic of so many great physicists.

What then, is in our opinion the value of natural science? I answer: Its scope, aim and value is the same as that of any other branch of human knowledge. Nay, none of them alone, only the union of them all, has any scope or value at all, and that is simply enough described. . . . In the brief impressive rhetoric of Plotinus, 'And we, who are we anyhow?'

Erwin Schrödinger in Cropper (1970, p. 98)

Typical professional examples

In the preface to his book *The Quantum Physicists*, Cropper (1970, p. viii) writes:

The theory [of quantum physics] emerges, from all the accidents, mistakes, and controversies which brought it into being, like a great painting materializing from the chaos of the artist's studio, with pure beautiful lines and magnificent vision.

Many theoretical physicists of world-class level have tended to do badly at school, fail A-level mathematics and in such ways show their distaste, disorientation or distance from what would usually be considered good or very good thinking function (as displayed by individuals who tend to do academically well within Eurocentric cultures who value this capacity).

Theoretical physicists, mathematicians or theoretical scientists in the new sciences of chaos and complexity theory are for many of us the quintessence of thinking types. Yet the road to achievement in this area runs notoriously, often and strangely enough, through heightened incremental development in feeling function and then a sudden leap into 'a way of thinking' which is described or experienced as strangely discontinuous with ordinary thinking, e.g. Schrödinger (in Cropper, 1970, p. 4):

As our mental eye penetrates into smaller and smaller distances and shorter and shorter times, we find nature behaving so entirely differently from what we observe in visible and palpable bodies of our surroundings that *no* model shaped after our large scale experiences can ever be 'true'. A completely satisfactory model *of this type* is not only practically inaccessible, but not even thinkable. Or, to be more precise, we can, of course, think it, but however we think it, it is wrong; not perhaps quite as meaningless as a 'triangular circle,' but much more so than a 'winged lion'.

When he read Planck's theory, Einstein (in Cropper, 1970, p. 7) said: 'It was as if the ground had been pulled from under me, with no firm foundation seen anywhere upon which one could have built'. This is a good description of the vertiginous experience of enantiodromia – in this case, when feeling reaches enantiodromia in thinking of a very superior order. It was clear from childhood that Einstein, a mediocre student, was hardly what we would now call a 'dominant thinking type'. His teacher was sure that he would 'never amount to anything'; he was refused admission to the Hochschüle in Zurich, and passed many of the next exams 'with the help of a friend'.

When he writes about his criticism of the educational system it is in feeling function terms. 'The coercion had such a deterring effect that, after I had passed the final examination, I found consideration of any scientific problems *distasteful* to me for an entire year . . .' [italics added] (Einstein in Cropper, 1970, p. 18).

One of the masterpieces of world literature – Marcel Proust's – *Remembrance of Things Past* sprang from fully feeling into the aroma of a piece of madeleine biscuit soaked in a cup of tea. The laborious and detailed writing down in novelistic form of several thousand pages, in three monumental novels, which resulted from one fully experienced moment, required sustained thinking and logical concentration of a very superior kind. In particular, it drew on the rich resources of memory which can be the downfall of the feeling type (Mann et al., 1968) but transforms what could be only a felt state into a work where beauty blends with logic, and the thoughtful and intelligent construction of a whole life emerges aesthetically, but also particularly intelligently.

It is salutary to reread the whole 'overture' to feel and empathize with his struggle of transforming feeling into a thoughtful act of creation. It is not an avoidance of the superior function of feeling, it is an immersion.

> What an abyss of uncertainty whenever the mind feels overtaken by itself; when it, the seeker, is at the same time the dark region through which it must go seeking and where all its equipment will avail it nothing. Seek? More than that: create. It is face to face with something which does not yet exist, to which it alone can give reality and substance, which it alone can bring into the light of day.
>
> Proust (1983, p. 49)

In more of his own words:

> And I begin again to ask myself what it could have been, this unremembered state which brought with it no logical proof, but the indisputable evidence of its felicity, its reality, and in whose presence other states of consciousness melted and vanished. . . . And then for the second time I clear an empty space in front of it; I place in position before my mind's eye the still recent taste of that first mouthful, and I feel something start within me, something that leaves its resting-place and attempts to rise, something that has been embedded like an anchor at a great depth; I do not know yet what it is, but I can feel it mounting slowing; I can measure the resistance, I can hear the echo of great spaces traversed. . . . Ten

times over I must essay the task, must lean over the abyss. And each time the
cowardice that deters us from every difficult task, every important enterprise, has
urged me to leave the thing alone, to drink my tea and to think merely of the
worries of to-day and my hopes for to-morrow, which can be brooded over
painlessly. And suddenly the memory revealed itself.

                                                                    Proust (1983, pp. 49–50)

Notice again the experience of 'emptying out', the enormous effort of will to
feeling – fully and the 'sudden-ness' of the transformation from this
apotheosis of feeling into very superior thinking in 'a higher octave'.

Joseph Beuys is also a very good example of a person with superior
feeling function whose apotheosis in thinking led to the eventual
recognition of his status as the seminal conceptual artist of our time. Much of
his art, too, drew from his memory of the past, the times when he was very
seriously burnt in a wartime aeroplane and people from a Tartar tribe found
him and kept him alive by wrapping his body in animal fat and felt until he
had healed. This became a fractal image for his art.

Beuys – the artist and the teacher of artists – displayed a clear superior
feeling function, finding and enabling transformation into thinking. Sacks
(1995) described how he helped students who 'were unlikely to have "made
it" as professional artists; in an exam system, measured on the quality and
quantity of their products they would have failed' (p. 57). But he reminded at
least one of them to begin with her pain, her depression, her feeling.

You can only begin with this, as you yourself have found. You cannot go beyond
this. The work that you are forcing yourself to do is contrived, without
motivation, unloved. Don't ask yourself where it will lead, don't pressurise
yourself, just enter your world. Write down, draw, document everything that you
think, that you do, that comes to mind. Write down what you feel and what you
see, what you imagine, what you hope for. Then let us see what happens.

                                                                    Sacks (1995, p. 56)

The works of art that Beuys produced relied heavily on an enjoyment of
evaluative contact with the unconventional materials he used (e.g. fat and
felt) significantly of value to him from his own past history – which he
himself always kept alive in significant ways in the materials he used for his
work. However, his prominence as a great innovator in twentieth century art
comes from his conceptual work which involved what appear as highly
developed, complex thinking processes such as the various 'happenings' –
staged events presented as works of art – where a strange leakage from the
unconscious into reality was allowed to occur. Bearing in mind that the
inferior function is that process which remains partially submerged in the

unconscious, Beuys' conceptual art can be seen in terms of these complex thinking processes manifesting at the superior extreme of his feeling function abilities. In his educational work we can see how he does not force the feeling person to develop their thinking, but he encourages, even prescribes, a total and complete immersion in feeling, trusting that from that something new might happen of far greater quality than had been made hithertofore.

Clinical example

She had always kept diaries, many dozens of them. Her attic held them, brightly covered in colourful pictures representing the phases and moods of the time in which they had been written; little locks and little keys kept them from prying eyes, and handmade ribbon stained with the blues and crimson of organic dye tied the bundles. She said she 'had written her heart out in these journals', her soul was contained in them. Of course she had been sexually abused as a child by her father since she was (perhaps?) four years old. Maybe he had used her mouth for fellatio since she was a baby. Her dreams told her these things, and her body ached in many places and was always hungry no matter what she ate or how.

She always acted on her feelings, judging friends and acquaintances by their taste, their beauty, their expression of the values she held dearest. If we were using astrological imagery, we might say that she had many planets in Libra and Venus rising. She was admired by all her friends for her exquisite and appropriate gifts at birthdays and Christmas time. Her previous marriage had been to a brilliant but ruthless man, large in the city, but very absent at home. He provided well for her and her children, but was painfully insistent on unloving sexual intercourse which, if she refused, seemed to abandon her to a desert of excusing phonecalls. None the less she needed him. 'I like being a wife', she said and was devastated when he finally left after another one of his numerous, nonsensical, 'unimportant' affairs.

Her reaction was cataclysmic and suicidal. She experienced the terrors of birth, of childhood abuse, of archetypal hurricanes obliterating the known and loved world – the destruction of the known universe. Often she could identify with the terrorists or the death-wreaking storms in active imagination. She painted and wrote in her diaries and spilled out her feelings in art therapy, but it always remained 'carthartic' art – an expression of affect, bold, beautiful even, but unworked, untransformed, unshaped in a peculiar way – attractive, but ultimately personal. Pictures of little girls left to die in the snow, pretty girls sitting on fences, androgynous amazons scaling mountains in cumbersome boots. Too personal to be shared by others, and not unconsciously collectively personal enough (so to speak) to be universal. She was beautiful and the first analyst she went to fell in love with her. Never had he experienced such beauty of feeling, such rawness of emotion, such translucence of soul in a woman. She wanted help, but she also wanted nurture and protection. Anyway there was always something wonderfully entrancing about being loved by a man who is for the very first time emotionally moved by the force of a sexually desired vulnerable woman – open to his influence in all ways. To be his anima. To help him find the woman in himself. Made him write poetry again. Took the pain away for a little. New feelings – well, same feelings new again.

When she became suicidal because the analyst would not leave his wife for her, he stopped the analysis. She phoned and wrote letters and poems and sent him pictures – but none of it seemed to matter any more. He felt she was demanding, trying to 'devour' him, expecting more from him than he could realistically commit to at this moment in his life. She ended up in a psychiatric ward. He did not come to see her or contact her at all; he had decided to pay more attention to his family and his wife was not very well. She kept their affair secret even though she had ECT in the hospital and lost consciousness many times. His collection of poetry came out, she lost custody of the children.

Hell. The abyss. The chasm. The place where God forsakes and is forsaken. The dark night at the centre of the world forever. Dreams of revenge from time immemorial. Burnt witches. Trapped in a body flayed but bandaged in barbed wire. Agony every day. A hand to hold on to. Don't try to be different. Be fully who you are. Now. Fully present in the pain. All of it. Time passes. More. Eventually a moment of illumination. An embarkation on a Ph.D. programme – a desire to know, to study, to discipline, to have some of those cool, clear boundaried frontiers, knowledge of how to protect and how to avoid falling. The power and potency of having fallen. Success. Great success. Life goes on of course, but reason carves it into international recognition for a particular expertise, a coolness more sleek than Siamese cats, but with all the fiery enchantment of Thoth.

The enantiodromia of the dominant sensation function becoming superior intuition

> Sensation, or sensing is that psychological function which transmits a physical stimulus to perception. It is therefore identical with perceptions.
>
> Jung (1944, p. 585)

Typical professional examples

A person who lives by sensation in the present, such as is often the case with sports professionals, shows their greater gifts not in simply being faster, stronger, more practised – although all these count, of course. Sherlock Holmes baffles Watson because the sense perceptions are there for both of them to experience, yet the moment of intuitively knowing appears almost magical and discontinuous with the few grains of sand on the living room carpet. Then, like all intuitive psychotherapists, there are impressive *post facto* justifications to be made. Great masters of the martial arts train fully in sensation, developing it to its utmost, and then through the gift of intuition, they may 'irrationally know' the danger, the source of it, and spontaneously engage in the required action.

Just imagine those pictures of old and frail men on the Aikido mats who can disable six or ten strong grown men attacking them at the same time. In the ultimate moment, when anticipation reaches unhesitatingly for the future opportunity and sensation transforms into 'knowing, in the way that highly developed intuitives know' for certain, suddenly and indisputably where the gap is, like the great goalscorers of footballing history. In a book devoted to the spiritual dimension of the martial arts (Payne, 1981) there is an illustration of the:

> . . . karate sparring exercise, developed by Master Egami, [in which] the opponents stand at some distance from each other. On the teacher's signal, they both attack; but the point of the exercise is that their actions should be simultaneous with the command of the teacher (not merely very shortly after it). This requires a spontaneity of action that transcends speed of reflex and approaches the telepathic. The participants do not react in response to some internal thought or external stimulus; their openness of mind allows a synchronistic harmony with their environment and thus a truly appropriate spontaneous action.
>
> Payne (1981, p. 93)

Sensation reaches enantiodromic perfection in a superior kind of intuition – one which is almost psychic. We know how psychics or clairvoyants often physically handle a ring, a photograph, yarrow-stalks, a hand or an astrological chart in order to enable them to 'see' the future. It is instructive to compare this with other times and other cultures.

> An American anthropologist with the magnificent name of Omar Khayyam Moore examined divination techniques used by the Indians in Labrador. These people are hunters, and failure to find food means hunger and possible death, so when meat is short they consult an oracle to determine in which direction they

should hunt. They hold the shoulder bone of a caribou over hot coals, and the cracks and spots caused by the heat are then interpreted like a map. The directions indicated by this oracle are random, but the system continues to be used, because it works. Moore reasons that, if they did not use the bone oracle, the Indians would return to where they had last hunted with success or where cover was good or water plentiful. This could lead to overhunting of certain areas, but the use of the oracle means that their forays are randomised; the regular pattern is broken up, and they make a better and more balanced use of the land, which means in the end that they are more successful. Some kinds of magic work.

Watson (1974, pp. 208-209)

Before we draw back too far, I also commend the reader to an introduction which Jung writes to Jaffé's (1979) *Apparitions: An Archetypal Approach to Death, Dreams and Ghosts*, in which prescience, premon-itions and prophetic dreams, amongst other perhaps 'psychic' phenomena, are explored.

An integral component of any nocturnal, numinous experience is the dimming of consciousness, the feeling that one is in the grip of something greater than oneself, the impossibility of exercising criticism, and the paralysis of the will. Under the impact of the experience, reason evaporates and another power spontaneously takes control - a most singular feeling which one willy-nilly hoards up as a secret treasure no matter how much one's reason may protest. That, indeed is the uncomprehended purpose of the experience - to make us feel the overpowering presence of a mystery.

Jaffé (1979, p. vii)

And in order to experience mystery the prophets of old go into the desert, and experience sensation's extremes, hunger, fear, pain, illness in order to return with illumined foresights. Here follows a story told by Meade which points to this.

The sweetness of life

Once many years ago, there was a great hunter who knew all the secrets of the bush and its inhabitants. When his wife told him she was pregnant, he knew that this would be his firstborn son. With the help of magic formulas, he lured the unborn boy out of the womb and took him hunting in the bush. He taught his son all his knowledge of the bush: which berries were edible, which flowers poisonous. He taught him about animals and birds, how they walk and fly, where they hide and when. When they came back, the hunter's wife was asleep, and he conjured the boy back into the womb; she didn't seem to notice.

The embryo was not taken out, no physical removal took place; the hunter, by means of his magical power, controlled the spirit of his unborn son. It was this spirit that accompanied him on his hunt, while the body went on growing in the womb. In this way, the spirit learned effortlessly while wandering the bush. Perhaps the spirit was really the hunter's father, about to be reborn as his son.

When the days were fulfilled for the son to be born, the women of the village assembled to sing songs in praise of the firstborn. And such a big baby! After a day or two, he could speak, and he refused his mother's milk, saying he craved meat, like all men of his rank. The third he began to creep; the next day he stood up, and after five days he could walk and run. He was grown up.

So the day after that, the son went hunting with his father, this time in the flesh. They heard the honey bird sing, and the father knew it would lead them to a tree where the bees had honey. They found it; the father told the son to receive the honeycombs as he took them from the bee's hive and put them in the calabash. 'But don't lick your fingers, for it is very bitter,' he said. The father wanted to control the honey himself, but he forgot that the son knew as much about the forest as he did. By the time the father climbed down, the son had eaten the honey.

The father was enraged. He decided to test the son's power. He knew the language of animals. He called the big beasts, the elephants, the buffalo, the lions. They all came charging at the son. The son did not blink. He took up a tree trunk and knocked all the animals to the ground. The father did not blink. He said, 'Not badly done. Now I would like a fire to roast all this meat. There's smoke on the horizon. That must be a village. Go get a burning log, while I guard our meat.'

The son went off toward the smoke. There was a village, but the villagers were big cannibal people, whose great noses always wished to smell delicious human meat. The son ran back as soon as he saw this tribe. But it was too late; a cannibal child had smelled him and seen him. The cannibal people all came running after him. The son came running into the clearing, shouting, 'Father, climb a tree and hide, monsters are coming after me!' The father thought, 'He is a boy, after all. What have I to fear in this forest?' The son managed to climb the tree unnoticed. But the cannibal people fell on the father before he could move. They feasted on him, every bit of him, enjoying it and licking their lips. Then they helped themselves to the pile of elephants, buffalo, and lions. When they were absolutely full, they returned to their village. There, they drank all the beer they had been brewing and settled down to a long satisfied sleep, as was their custom.

The son climbed down and followed them to the village. Once they were snoring away inside their huts, he tied shut the doors and set fire to them. They all died in the flames.

Nearby, the son found men and women prisoners who were being fattened for consumption by the cannibal tribe. He released them all. They made him their king. He married one of the women he had saved. They built new huts. The queen became pregnant. The new king knew it would be his firstborn son. He lured the unborn son out of the womb and took him hunting in the bush. He taught his son all he knew of the bush.

Meade (1993, pp. 70–72)

Clinical example

He was a scientist born and bred. His mother was a behavioural psychologist, his father dean of the faculty of engineering at a prestigious university. Exciting early outings which he remembered with delight were to the Museum of Natural History, early experiments the dissection of rats and insects to 'see how they worked'. As a boy, he excelled in sports and sciences. If he could not experience something through his senses, such as fairy stories and church, he was vociferously contemptuous of it. His greatest fears were 'being made a fool of' and 'being found out to be a fraud', notwithstanding his superior grades at school and university. He said that empiricism, in the sense of one who learns only from trial and error and rejects all '*a priori* knowledge [and whose knowledge, skills and authority] rests solely on experience and induction' (*Chambers' Twentieth Century Dictionary*), was his religion, if he had any. He even belonged to the Rationalist Society. In time he married a fine 'upstanding young woman' and his career progressed with due satisfaction until his wife was ready to go into hospital for the delivery of their baby.

He was in the delivery room when after several painful hours of labour his wife gave birth. The experience of that bundle of blood and life from the body of his wife shocked him into ecstasy. 'I experienced awe, wonder, miracles, the transcendent knowing that the meaning of life was beyond the senses.' The synchronous event of his laboratory being closed down seemed to him to be the very perfection of a higher plan. He yielded in some fundamental way and never quite returned to the man he was before. He turned toward the study of synchronicity and what is quaintly called 'wondrous events' in psychology, and eventually became an archetypal Jungian psychotherapist well known for his remarkable diagnostic powers – bordering on clairvoyance. In his society, he became the acknowledged expert in the selection of students and in the most effective matching of prospective patients and potential trainee psychotherapist/analysts or their more experienced colleagues.

The enantiodromia of the dominant intuition function becoming superior sensation

Here is a description of dominant intuition according to Jung (1944, pp. 567–568):

> It is that psychological function which transmits perceptions *in an unconscious way*. Everything, whether outer or inner objects or their associations, can be the object of this perception. . . . A kind of instinctive apprehension irrespective of the nature of its contents.

Typical professional examples

It is classically the dominant intuitive type of personalities who have inferior sensation function. They can't read maps, lose their keys, their glasses, their umbrellas. But, if they 'listen to their intuition', they often appear to be quite successful in our sensational world. Indeed it is said of Richard Branson that he is 'accident-prone' and loses his way when he is driving his car to a new destination. Apparently things to do with the sensational world often go wrong for him. This clearly has never seriously impeded his ability, indeed extraordinary talent, to make money, to find inventive and unusual ways of increasing his fortune and thereby also create many jobs and opportunities for others. He knows what should be done in the real world, the sensational world.

Many studies, of which Agor's (1984) is only one, have shown that one of the qualities effective managers rely on most seriously is their intuition. The particular quality which is valued is the capacity of intuitives to read the emerging conditions from the chaotic turbulence of world conditions, sense the shape of things to come. Body Shop managers have intuition on their lists of capabilities. It is obvious that it is the intuitives who usually 'just know' what the next fashionable colour, car shape, film genre will be, often long before and against all the advice of the thinking type accountants or bank managers. Although intuition is often spoken of in a derogatory (or envious) way as 'women's intuition', it is the function which distinguishes great strategists of war, captains of industry, the detective such as Sherlock Holmes who makes out that he 'deduces' facts from observation or the police officer who 'just smells out' whether someone is telling the truth or not. Reading the life stories of transformed criminals such as Jimmy Boyle (1977) we can also hear echoes or indications of the transformation from dominant sensation function to gifted intuitive – often the result from a sudden 'conversion'-type experience following immersion in sensation.

I have simply been on a journey and experienced terrible pain of a physical, spiritual and emotional nature and I want to stop those of my ilk from doing the same. . . . It was all of these thoughts that were racing through my mind and I hasten to add they were not all of an altruistic nature, but the complexity and intensity of them were giving me a hard time [pp. 239–40]. . . . If it was the opposite and someone needed support due to some problem, then everyone would reach out and touch him, and by that I mean help him over the bad patch. Either way the group meeting was a very powerful force [p. 245]. . . . I was concerned with helping myself and building for my own future but there was the wider issue in that I was now committed to helping the general situation on the penal and social fields. It was now that I was tasting a short spell on the outside that I realised just how committed I was to proving that people in hopeless situations like myself, who are serving very long sentences, can act responsibly and through their own experience, give something back into society [p. 257].

Usually by the time they know the facts, the moment for action, decision or 'the window of opportunity' has already passed. The more gifted and successful the intuitive, whether stockbroker or psychotherapist, the less likely they are to give concurrently good rational reasons for the actions they are certain should be taken at the time of their 'irrational knowing'. If the insurance is not taken out at the time they first say so, the burglary tends to happen anyway; if the flowers are not sent to the sick friend when the impulse arises, by the time it comes again they may have died; if the phone call to school is not made, something may go wrong – there are many examples of the effective and gifted use of intuition when it crosses the barrier from irrational knowing to knowing what to do, and where and how to act to accomplish what reason has not yet had time to explain. Gifted bodyworkers and healers of all persuasions work like this when they 'just know where and how to touch', as do inventors such as Pasteur and Edison when they suddenly know to what insignificant part of the field attention should be paid. (Frequently the observers, the collective or 'the establishment' reject them. Sometimes they are simply hounded to death by disapproval like Semmelweis, excommunicated like Galileo, or called 'crazy' by the state psychiatric system or their diagnostically-minded, more mediocre colleagues. By the time that time catches up with the truth of Cassandra's prophesies, those who disbelieved her may have had their humanity or their lives destroyed.)

Clinical example

She was a pretty 'average', middle-class, 'county' woman who cared for her children and husband with the Demeter-like concern expected from her culture. She used to be good at maths, but lost interest around the time she started menstruating and her interest turned to English literature. She did reasonably well at university, but never excelled. She was 'averagely' happily married. She was also very sensitive to her husband's life and her babies from the beginning – as many women like her are. She would often feel sure that he was on his way home from work – and it frequently turned out to be correct. She was so empathically attuned that she even experienced the physical sensations of her children, particularly the enuretic one. She would spontaneously wake up in the middle of the night when her child needed to go to the toilet. And she was right. Her psychotherapist took a dim view of this symbiosis. When her husband appointed new staff, he consulted her and she was usually right. When they argued, he said: 'You always want to be right without giving any reasons!' But the next day when he was cooler, he felt not only the 'injustice of the position' but also the injustice of not having her talent. When she said 'get the washing in before the storm', he learnt not to question, but to do it, even though there wasn't a cloud in the sky. When she said 'we'd better take out new private health insurance' even though they could hardly afford it, he did it, having learned from experience that most likely it would become clear in time why and how this had been the right thing to do at that time. When intuition reaches enantiodromia, it happens in superior sensation.

When her husband died she mourned for several years. She felt she would never truly overcome her grief, but eventually it faded. She became a stockbroker because her son was studying for his MBA and living with her at home during his finals. She made millions. She built a blue-chip company. She enjoyed that too. This is the dream foreseeing the end of her analysis.

> I was in the presence of two older women. One of them seemed to be my 'difficult' grandmother. But she faded into the background immediately. Both women were engaged in religious and spiritual pursuits. But the stranger definitely was more level-headed. She suggested I should do an 'exercise'. I was puzzled. She called it shedding of the skin. As she was explaining it to me a young woman was in fact performing the exercise. She put her head on to her chest. And it disappeared into her body. That's all I saw. Although I was slightly scared and apprehensive I told the woman I wanted to do the exercise. So I put my head on to my chest. . . . [It] entered my body. And from then on I had to completely trust the woman. I felt her hands curling my skin across my bones. I was completely soft. Even my bones. She proceeded to peel me, turn me inside out. I felt like a sausage, with an unsavoury skin. I felt this as I was 'peeled'. I remember thinking, 'How nice to get rid of that skin'. But at the same time I still didn't know if I'd ever get out of this very awkward situation! I could get completely stuck halfway through. . . . Those fearful thoughts crept through my mind as I felt my skin being pushed on my outside. I was still inside. It was awfully dark. . . . And then I felt a hand quite hard pushing at my head. And I saw light. I saw it from the inside of my own vagina. And I realised I was actually born from myself. I saw the shedded skin and even the umbilical cord, which had been cut off. I can't remember how I got 'out' – but when I was OUT I had a new skin and felt very fresh all over. And glowing . . .'

Conclusion

This chapter has reviewed Jung's typological differentiations (the feeling, thinking, intuitive and sensation functions, whether introverted or extraverted in attitude) as dynamic structures which contain the seeds of their opposites. Contrary to the usual counsel of concentrating on the development of the inferior function, this chapter suggests a reversal of (or alternative) attitude which suggests that if the superior function is developed to its fullest extent, it will tend to an enantiodromia – a turning into its opposite. This means that there can come into being a natural and even superior manifestation of the inferior function which is more the hallmark of gift or genius or extraordinary talent than the prescription for the linear and incremental development patterns more usually associated with the development of the inferior function itself.

This hypothesis was explained by means of general examples of professionals and historical figures as well as fictional clinical examples to explore cases where dominant function is not inhibited, but allowed to flourish in its extremity. The examples indicate possibilities that the so-called 'inferior function' may manifest at a higher order of complexity, functionality and excellence. Thus thinking function may manifest as feeling function *in excelsis* in its apotheosis. Similarly, feeling function transforms into a higher order of thinking when fully unfolded. Sensation likewise yields in its extreme the development of intuitive or even psychic insights, and intuition finds its enantiodromic peak in sensation function outcomes of remarkable acuity.

These conclusions may be of value to all people who wish to nurture their individual genius, but in particular may prove helpful to other clinicians working with those of exceptional gifts or those whose gifts and talents as children were limited, handicapped or punished.

References

Agor, W. (1984) Intuitive Management. Englewood Cliffs, NJ: Prentice-Hall.

Boyle, J. (1977) A Sense of Freedom. London: Pan.

Cropper, W.H. (1970) The Quantum Physicists: And an introduction to the physics. London: Oxford University Press.

Douzinas, C., Warrington, R. and McVeigh, S. (1993) Postmodern Jurisprudence: The law of text in the texts of law. London: Routledge.

Dworkin, R. (1986) Law's Empire. London: Fontana.

von Franz, M-L. (1971a) The four irrational types. In: von Franz, M-L. and Hillman, J. (eds), Lectures on Jung's Typology. New York: Spring Publications, pp. 22-37.

von Franz, M-L. (1971b) The role of inferior function in psychic development. In: von Franz, M-L. and Hillman, J. (eds), Lectures on Jung's Typology. New York: Spring Publications, pp. 54-72.

Jaffé, A. (1979) Apparitions: An archetypal approach to death, dreams and ghosts. Irving, TX: Spring Publications.

Jung, C. G. (1944) Psychological Types: Or the psychology of individuation (H.G. Baynes, trans.). London: Kegan Paul, Trench, Trubner.

Jung, C. G. (1954) Collected Works, Vol. 17. (eds Read, H., Fordham, M., Adler, G., trans. Hull, R.F.C). London: Routledge & Kegan Paul.

Mann, H., Siegler, M. and Osmond, H. (1968) The many worlds of time. Journal of Analytical Psychology 13(1): 33-56.

Meade, M. (1993) Men and the Water of Life: Initiation and the tempering of men. San Francisco, CA: Harper.

Payne, P. (1981) Martial Arts: The spiritual dimension. London: Thames and Hudson.

Proust, M. (1983) Remembrance of Things Past. Harmondsworth: Penguin. (First published in French in 1913.)

Sacks, S. (1995) Joseph Beuys' pedagogy and the work of James Hillman: The healing of art and the art of healing. Issues in Architecture, Art and Design 4(1): 52-73.

Watson, L. (1974) Supernature: A natural history of the supernatural. London: Coronet.

Watts, A.W. (1960) The Spirit of Zen: A way of life, work and art in the Far East. New York: Grove Press.

Chapter 4
In Praise of Speed, Experimentation, Agreeableness, Endurance and Excellence

This chapter reviews definitions of counterscript drivers and allowers in terms of the underlying values towards which self-actualizing people may aspire. Thus, the values of being fast, energetic, pleasing, strong and excellent, as prized qualities of the autonomous individual under the influence of physis (the generalized creative force of nature, which eternally 'strives to make things grow and to make growing things more perfect' [Berne, 1968, p. 89]) are differentiated from the counterscript drivers of 'be perfect', 'try hard', 'hurry up', 'please me' and 'be strong' under the influence of the script.

Kahler and Capers (1974) made a valuable contribution to transactional analysis (TA) in their formulation and explication of counterscript drivers and the concomitant allowers or permissions. They found five broad psychological patterns underlying compulsive and repetitive dysfunctional behaviour. However, as often happens with good ideas, eventually these concepts suffer from their popularity because the thought and care put into the original formulations are not always maintained in professional practice, e.g. traditionally, transactional analysts (whether in educational, organizational or clinical work) have worked to eliminate driver behaviours. In so far as a driver limits living life to the fullest, this goal has, to many psychotherapists, seemed worthwhile and important for script cure, growth or whatever other goal they and their clients had identified. However, over the years, as the theory has sometimes become embedded in and sometimes sullied by practice, prejudice and habit, this has occasionally led to some preventable misunderstandings.

Kahler (1975, p. 280) defined drivers as:

> . . . behaviours that last from a split second to no more than seven seconds. There are no feelings related to them. There is no way to feel a racket or play a stopper

tape without first going through driver behaviour (this is demonstrated behaviourally). Just as the stopping of the driver behaviour prevents the stopper tape from being played and the racket being felt, the stopping of the driver behaviour also prevents the concurrent script sentence (thought) patterns.

Counterscript drivers

Kahler and Capers (1974) identified the five basic counterscript drivers: 'hurry up', 'be perfect', 'try hard', 'please me' and 'be strong':

The 'Hurry Up' counterscript driver invites a person to do things faster, talk rapidly or more quickly. The person, when under this driver influence, believes that he must do everything right now. He may interrupt people, thus hurrying them up to finish their sentence, glance at his watch frequently, or tap his fingers impatiently. When he is demanding others to hurry, he is under this Hurry Up influence . . .

(p. 32)

When a person is under the influence of his 'Be Perfect' counterscript driver, he strives for perfection, or expects others to do so. He may use big words, tell more than he is asked to tell, or cover all the bases. He believes he has to give a great deal of information so that people will understand him just right. He is under the misconception that if he is not perfect, that means he is not-OK . . .

(p. 32)

When a person is under the influence of his 'Try Hard' counterscript driver, he invites others to try hard with him. He may not answer questions directly, may repeat questions, pause, go off on tangents, or say things like It's hard for me, or I don't know (when he actually does) . . .

(p. 32)

When a person is under the influence of his 'Be Strong' driver, he is stoic, holding in his feelings. He may talk in a monotone and evidence few signs of excitement . . .

(p. 32)

When a person is under the influence of his 'Please Me' driver, he feels responsible for making others feel good. He may freely agree with others. It may be important for him to be liked, and he may have an investment in getting the approval of others. He may look away before he answers questions, nod his head frequently, raise his eyebrows, say um humm often, or be interested in knowing How am I doing?

(p. 33)

This chapter is not intended as a criticism of Kahler's counterscript driver theory: he made it clear that there is more to psychotherapy than simply 'stopping counterscript drivers.

Allowers

Capers (Kahler and Capers, 1974) elaborated the OK miniscript in order to answer the question 'What can you substitute for the driver?': 'These reparenting messages selected by the patient, who knows his own needs, form the specifics for his allowers that are the antitheses to his drivers' (p. 33). For each driver, there is therefore an allower, as in Table 3.1.

Table 3.1 Drivers and allowers

Drivers	Allowers
Be perfect	It's OK to be yourself
Hurry up	It's OK to take your time
Try hard	It's OK to do it
Please me	It's OK to consider yourself and respect yourself
Be strong	It's OK to be open and to take care of your own needs

From Kahler and Capers (1974, p. 33).

These allowers are extremely important antitheses to the not-OK or dysfunctional life script, and they are often used effectively in psychotherapy and training. Allowers, as 'permissions' of a kind, can open psychological doors, provide options and be used in ways conducive to psychological health and growth. When used *ineffectively* such messages may be formed into a new counterscript, thus forming part of a 'counter-script cure' (Clarkson, 1988) that, despite the illusion of autonomy, maintains the script. By this I mean that people can make some superficial behavioural or cognitive changes that rapidly collapse under pressure or stress, such as the unreliable changes obtained by simplistic 'positive thinking' cognitive restructuring if they are not otherwise supported. However, the notion of 'stopping driver behaviours' may perhaps be misused as disguised opposition to people's natural drive to develop, grow and liberate themselves from the constraints of script (or repetitive dysfunctional life patterns).

Context

Drivers are occasionally interpreted as supporting the person's script or composing a new counterscript – neither of which is conducive to lasting script cure. In the permissive 1960s, a psychological refutation of oppressive collective Parent messages afforded, I believe, a necessary and important rebalancing for our society. However, as new, more liberating and permissive ethics have become part of our consciousness and clinical practice, there has often been another kind of imbalance. Certainly the concept of drivers is sometimes misunderstood and perhaps even abused by well-meaning and well-motivated clients (or trainees).

When parents (or other significant others such as teachers) originally give the counterscript messages such as 'be perfect', 'try hard', 'hurry up', 'please me' and 'be strong' to a child, they probably do so with the best of intentions. Of course few parents, teachers or religious leaders actually use precisely these very words. They may couch their advice in all kinds of verbal and non-verbal expressions, which children accurately or inaccurately decide to adopt in or out of awareness.

> The 'natural' Parent in the mother and father (as distinguished from the controlling Parent) is biologically programmed to some extent, and is naturally nurturing and protective. Both parents, whatever their inner problems, fundamentally wish Jeder [every person] well. They may be badly informed, but as 'natural' parents they are well-meaning, or at least harmless. They encourage Jeder in ways which, in their picture of the world and their theory of living, are meant to bring him well-being and success.
>
> Berne (1972, pp. 117–118)

It is only when these messages became linked conditionally to 'You are only OK if . . .' that they became destructive and part of the supporting structure of script. However, these messages are sometimes misunderstood or misinterpreted to mean that there is something wrong with a person's 'autonomous aspirations' (Berne, 1972, p.130) to be fast, energetic, pleasing, strong and excellent. Stated this way, it may appear obvious, but in practice it seems that some reminder of the original good intention behind these counterscript messages seems necessary. Also, as we know from TA re-decision theory, a child can make a decision to accept these drivers either as conditional limitations of OK-ness as a person *or* as guiding values that support the unfolding of his or her personhood.

Being fast, energetic, pleasing, strong and excellent is *not* the same as being in driver behaviour. However, these qualities can be mislabelled in such a way as to blunt the distinctions between driver behaviour and the autonomous Adult integration of parental values.

One reason for this may be the ubiquitous confusion between *being* and *doing*. I understand Berne's intentions as being to validate the essential OK-ness, worth or value of every human being separate to his or her doing, contribution or performance. Yet this does not mean an abrogation of the responsibilities of judging adequacy, competence and excellence in terms of performance.

The TA examination process

This distinction between being and doing, or personhood and performance, is well enshrined in the examination process of transactional analysts worldwide. Although someone taking an examination is considered to be OK as a person, his or her performance is assessed separately according to performance criteria. However, the psychological contamination between OK-ness for *being* and values about *doing* is often vividly experienced or enacted before or during examination situations.

This provides another opportunity for doing, re-doing or re-affirming the psychotherapeutic work that supports the *existence* of the person as separate and more fundamental than his or her performance. Thus, everybody is OK, and yet not everyone who starts training passes a TA examination. However, the person is *not* the performance and should never be subject to judgements that relate more appropriately to performance.

Steiner (1984) provided an important foundation for this in TA theory and practice with his concept of emotional literacy, which helps people to give negative feedback (conditional negative strokes) while discriminating such feedback from 'pigging' (the unconditional rejection of another person) (L. Collinson, personal communication, March 1985).

You may have heard the phrase 'reject the sin and not the sinner'. Most people can feel the difference between, for example, being shamed as a person because of a failure to live up to parental expectations in an exam *or* being particularly shown strategies on how examination marks can be improved.

Not everybody wants to run in the same races and not everybody wants to win the same prizes. 'Winning' or 'success' for Berne meant success in what you set for yourself as a goal, not in living up to other people's expectations. People who are learning disabled can be as or more successful by these definitions than a London City businessman – if they live the kind of life that they like and achieve their own goals. Life in itself is valuable and worth respect and dignity – whether or not the person is successful, performing or producing.

That is one principle, but it is not the only one. There is also a separate and different delight in performing, producing and being creative – and learning to become better and better according to certain other values. By exploring the values embedded in the original positive uses of drivers, we may learn something to our advantage.

Drivers and values

The 'hurry-up' driver

Dictionary definitions of the five counterscript drivers provide positive denotations for all but the 'hurry-up' driver. Hurry is defined as 'to carry, convey or cause to go with excessive haste; to carry or drive with impetuosity or without deliberation to some action, conduct or condition of mind' (Onions, 1973, p. 999). Yet the connotation of speedy efficiency used to be a TA examination criterion (crispness). Berne (1971) exhorted transactional analysts to cure as fast as they can. Another term used in teaching member examinations is pacing – balancing speed and intended content of teaching. The problem with hurrying is not speed, but the fact that it is usually ineffective in terms of outcome.

Other drivers

Onions (1973) defined *to please* as: 'to be agreeable; to give pleasure' (Onions, 1973, p. 1605). *Strong* is defined as: 'physically powerful; able to exert great muscular force; maintained with vigour that does not flag . . . having great moral power for endurance of effort firm in will or purpose; brave, resolute, steadfast . . . having great controlling power over persons and things, by reason of possession of authority, resources, or inherent qualities' (p. 2155). *Try* is honourable enough in meaning: 'an act of trying; an experiment, attempt, effort' (p. 2375).

Some of the dictionary definitions of perfect are:

> Thoroughly made, formed, done, performed, carried out, accomplished . . . free from any imperfection; faultless. Often used as a near approach to such a state, and hence capable of comparison . . . exact, correct. To complete, to carry through, accomplish . . . to bring to full development . . . to make perfect or faultless . . . to bring nearer to perfection; to improve.
>
> Onions (1973, p. 1553)

Distinguishing drivers from values

- What distinguishes *fast* from *hurry* is that fast gets things done on time *without* feeling rushed, e.g. the training material is well paced so that all parts are covered at optimum speed for understanding and assimilation.
- What distinguishes *pleasing agreeableness* from *compulsive adaptation* is that such pleasing is not compulsorily extended to everyone. Thus, the

person can tolerate not being pleasing without feeling a threat to his or her basic survival.

- What distinguishes *strong* as a value in favour of *endurance* or *vigour* is flexibility and appropriateness. Sometimes it is good to be strong and stoic, and to endure. It is only driver behaviour if the person believes that he or she has no other choices in different circumstances or with other people.
- What distinguishes *trying in the driver sense* from *trying in the experiential sense* is whether the effort succeeds in achieving the person's stated goal.
- What distinguishes *being perfect* from *striving for excellence* is whether excellence is achieved. Compulsive behaviour in a 'be perfect' driver does not lead to excellence, just as obsessive–compulsive symptomatology does not lead to mental health. In fact, the achievement of high standards is probably incompatible with a 'be perfect' driver.

These distinctions are meant to be indicative, not exhaustive. Drivers are not to be 'diagnosed' by content, but by a combination of behavioural, physical and psychological clues that indicate compliance with the driver. In the same way, psychotherapists need to invite clients out of driver behaviour in order to become genuinely healthy (or script-free), not simply coerce people out of driver contents or deny people the right to aim for betterment of themselves and their lives in ways that they choose and that are not harmful to others.

It is hoped that transactional analysts and their clients may sometimes remind themselves of these distinctions and work together to differentiate and discriminate further between *values* that are aspired to in the physis sense of a 'general creative force' (Berne, 1968, p. 91) and *oppressing messages* that are used to constrain and limit precisely these creative urges – our needs to aspire towards fuller selfhood as people and as professionals

It is important that we guard against calling 'script' that which we don't like in other people. For them it may not be a limitation of their potential or a restriction of their autonomy – in fact it may be a script-free celebration of their talent and ability. In the same sense, clients and trainees have found it helpful to be more discriminating and selective in terms of what we call 'counterscript' or 'drivers'. Sometimes what is called driver behaviour may be that which is envied in the other person.

To emphasize, a driver is defined by a specific set of behaviours which are observable and which 'reinforce an existential position of "I'm OK if . . ."' (Kahler, 1975, p. 283). One word, or even a few, from the miniscript chart (Kahler and Capers, 1974, p. 37) does not necessarily identify a driver. *A set of several such important behaviours occurring together relating to words, tones, gestures, posture, and facial expressions combined with physical feelings, beliefs and psychological or internal discounts, can be used to identify a driver. Furthermore, a driver 'structures a sequence of not-OKness' (Kahler and Capers, 1974, p. 29) and rackets are used to reinforce the script, i.e. lead to a limitation of the individual's potential.*

Being fast, enduring, pleasing, strong and excellent, or any combination of these, in achieving the individual's own stated goals by his or her personally chosen criteria, contraindicates driver behaviour because the essence of drivers seems to be the inherent ulterior intention to fail. Script-ridden individuals repeat the desire to achieve the scripted parental value (e.g. to please) but they do so in a way guaranteed to fail again – just as it did originally (Steiner, 1974).

I believe that humanistic existential psychotherapies such as TA have an important role in influencing the collective consciousness (or cultural Parent) as we move forward. What is necessary is to combine the passion, permissiveness and iconoclastic qualities of our heritage with precision, discipline and a respect for standards and excellence.

The aspirations to be fast, energetic, pleasing, strong and excellent are fine goals, profoundly compatible with a value base that places the fulfilment of human potential as a cornerstone of all its efforts, knowledge, practice, epistemology and ethics. That the pursuit of these values may be used to suppress potential or oppress individuals is undeniable, but there is often reason to guard against over-generalized caution against values that are, in fact, healthy and aspirational.

To aspire, according to MacDonald (1972, p. 75), means 'to desire eagerly; to aim at or strive for high things'. Surely this is one of the core ideas of the humanistic existential endeavour: to liberate human beings whether through education, example or psychotherapy, to become more fully themselves and, in Berne's (1968, p. 89) words, 'to make things grow and to make growing things more under the influence of Physis'.

This is *not* the perfection that is cautioned against by the counterscript drivers. This is the perfection that is already inherent in every human being according to his or her capacities or gifts. Every human being is at this moment being as perfectly him- or herself as is possible. Psychotherapists must realize that clients and colleagues are at any moment already manifesting the most perfect behaviours of which they are currently capable. In this way, perfection and aspiration become paradoxically reconciled. Only by accepting the perfect solution to the existential dilemma that is the script may it become possible, but not necessary, for an individual to get on their 'aspiration arrow' and change (Berne, 1972, p. 128).

Summary and conclusion

Berne pointed out that counter-injunctions (the prescriptions issued from Parent by the parent) originally had a benificent intent. An individual may make a set of decisions in compliance with the counter-injunctions, which then become the counterscript and begin to limit life by seeming to enforce controls and strictures that prevent its fullest blossoming (Stewart and Joines, 1987, p. 328).

In so far as the counterscript is used to limit the fulfilment of an individual's potential and awareness, and to eliminate driver behaviours, it is desirable and usually necessary for what has been called 'script cure'. However, the *values* of being fast, energetic, pleasing, strong and excellent need not be sacrificed in order to become script free. Indeed all these qualities are often reflected in the behaviour of the autonomous individual without it necessarily being counterscript. Aspiration (Berne, 1972, p. 130) to improve any of these qualities is part of the quest for the fulfilment of human potential (which was so close to Berne's heart).

To prevent this aspiration from becoming a new oppression, the psychotherapist would do well always to bear in mind the idea that people are already as perfect as they can currently be. This may remove some of the judgemental implications and conditionality of earlier prescriptive messages, but *without* sacrificing the aspirational drive of human beings towards self-actualization, self-fulfilment and responsibility.

References

Berne, E. (1968) A Layman's Guide to Psychiatry and Psychoanalysis. New York: Simon & Schuster.

Berne, E. (1971) Away from a theory of the impact of interpersonal interaction on non-verbal participation. Transactional Analysis Journal 1: 6–13.

Berne, E. (1972) What Do You Say After You Say Hello? New York: Bantam Books.

Clarkson, P. (1988) Script cure? A diagnostic pentagon of types of therapeutic change. Transactional Analysis Journal 18: 211–219.

Kahler, T. (1975) Drivers: The key to the process of scripts. Transactional Analysis Journal 5: 280–284.

Kahler, T. and Capers, H. (1974) The miniscript. Transactional Analysis Journal 4: 26–42.

MacDonald, A.M. (1972) Chambers Twentieth Century Dictionary. Edinburgh: W. & R. Chambers.

Onions, C.T. (ed.) (1973) The Shorter Oxford English Dictionary: On historical principles. Vols 1 and 2. Oxford: Clarendon Press.

Steiner, C.M. (1974) Scripts People Live: Transactional analysis of life scripts. New York: Grove Press.

Steiner, C.M. (1984) Emotional literacy. Transactional Analysis Journal 14: 162–173.

Stewart, I. and Joines, V. (1987) TA Today: A new introduction to transactional analysis. Nottingham: Lifespace Publishing.

Chapter 5
Reclamation of the Child I: phenomenology and the definition of ego states

Chapters 5 and 6 review transactional analysis (TA) as a *phenomenological* psychology according to Berne's stated intention, and recapitulate the understanding of ego and ego states, emphasizing the reality of the latter. Phenomenology is discussed, as well as the central role of time in psychic life. This is supplemented by understandings from modern physics. Definitions of structural (or phenomenological) Child ego states are then retrieved from Berne as well as other major TA theorists, and it is shown from both literature and subjective experience that there are at least two varieties of such Child ego states – fixated and accessible.

Although the functional (behavioural) model of ego states is specifically excluded from this discussion, making such a conceptually and theoretically coherent integration has advantages for whichever model of ego states is used. Psychoanalytic definitions of fixation are re-examined, and repression as a defence mechanism is differentiated from the evolutionary healthy process of orthriogenesis. A reminder of the nature of the Adult ego state, particularly in terms of its executive function, is followed by consideration of Child ego states in healthy functioning and creativity. This is followed by a summary showing how Child ego states are accessed in psychotherapy in order to focus on confusion, conflict or deficit models of treatment of the Child.

Introduction

The ultimate aim of transactional analysis is structural readjustment and reintegration. This requires first, restructuring, and secondly, reorganization. The 'anatomical' phase of restructuring consists of clarification and definition of ego boundaries by such processes as diagnostic refinement and decontamination. The 'physiological' phase is concerned with redistribution of cathexis through selective planned activation of specific ego states in specific ways with the goal of establishing the *hegemony of the Adult* [italics added] through social control. Reorganization generally features *reclamation of the Child* [italics added], with emendation or replacement of the Parent. Following this dynamic phase of reorganization, there is a secondary analytic phase which is an attempt to deconfuse the Child.

Berne (1975, p. 224)

I consider that the above and the following quotations from Berne and others should be reproduced at length to facilitate comparison and understanding of certain key concepts, such as the Child ego state, in the literature of TA and its psychoanalytic sources and contemporary systems. From some discussions (e.g. Erskine et al., 1988), an unfortunate either/or position could be allowed to evolve into our theoretical literature – a position where, on the one hand, all Child ego states are viewed to be fixations and, on the other, although some are fixated, other Child ego states are not. Obviously psychological difficulties are caused by the few Child ego states that have been fixated.

However, from a viewpoint focusing on pathology, an interest in these may blind us to the usefulness of those Child ego states that are not fixated. This could lead to unnecessary alienation from colleagues favouring the behavioural or functional model of ego states who experientially and in clinical practice recognize that behaviours from an individual's Child, optionally cathected under Adult control, are fruitful, deepening and enjoyable parts of Adult life. Some theoretical clarification could bridge this gap.

Throughout Chapters 5 and 6, I discuss the structural (also sometimes called phenomenological) Child ego state, not the behaviourally defined Child of the functional model. Study of the excerpts below, as well as other sources, could encourage transactional analysts to question some of the assumptions that may have become ingrained and, even more, dogmatically asserted the further away they drift from the original definitions and surrounding intellectual contexts.

It is hoped that this chapter can contribute to some reconciliation of apparently contradictory statements of Berne himself – in particular, what appears to be a polarity between the idea that all Child ego states are fixated and a wider and more inclusive definition, which makes room for some Child ego states to be beneficial contributors to life, psychotherapy and creativity when they are cathected under the hegemony of the Integrated Adult.

Federn – a psychoanalyst and a great friend of Freud – was Berne's analyst and teacher, and Weiss – another important influence on Berne – was a major exponent of Federn's theories. It appears to me, from a close reading of these sources in relation to Berne's theories, that when the relevant definitions are understood in context – whether Berne was discussing psychopathology or healthy functioning – the apparent contradictions turn out to be a matter of differential emphasis.

An inclusive appreciation of the Child ego state (always archaic, sometimes fixated, sometimes accessible and beneficial) takes into consideration and respects the extensive literature and clinical experience of transactional analysts of the last 40 years. This chapter is an account of the mutual complementarity of the varied concepts that become intelligible when understood as a whole, especially when taking into account Federn's (1977) phenomenology and his notion of orthriogenesis.

I hypothesize that the accent on fixated Child ego states was important, particularly in drawing attention to the integrated Adult ego state in a structural or phenomenological model (Trautmann and Erskine, 1981). (In this respect James and Jongeward [1971], following Berne, first described the integrated Adult as containing *Adult feelings* that are genuine responses 'to an actual situation happening now' [Berne, 1975, p. 271]. The model under examination here is seen as different from, but complementary to, a behavioural or functional model of ego states.) This author wants to present an integrative view – a focus on pathology, but also on normality. This is in the tradition of Berne, Federn and Weiss, and also in keeping with the cultural and theoretical re-emergence of interest in the *inner child*.

Reclamation – 'to call back (as a hawk): to win back: to win from evil, wildness, waste, submersion: to claim back' (Macdonald, 1972, p. 1128) – originates from the Latin verb *clamare*, to cry out. It is aimed in this chapter to call back the Child ego state from being submerged or wasted in the wild, from being considered only evil (or pathological), and to win it back also on the side of health, growth and creativity.

With Kohut (1987), I wish to question a 'maturity morality' in psycho-therapy that *necessarily*, under all circumstances, considers earlier or regressed developmental stages as less valuable than later, more mature ones. This chapter is an exhortation to cry out for the healthy inner Child and restore it to its proper place in the psychic constellation of the here-and-now, well-functioning, creative and self-actualizing adult.

As developed elsewhere (Clarkson and Gilbert, 1988), the pheno-menological approach to ego states is Berne's (1975) development of Federn's (1977) phenomenological or subjective description of psychic life. Honouring the phenomenological perspective of Berne and Federn, structural ego state analysis is considered to refer to Berne's postulated psychic organs, and phenomenological ego state analysis refers to ego states as phenomenological realities. 'The ego must be conceived of as a continuous experience of the psyche and not as a conceptual abstraction' (Federn, 1977, p. 283).

Fairbairn's (1952) concept of the tripartite ego was examined in Clarkson and Gilbert's (1988) paper. Here, however, for the sake of simplicity, the concentration is on the contributions of Federn and Weiss to TA, with a clear statement of a phenomenological perspective supported by extracts from the writings of these other authors, and incorporating Berne's phenomenological approach to ego states.

Phenomenology

Phenomenology is a philosophical approach, often associated with existentialism and also originating in Europe, that has had an enormous impact on psychologists, psychiatrists and psychotherapists, including Berne, Federn and Weiss. Along with others, such as Binswanger (1958) and May, Angel and Ellenberger (1958), they wanted to validate and use people's direct subjective experience rather than impose assumptions, interpretations or categories, and as such saw themselves engaged in a phenomenological endeavour. 'One might look on the whole development of ego-psychology as a return from hypothetical constructions, as in the case of the superego and id, to the level of experiential description' (Spiegelberg, 1972, pp. 134-135).

Empathy as a method of obtaining knowledge of another's inner world was one of the first applications of the phenomenological approach to psychology exemplified by Berne and Federn's intellectual and epistemological predecessors. The phenomenological psychiatrist Jaspers (1913/1963) was thus engaged early in the twentieth century. He 'defined descriptive phenomenology as a careful and accurate description of the subjective experience of mentally sick patients with an effort to empathize (*einfühlen*) as closely as possible with this experience' (May et al., 1958, p. 97).

Weiss's notion of empathic resonance (discussed later) also appears to be derived from Jaspers. (As is clear to the student of phenomenology in psychology and psychiatry, the work on empathy by Jaspers and other Europeans preceded that of Rogers [1951] and Kohut [1959] by at least 38 years and was a direct tributary to TA.)

Although phenomenology was thus an important notion for the fathers of ego psychology and therefore TA, it has since sadly been misunderstood or neglected in the TA literature. Phenomenology (which is generally considered to have been originated by Husserl [1913/1983], also a major source for Federn) has been defined as 'the descriptive analysis of subjective processes' (Runes, 1966, p. 231). The descriptive analysis of subjective processes is precisely what Federn, and subsequently Berne, set out to do, as shown below.

Phenomenology is articulated as an alternative epistemology to Cartesian intellectualism, on the one hand, and empiricism, on the other. It is not only a philosophy, but also *a way of doing* philosophy and psychology by describing phenomena without preconceptions or presuppositions, which puts the person's own subjective experience first. Phenomenology concerns itself with things or states as they are experienced, as they are perceived subjectively. By definition it is *not* concerned with proving phenomena to be true or false. Phenomenological psychology was developed as an alternative to experimentally based behaviourism, on the one hand, and the theoretical constructs of the psyche and external interpretations of the unconscious mind in classic psychoanalysis, on the other.

Schilder, a psychiatrist and phenomenologist who influenced Federn profoundly, particularly in terms of his work on body image and ego feeling, also rejected the Freudian hypothetical construct of the unconscious and provided a phenomenological perspective that sees 'repression being not necessarily repression into the unconscious' because conscious experiences 'are still available there in a corner of consciousness' (Spiegelberg, 1972, p. 330).

After Schilder, the phenomenologist who appears to have influenced Federn's ego state psychology most was Minkowski. He (Minkowski 1933/1970) saw phenomenology's task as offering a closer contact with reality – the immediate data of consciousness which he saw as final authority. For Berne (1975) as well, 'the phenomenological diagnosis' (p. 76) was the final authority in the complete diagnosis of an ego state (after the behavioural, social and historical diagnoses).

> The diagnosis [of an ego state] is validated if the individual can finally re-experience in full intensity, with little weathering, the moment or epoch when he assimilated the parental ego state.

Through Federn, Berne must have inherited some of Minkowski's (1933/1970) preoccupation with *lived time* and the temporal structure of psychological life. The phenomenon of the present, which is an unfolded, extended 'now' (p. 36), appears later in TA as 'feelings, attitudes, and behavior patterns which are adapted to current reality' of the Adult ego state (Berne, 1975, p. 76) and Minkowski's lived continuity echoes in Berne's (1973) sense of a continuing Self, which can nevertheless maintain a sense of personal identity even as the 'moving self' (p. 248) shifts over time. In this regard, Weiss's (1950, p. 15) discussion of the term 'ego' is illuminating:

> While no one can recall all conditions and events in his or her own life, every normal human being has a feeling of 'selfness', or identity, and can establish

connections, by means of 'associations', between single experiences in his or her own past. We do not know how the phenomenon of 'experiencing' comes into being, but every self-experiencing, acting, reacting subject – aware of its identity as an 'experiencing' organism – calls itself 'I', and by the substitution, in philosophy and psychology, of the corresponding pronoun in Latin, we arrive at the term *ego*: 'something which experiences itself and maintains its identity throughout its continuous changes.' The word 'I' indicates the *experience unity* of the self: we say 'I' of both our bodies and our minds.

Of course, in both Dutch and German, ego states are translated as 'I-states', i.e. conditions of the I. Berne (1975) states that he uses the term 'ego state' 'to denote states of mind and their related patterns of behavior as they occur in nature' (Berne, 1975, p. 30). This is a profoundly phenomenological approach, neither metaphorical nor empirical. He also explicitly intended his approach to be a systematic phenomenology:

> Freud does not raise any question of systematic phenomenology, and it is here that structural analysis can usefully fill a gap in psychological theory, just as transactional analysis fills a gap in social theory by setting up elementary units (transactions) and larger units (games and scripts) of social action.
>
> Berne (1975, p. 244)

It was Federn who in the interim approached the study of the ego as:

> the precise and minute description of inner experience, rather than theoretical hypotheses. In his assertion that the medial-narcissistic libido is actually *felt*, for example, he gives a description of the ego which is accurate in both phenomenological and metapsychological terms. Similarly, in his statement that the ego is felt as a single coherent unit, he correctly describes another essential feature of the ego experience and derives the concept of a 'coherent ego cathexis'.
>
> Weiss (1950, p. 39)

Berne did not base his ego state psychology on objective, logical, positivist, laboratory processes grounded in hypotheses and proofs, nor did he primarily seek to create theoretical unconscious mechanisms or hypothetical constructs.

Transactional analysis is not concerned with reification of metaphor (Loria, 1990) or theoretical constructs, as Berne (1975) repeatedly pointed out. Berne was concerned with phenomenology in action – people's actual experience of their subjective realities. For phenomenologists the most fundamental aspects of human experience are non-rationalistic and non-quantifiable – they concern themselves with the way in which the fundamental categories of life are *lived*.

Although such a brief summary does not claim to do it justice, one can say that in phenomenology the acquisition of knowledge through the traditional means of philosophy and scientific proofs of conventional psychology is rejected. Of value instead are experiential dimensions such as body–mind wholeness, subjectivity, our intrinsic interconnected communication with others, and the vital role of space, and especially time, in psychology and philosophy. Particularly as it developed in Europe, the principles of a phenomenological approach to psychology and psychiatry would influence all the ways and times in which we live, and move, and have our being as persons. Spinelli (1989) assesses the influence of the approach thus:

> As is now generally agreed (Giorgi, 1970; Misiak and Sexton, 1973; Shaffer, 1978), phenomenological psychology is principally concerned with the application of the phenomenological method to issues and problems in psychology so that an individual's conscious experience of the world can be more systematically observed and described. Any conscious act - such as perception, imagery, memory, emotion, and so on - falls under the scrutiny of phenomenological investigation. In keeping with the rules of the phenomenological method, the focus of such a psychology is placed on the description (and acceptance) of current experience as a result of 'bracketing' as many assumptions, suppositions, theoretical explanations and habitual psychological biases as possible.
>
> Spinelli (1989, p. 30)

In this chapter, the reader has an opportunity to conduct a phenomenological experiment by reading and considering the material that I have brought together as if for the first time. Such a phenomenological investigation requires a bracketing (epoch) or putting aside of preconceptions, assumptions and preconceived notions based on past theoretical beliefs or external authorities, and allowing the ideas to unfold themselves so that one can find the realities of one's own experience.

Federn, Weiss and Berne tried to go directly to the I (or ego) phenomenon 'with full acknowledgement of their reality' (Federn, 1977, p. 161). Lack of a thorough understanding of the phenomenological epistemological orientation of Berne, Weiss and Federn, and the philosophical context in which they were working, can easily lead to suggestions that they were reifying metaphor or unconsciously using figurative language.

However, this would precisely commit the error of confusing different universes of discourse (Ryle, 1954), similar to criticizing roses for not being better dishwashing machines. The only epistemologically correct way of establishing *true knowledge* in phenomenology is one's own experience. Do you sometimes re-experience the Child you once were, or suddenly recognize your own unedited Parent in your current actions? Do you experience such changes in others? This is Berneian phenomenology.

Definition of ego states

> An ego state is the phenomenological and behavioral manifestation of the activity of a certain psychic organ, or organizer.
>
> Berne (1975, p. 240)

Berne sees ego states as phenomena (Berne, 1975, p. 239), e.g. a person who is crying could be described in functional or behavioural terms as exhibiting Child ego state behaviour, but in phenomenological terms it may not necessarily be a Child ego state that is being experienced.

Whether categorized as a Parent, Adult or Child ego state, diagnostically and operationally, will depend on accurate application of behavioural, social, historical and phenomenological diagnostic criteria. The phenomenological diagnosis is dependent on whether the individual can subjectively relive or re-experience the relevant psychological epoch in the sense in which phenomenology has been explained above.

Berne stressed that these Parent, Adult and Child ego states are three types or categories of existential phenomena, not theoretical constructs or metaphors. 'Parent, Adult, and Child represent real people who now exist or who once existed, who have legal names and civic identities' (Berne, 1975, p. 32). These have a phenomenological reality, as do Penfield's (1952) individuals under cortical stimulation, and the subjectively real experiences of people under hypnosis (Erickson, 1967; Watkins and Watkins, 1986).

According to Berne, Parent or Child ego states can be voluntarily or involuntarily activated by external stimuli or autonomous cathexis at any moment in time and experienced as a current reality with the same vividness that attended the original experience. Such a reliving of a psychological epoch of the past in the present can be to the detriment or enhancement (e.g. intuition) of accurate Adult reality testing in the here and now of a person's life.

'The ascendancy of archaic mental processes' must be accompanied by a 'different kind of reality testing' (Berne, 1975, p. 78) – called a fixation. Directly in Berne's own words:

> It is the proper function of the 'healthy' Child to motivate the data-processing and programing of the Adult so as to obtain the greatest amount of gratification for itself.

So, even here Berne makes allowance for a healthy Child ego state that influences the executive Adult.

Berne (1975) identified the three types of ego states as 'manifestations of the corresponding psychic organs: exteropsyche, neopsyche, and archaeopsyche' (Berne, 1975, p. 75). Sometimes he used the terms 'ego states' and 'psychic organs' interchangeably; at other times he distinguished psychic organs as the structural organizers and ego states as the phenomenological manifestations of the activity of these organs. It would appear most useful to consider the psychic organs as structural concepts and the analysis of ego states as phenomenological.

In other words, Berne considers the structural organizers as theoretical constructs and ego states as experiential realities. This both corresponds to and is congruent with the psychoanalytic, scientific and phenomenological subjective epistemology from which TA as a psychotherapy grew. Each of these ego states has 'its own idiosyncratic patterns of organized behavior [executive power]. . . . Each is capable of adapting its behavioral responses to the immediate social situation' (adaptability), the responses of each are "modified as a result of natural growth and previous experiences" (biological fluidity) and each "mediate[s] the phenomena of experience"' (mentality) (Berne, 1975, p. 75).

It seems clear from Berne's synopsis here that each type of ego state (i.e. Adult as well as Parent or Child) is capable of adapting to the immediate social situation, as well as being modified over time. Therefore, Parent, Child and Adult ego states are open to growth, development and change for the duration of an individual's life. This is consistent with the work of major TA theorists, such as Goulding and Goulding (1979), Schiff et al. (1975) and James (1974), who all describe techniques intended to change existing ego states. This concept is also developed further in the rechilding material of Clarkson and Fish (1988).

> Every ego-state is the actually experienced reality of one's mental and bodily ego with the contents of the lived-through period. Some ego states are easily remembered and revived even after many years, some are difficult to recall, some are strictly repressed.
>
> Weiss (1950, p. 141)

Perhaps the greatest psychological phenomenologist of the century was Merleau-Ponty (1962), from whom transactional analysts working now can learn a great deal. Here he is referred to in order to supplement notions of the bodily ego and the temporality of existence. His illumination in terms of subject relations, the existentialist reworking of object relations within an existentialist philosophy of freedom and responsibility *with* others, must be left to another paper.

According to Merleau-Ponty, the body comprises both the 'habitual body' and the 'present body': '. . . our body comprises as it were two distinct

layers, that of the customary body and that of the body at this moment'
(Merleau-Ponty, 1962, p. 82). Langer (1989), a major exponent of Merleau-
Ponty's theories, continues:

> As such, it [the body] draws together a comprehensive past which it puts at the
> disposal of each new present, thereby already laying down the general form of a
> future it anticipates. With its 'two layers' the body is the meeting place, so to
> speak, of past, present and future because it is the carrying forward of the past in
> the outlining of a future and the living of this bodily momentum as actual present.
>
> Langer (1989, p. 32)

Federn has a matching conceptualization:

> Federn emphasizes the flexibility of the ego boundaries, which undergo
> progressive changes from birth on, and include, at various periods, various
> contents. Some changes of the dynamic ego boundaries also occur during the
> everyday life of the individual, in different situations. Throughout these changes,
> however, the ego constitutes a continuity and struggles to establish and maintain,
> in every state, its coherence and integration. The specific contents which are at
> any given time included within the ego boundary determine the specific ego state.
> Different ego boundaries are correlated with different ego states.
>
> Weiss in Federn (1977, p. 14)

A more modern realization of this concept, also drawing attention to the
coexistence of different ego states, follows for comparison:

> You'll realize that it is possible at times for a person to have some active cathexis
> in *all three* ego states at once. For instance, I might continue to keep executive
> power in Adult, exchanging technical information with my colleague. While
> doing so, I might also unbind some cathexis in Parent and start criticizing myself
> internally for not understanding the task well enough. At the same time I might
> unbind some Child cathexis and begin feeling ashamed that I was not complying
> with those Parental demands.
>
> Stewart and Joines (1987, p. 49)

Reality of ego states

The phenomenologist Minkowski (1933/1970) differentiates between
remembering (an Adult ego state function) – reliving past experiences while
remaining in contact with the current reality – and re-experiencing 'when
we feel it [the experience] still present in the very fibers of our being, when
we feel it thus become a part of our present *even more than the actual
present* [italics added]' (p. 38). It is true that all graphic depictions of ego

states (e.g. the three stacked circles) are static visual metaphors and cannot replicate accurately the life experiences of an individual. Whether the past is remembered, relived in the present or becomes more real than one's current reality, these modes are intensely subjective phenomena.

Berne (1975) considered each ego state to be a phenomenological entity representing 'natural psychological epochs' of a person's life (p. 52). Federn and Berne's use of the word epoch refers to the profoundly temporal experience of ego states within their psychological phenomenology. It is interesting here to note the dictionary definition of epoch: 'the particular time, used as a point of reference, at which the data had the values in question . . . a precise date; a time from which a new state of things dates' (Macdonald, 1972, p. 441).

> It seems that ego states can be described as 'chunks of psychic time' – complete and discrete units of psychological reality. These natural 'psychological epochs' do not disappear but are preserved throughout the person's life, potentially available for the vivid re-experiencing of those ego states with their corresponding affects.
>
> Clarkson and Gilbert (1988, p. 21)

A corresponding Jungian perspective states it thus:

> At any one moment, earlier *phases of development, or rather of experience* [italics added], have the possibility of becoming operative within a person. . . . These phases-become-autonomous contents influence each other . . . cores around which adult events cluster, and which dictate the emotions and feelings such events engender.
>
> Samuels (1985, p. 145)

At the beginning of *Transactional Analysis in Psychotherapy* (1975), Berne discussed ego states as:

> . . . states of mind and their related patterns of behavior as they occur in nature.
>
> Berne (1975, p. 30)

> An ego state may be described phenomenologically as a coherent system of feelings related to a given subject, and operationally as a set of coherent behavior patterns; or pragmatically, as a system of feelings which motivates a related set of behavior patterns.
>
> Berne (1975, p. 17)

> One of the most difficult aspects of structural analysis in practice is to make the patient (or student) see that Child, Adult, and Parent are not handy ideas, or interesting neologisms, but refer to phenomena based on actual realities.
>
> Berne (1975, p. 34)

This corresponds acutely with the psychological phenomenology of Minkowski (1933/1970) and Merleau-Ponty (1962). As Langer (1989), for example, says of Merleau-Ponty's position:

> Since emotion and memory can bring about the phenomenon of the phantom limb, it is evident that the patient is experiencing 'a former present' rather than merely recollecting it or having an idea or image of it.
>
> Langer (1989, p. 33)

> All explanations of my conduct in terms of my past, my temperament and my environment are therefore true, provided that they be regarded not as separable contributions, but as moments of my total being.
>
> Merleau-Ponty (1962, p. 455)

It is these moments of a person's total being that are the I-states or ego states. Weiss (1950) stresses that:

> Federn is convinced that the ego is more than the integrative function of the mind, or a mental abstraction, or the sum of all conscious interrelated mental phenomena; he believes that it is an experienced reality, constituted by mental and bodily ego feeling – 'an actual continuous mental experience'.
>
> Weiss (1950, p. 18)

The Adult ego state

> The Adult ego state is characterized by an autonomous set of feelings, attitudes, and behavior patterns which are adapted to current reality.
>
> Berne (1975, p. 76)

The integrated Adult draws from Child and Parent ego state reservoirs. Their content can act to enhance or support healthy functioning. Conversely, such ego state programming, if based on pathological introjects or archaic fixations, will diminish appropriate Adult functioning in the here and now (Clarkson and Gilbert, 1988, p. 25).

The integrated Adult ego state therefore represents a biologically mature person with a fully developed adult intellectual functioning, full emotional responsivity (pathos) and a guiding set of considered values (ethos), all of which moderate a person's needs in response to the resources available in the environment (Berne, 1975). A person who has Adult executive control 'learns to exercise Adult insight and control so that these child-like qualities emerge only at appropriate times and in appropriate company' (Berne, 1966, p. 306). Berne's conceptualization of the Adult corresponds with considerable accuracy to Federn's (1977, p. 218) formulation:

> Integrated personality, therefore, means maintenance of control not only of the partial ego reactions but also of different ego states. This maintenance requires the reliable and strong cathexis of the lasting, mature ego state. All psychosis is

ego disease, so all psychopathology is due to characteristically abnormal psycho- and organo-genesis of the ego.

Fairbairn's description (1952) of some of the functions of therapy also sounds like an integrated Adult: 'to reduce the split of the original ego by restoring to the central ego a maximum of the territories ceded to the libidinal ego and the internal saboteur' (Fairbain, 1952, pp. 129-130).

Berne (1975) uses the metaphor of the barnacle to great effect in regard of ego interference. It is true that the interior of a ship is not damaged by barnacles early on, although they can ultimately erode the interior of a ship. Also, a ship cannot move freely if it has acquired too many barnacles, for it may be slowed down, and an unequal distribution of barnacles can affect the steering. The Adult is indeed altered as a consequence of contamination – the intrusion by the past or foreign egos.

> Ego regression (primitivization of ego functions) occurs not only when the ego is weak – in sleep, in falling asleep, in fantasy, in intoxication, and in the psychoses – but also during many types of creative processes. This suggested to me years ago that the ego may use the primary process and not be only overwhelmed by it. This idea was rooted in Freud's explanation of wit (1905a) according to which a preconscious thought 'is entrusted for a moment to unconscious elaboration,' and seemed to account for a variety of creative or other inventive processes. However the problem of ego regression during creative processes represents only a special problem in a more general area. The general assumption is that under certain conditions the ego regulates regression, and that the integrative functions of the ego include voluntary and temporary withdrawal of cathexis from one area or another to regain improved control (Hartmann, 1939a, 1939b, 1947).
>
> Kris (1952, p. 312)

Hartmann here assumes, as I do, that the ego regulates regression as part of its integrative function and that such regulation can lead to improved control of adult functioning. The function of ego regression in making a new beginning by reinventing childhood, as well as its function in creativity, will be dealt with in Chapter 6.

> Coherence is the property of investing simultaneously all of a given area so that the resulting experience is felt as a unit. It is only by means of such an investment of energy by the ego cathexis that the ego is appended as a unit . . . both *subject* and *object* . . . a *bodily* [italics added] thing.
>
> Weiss (1950, pp. 39-40)

It is not only intrapsychically that we observe this process, but also in science:

> At that crucial point, the point of a 'phase shift' into the condensed phase, the movements of the synchronized molecules within neurone cell walls (or photons

emitted by them) would take on quantum mechanical properties - uniformity, frictionlessness (and hence persistence in time), unbroken wholeness.

Zohar (1990, p. 68)

As quantum systems are always undulating, their boundaries shifting and changing, the extent to which the self is integrated at any one time may change from moment to moment. The act of paying attention focuses our mental energy, so through the mechanism of selective attention we can channel more energy into a particular aspect of the self, thus lighting it up (giving it more coherence) while others recede more into the background. We may even at times be taken over by one of our sub-selves - as, for instance, when an angry person can think of nothing good about the person he loves during a row, or when a depressed person can think of no reason to be happy while suffering his affliction. When this happens, we say the person is unbalanced, an apt description given the quantum dynamics of the personality.

According to psychologists, 'now' (William James' 'specious present') is a span of time lasting for anything up to twelve seconds, and represents the breadth of experience that our awareness can digest as a unified whole.

Zohar (1990, p. 101)

This is analogous to Minkowski's span of lived time and the naturally occurring psychological epochs of Federn, Weiss and Berne.

Adult is not a circle or a container; it is a function. Thus, the Adult is most naturally and consistently seen as the most recent event or time period that can be contained within the ego boundary of the present chunk of psychic time, with its mental, emotional and bodily concomitants. In this conceptualization, it is therefore like an empty readiness concerning a naturally occurring epoch of time: for Federn and Berne this could be a day, for James a span of time not exceeding 12 seconds.

The following excerpts from a quantum physics writer (Zohar, 1990) need reading in this context, because her explanations fit so well and so closely with the phenomenological apprehension and subjective experience of the Adult ego state ever changing through time. For most people, the Adult ego state of today is experientially not the same Adult ego state of yesterday:

For a quantum self, 'now' is a composite of already existing (but ever-fluctuating) sub-selves - our selves as we were *before* 'now' - and various inputs from the external world (new experiences), each of which forms its own wave pattern on the ground state of consciousness - the Bose–Einstein condensate. Personal identity on a moment-to-moment basis is formed by the *overlapping* wave functions of all these things which cause ripples and patterns to appear on the condensate - our thoughts, emotions, memories, sensations, etc. [Condensate is conceived of as similar to an ego state - a state condensed in time.]

Zohar (1990, pp. 101-102)

As 'now' fades into the past, the self which I was then is recorded in the brain's conventional memory system as 'a memory of the past'. It becomes a new set of neurone pathways which in turn can feed patterns of energy back into the condensate. This is the familiar sense of memory, the kind spoken of by Parfit and other philosophers. But on a quantum view, the self I was a moment ago is also woven into the next 'now', into my future self, by the overlapping of *its* own wave function with all the new wave functions just appearing as the result of new experience. In quantum physics, particle systems can overlap in both space and time.

Thus each self that I was, moment by moment, is taken up into the next moment and wedded to all that is to come – wedded both to old memories, in the conventional sense of memory, as these are fed back into the condensate, and to new experiences. The dynamics of this ongoing dialogue between past and present are very like those by which the wave functions of two elementary particles overlap to form a new quantum system, only in this case what is being formed is a new quantum self.

Zohar (1990, p. 102)

The quantum self, then, the 'I' that we take ourselves to be, is real enough, but from moment to moment it is a shifty thing with fuzzy and fluctuating boundaries. We can talk about its dynamics, but we can't really pin it down, no more than we can pin down both the position and the momentum of an elementary particle. It has substance, but in many important ways that substance eludes us. I can say with some certainty that I am, but if this were all there is to the self it would be difficult to say *who* or *what* I am.

Zohar (1990, p. 99)

This awareness of 'the moving self' was familiar to Berne (1973, p. 248) and could be a restatement of a phenomenological point of view distinguishing between 'lived succession' and 'lived continuity' (Minkowski, 1933/1970, p. 27) and that of the 'Present' and the 'Now' (Minkowski, 1933/1970, p. 32).

Like particle systems, our selves are partially integrated systems of sub-selves that still, from time to time, assert their own identities. Their boundaries shift and merge as the boundaries of patterns (excitations) within the Bose–Einstein condensate shift and merge. We are at times more fragmented – more child or adult, more conventional or rebellious, more tormented or at peace – and at times more 'together', some more integrated self that binds together the sub-selves more completely.

Zohar (1990, p. 96)

And the strength of the self at any moment, the amount of awareness and attention that 'I' can bring to bear on my environment or my relationship with others depends entirely upon the extent to which my sub-selves (my many pockets of awareness) are integrated at that moment. This is purely a matter of energy and can be understood in terms of the physics of the self. . . . People who are in conflict, and this is most of us to some degree, who have many poorly integrated sub-selves – pockets of childhood pain, pockets of immaturity, pockets of personality which have developed in different directions – have much less energy available to their main personality (their highest unity) than people who are more integrated.

Zohar (1990, p. 98)

The correspondence with English's (1977) formulation above is clear.

> The concept of the ego as a dynamic entity and of the ego boundary as its
> peripheral sensory organ, which I introduced, is not included in Freud's
> assumption and is not made superfluous by it. The combined assumptions are
> fitted to explain the fact that the mental ego boundary usually consists of the most
> recent [sic] and conscious ideas. These assumptions direct passive attention to
> related perceptions and associations.
>
> Federn (1977, p. 225)

According to Berne (1966), a person who has Adult executive control can
learn to use Adult cognitions, awareness and autonomy to ensure that Child
ego states emerge with timely appropriateness. 'Making a conscious [Adult]
choice involves controlling the psychic energy so that a person can actually
shift from one ego state to another when it is appropriate' (James and
Jongeward, 1971, p. 236). 'The integrative functions of the ego include self-
regulated *regression* [italics added] and permit a combination of the most
daring intellectual activity with the experience of passive receptiveness'
(Kris, 1952, p. 318). *Self-regulated regression* will be discussed in a
subsequent volume in this series as Adult-monitored accessing of archaic ego
states, or earlier developmental levels as in rechilding. Weiss also refers to
the 'integrative and mastery functions of the ego' (Weiss, 1950, p. 42).

> My hold on the past and the future is precarious, and my possession of my own
> time is always postponed until a stage when I may fully understand it, yet this
> stage can never be reached, since it would be one more moment, bounded by the
> horizon of its future, and requiring in its turn further developments in order to be
> understood. My voluntary and rational life, therefore, knows that it merges into
> another power which stands in the way of its completion, and gives it a
> permanently tentative look. Natural time is always there.
>
> Merleau-Ponty (1962, pp. 346–347)

A definition of Child ego states

> Thorn looked back to her. 'Listen, what're the words you're looking for? I
> apologize? I'm sorry? I wish it hadn't happened? . . . When it happened, I was
> nineteen years old, for godsakes.'
>   'Nineteen is old enough. You knew what you were doing.'
>   'Did I?' Thorn said. 'Think who you were at nineteen.'
>   'I'm still nineteen,' Sarah said. 'In here.' She tapped her left breast with the butt
> of the Colt. 'Nineteen. Ten. All of it.'

In this extract from a popular novel (Hall, 1989, p. 286), the *phenomenological reality* of the continued existence of earlier I-states is vividly realized.
As has been mentioned in Volume 1 in this series, Berne recognized subjective
knowledge from clinical practice or the individual's experiences of everyday
life as the final authority for the reality of the phenomena of ego states.

Ego states are subjectively experienced as real as anyone who has experienced the eruption of an earlier ego state with or without Adult control knows. This may be partial as in the remnant of a childhood anxiety overlaying the pleasurable anticipation of a public speaking engagement (contamination), or the full and vivid reliving of terror from an earlier scene that hitherto had been safely excluded.

Federn (1977), along with Freud, maintained that ego configurations of earlier age levels are potentially available in intact adult personalities. He used the concept of 'engrams' (Federn, 1977, p. 218) to connote the continuous retention of ego units related to important events, intellectual interests or personal emotional reasons, which are continuously retained in the succession of ego states in the individual. These remain available to influence the person's ordinary life for good or for ill.

'The Child ego state is a set of feelings, attitudes, and behavior patterns which are relics of the individual's own childhood' (Berne, 1975, p. 77). Relics may be worthless or damaging, like asbestos roofing or, like a Ming vase, they may be valuable and add to the beauty, efficiency or poignancy of life. When Berne wrote about the Child ego state, he was technically referring (in the Penfield and Federn sense) to the multitude of such Child ego states that represent the entire earlier history of an individual in vivid, phenomenologically real, sensorily alive, psychological units.

Certain Child ego states could be distinct and circumscribed by traumatic fixations which may or may not interfere substantially with secondary process reality testing. As a psychotherapist, Berne's main concern was with these traumatic or repeated subtraumatic fixations as they interfered with the person's social and occupational functioning. His examples of fixated Child ego states may have encouraged some interpreters to use part examples as definitions. Such non-contextual interpretations divorce the fundamental idea of Child ego states from their phenomenological origins. Ego states were initially conceived as vividly available temporal recordings of past events with the concomitant meaning and feelings that 'are maintained in potential existence within the personality' (Berne, 1975, p. 19).

Within the multitude of Child ego states (which he also sometimes called archaeopsychic types of ego states), Berne distinguished between (1) Child as archaic ego states and (2) Child as fixated archaic ego states. Both categories are accessible to being relived, as such, in the present by the adult person.

Berne's idea of the Child ego state was, of course, based on the ego states identified by Federn in the first instance. Berne himself considered that 'each ego state is a kind of entity which is differentiated in some way from the rest of the psychic contents, including other ego states which existed many years ago or *a few moments previously* [italics added], or which are active simultaneously' (Berne 1975, p. 39). Goulding also says: 'And the Child as "chunks of time" for me is as of this moment. Anything that happened yesterday, in terms of the theoretical understanding of the Child, is in the Child ego state' (Erskine et al., 1988, p. 8).

New ego states, both fixated (e.g. in response to a rape at 60) and non-traumatic (e.g. a first real friendship at 40), are continuously being formed on a day-by-day basis for the duration of a person's life. Child ego states may be a misnomer, because it suggests a repository of experiences only relating to a person's childhood, whereas ego states – as normal psychological epochs – continue to be formed for the duration of a person's life. One's vivid experiences of today will be stored in natural psychological epochs, archaic by tomorrow.

However, for the sake of general recognition, the term 'Child ego state' will be used here. As pointed out by Clarkson and Gilbert (1988), Child ego states would more accurately be called historical ego states because they are the 'reservoirs' (Berne's term, 1975, p. 244) of all our previous experiences.

This has similarity with the position of Goulding and Goulding (1979, p. 20):

> We see the Child as ever growing and ever developing, as the sum total of the experiences he has had and is having in the present. A man of 45 may be behaving in a perfectly appropriate way until he sees a person who looks like the torturer who held him in captivity in Viet Nam; he may suddenly curl up in terror, or feel his heart pound and his hands sweat, and be overcome with fear.

Thus ego states may become fixated at any age and subsequently interrupt appropriate Adult functioning.

In many cases in his books, Berne did not necessarily equate fixated ego states with archaic ego states. It is instructive to find him using three adjectives when he wrote that 'the number of fixated pathological archaic ego states (or series of ego states) in any one individual is very limited: one or two and in rare cases perhaps three' (Berne, 1975, p. 54). In Berne's glossaries or indexed definitions of Child ego states, he referred only to their archaic nature. (Archaic is defined in *The Shorter Oxford Dictionary* as 'marked by the characteristics of an earlier period' [Onions, 1986, p. 99].) Archaic ego states are memories retained in their natural form: 'the temporal recording carries with it important psychical elements, such as an understanding of the meaning of the experience, and the emotion it may have aroused' (Berne, 1975, p. 18).

> Often there are several infantile ego states existing *facultatively* [italics added] at the same time; these must be recognized in order that one may establish contact

with them, as one does with a child. Many newer – that is, more lately acquired – stages and contents have lost their narcissistic cathexes in part, or even completely, and have become material accessible to psychoanalysis, while the unconscious has become more accessible and yields, without resistance, much material no longer repressed.

Federn (1977, p. 327)

Facultative is defined as 'optional; incidental; of or pertaining to a faculty; conferring *privilege* [italics added]; permission or authority; able to live under different conditions' (Macdonald, 1972, p. 468). Thus, Federn means that several infantile ego states are able to exist under different conditions, optionally and by permission or authority (not necessarily compulsively or unconsciously).

As well as Federn, Kohut (1987) recognizes the residual emotional 'baby', which persists through life and he warns against a 'maturity morality' (p. 6) that would negatively value this experience. In the words of Holmes and Lindley (1989, p. 230), this residual emotional baby in each one of us:

needs to be held and recognized in intimate relationships at whatever age. It is one of the functions of the psychotherapeutic relationship to provide such recognition and holding, without which there is a danger of emotional and spiritual death, and certainly no prospect of emotional autonomy.

The continuing existence of the inner child, as recognized by Kohut, is represented in the TA literature as follows:

Everyone carries within his brain and nervous system permanent recordings of the way he experienced his own impulses as a child, the way he experienced the world, the way he felt about the world he experienced, and the way he adapted to it. In the Parent ego state are incorporated the personalities of emotionally significant authorities, in the Child ego state is his inner world of feelings and experiences and adaptations. When a person responds as he did in childhood – inquisitive, affectionate, selfish, mean, playful, whining, manipulative – he is responding from his Child ego state.

James and Jongeward (1971, p. 127)

'The Child ego state is the part of people that thinks, feels and behaves as they did in the past . . . particularly as children, but sometimes as grown-ups' (Goulding and Goulding, 1979, p. 12). Schiff et al. (1975, p. 24) define it as follows:

The Child is experienced by healthy persons as the most real part of their personalities. It contains all of the experiences that people have had. It is also the storehouse for the games which he learned from his parents. The Child is the most clever ego state. Its primary concern is how to maximize gratification or comfort and minimize discomfort.

I agree with English, who suggests that 'It is misleading to diagram the second order structure of the Child as C_1, A_1, P_1, since these appellations imply structural subsistence when they actually correspond to functional aspects of the total Child' (English, 1977, p. 301). English stresses that, within the Child ego state system, which continues to exist within the grown-up as a separate system of thought and feeling, there are several coherent subsystems which may be very different from one another with separate phenomenological existences.

> The next step is to remember that the age differences, which we distinguish from one another when we watch live children, maintain themselves later as separate entities within the Child ego state of a grownup. These entities do not transform themselves from one into another, the way a child's small bones grow into larger ones. Rather, they remain as separate systems complete with their own idiosyncratic Gestalten of combined feelings and thoughts. These, then, exist as conclusions that are stored within each Child system like so many favorite rattles, teddy bears, dolls, and toy trains that indispensably belonged to the Child at each separate period of his life. They remain there with all their accrued importance, ready to be picked up at moment's notice as the tried and true basic tools for comfort and excitement in response to one stimulus or another that may appear later in life.
>
> English (1977, pp. 308–309)

English suggests a new structural diagram of the Child to show how different layers of the Child ego state, similar to the cross-section of a tree trunk, potentially coexist in the chronological adult. This diagram, which has proved most useful in clinical practice based on a Federnian/Berneian phenomenological understanding of ego states, is reproduced in Figure 5.1.

> The inner core represents infancy and the subsequent rings represent separately identifiable subsystems that added themselves on as the child grew . . . if we want to we can visualize adding more circles to represent later stages of the Child ego state's development beyond age seven, even all the way up to our present age.
>
> English (1977, pp. 304–305)

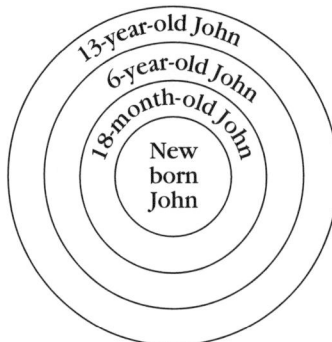

Figure 5.1 A new structural diagram of the Child (English, 1977, p. 305).

It is true that, after certain ages, neurophysiological development slows down, e.g. childhood amnesia rarely continues after age 7. However, people continue to grow, and the ego states of a person ending psychotherapy are often very different from those when they began. The greater range of resources available in adulthood may lessen the chances of traumatic fixations, compared with childhood. But pathological fixation may nevertheless occur, particularly under extreme conditions.

Common examples from working with clients suffering from post-traumatic stress disorders show how experiences well past the ages of 7, 12 or 19 years can become repressed and fixated, and subsequently act as archaic disturbing influences on a person's neopsychic functioning, e.g. a woman who as result of a rape at 37 (of which she has little memory) recoils and relives the fears and injuries in her body whenever her husband reaches out to her. *Ego units well past age 7, 12 or 19 can become fixated* – they are archaic when played out disconnected from real time (as if the past were now), they do interrupt current life, and current relationships are fixated until they can be fully brought into Adult consciousness, while the archaic terror and pain are discharged and the healing can begin.

An 'epoch', as Federn (1977) used it, is a natural time period or ego unit of a day, the foregoing diagram captures the essence of many naturally occurring time periods that potentially coexist and which, again according to Federn, can be used for good or ill. The position of Goulding and Goulding (1979) that the Child ego state includes yesterday is consistent with this idea of English's (1977).

To decide that Child ends at a certain date, after which it can no longer be added to, would be asking each person to draw a frontier at some arbitrary date in the past after which his or her current Adult existed, with all epochs available and none fixated. Adult starting suddenly at 12 or 19 years old, or cutting off one particular yesterday as more archaic than all his or her other natural time epochs, seems arbitrary and contradictory to both phenomenological experience and understandings of time in modern physics. In this respect, very recent theorists in physics, such as Zohar (1990, p. 106), can be particularly useful for comparison:

> The quantum self is simply a more fluid self, changing and evolving at every moment, now separating into sub-selves, now reuniting into a larger self. It ebbs and flows, but always in some sense being itself. I am the person who was an infant in my mother's arms, who was a teenager, a young woman, etc., but each of these past aspects of my being was also me as I am now.

It appears that, instead of TA becoming redundant, it continues to find new corroboration from adjacent workers in science and philosophy.

Perhaps as it reclaims its heritage and its position as a phenomenological approach, Minkowski's *lived time* (1933/1970) or the 'temporal structure of life' (Spiegelberg, 1972, p. 245) will come to be appreciated more, not as a failed epistemology, or reified metaphor, but as a unique and precious way of being-in-the-world.

Child ego states in healthy functioning are examined in Chapter 6, but I wish here to draw attention to at least three textual references on the vitality and choicefulness of Child ego states in Berne's own work, as reminders of his positive valuation of the Child and the extreme unlikelihood that he meant that all archaic ego states were either pathological and/or fixated:

> The Child is in many ways the most valuable aspect of the personality, and if it can find healthy ways of self-expression and enjoyment, it may make the greatest contribution to vitality and happiness.
>
> Berne (1975, p. 187)

> Child ego states are relics from the individual's childhood and reproduce his behavior and state of mind at a particular moment or epoch of his development, using, however, the increased facilities at his disposal as a grown-up.
>
> Berne (1966, p. 220)

Note that there is a difference between the reproduction of a particular moment or epoch of development and the memory thereof.

> The transactional Child is highly organized, is not necessarily seething, and is quite able to say 'No'; and in fact has a strong tendency to do so when this suits his unified will. Thus the Child is a well-organized ego state, in contrast to the unorganized cauldron of biological drives which is the id.
>
> Berne (1966, pp. 297–298)

References

Berne, E. (1966) Principles of Group Treatment. New York: Grove Press.

Berne, E. (1973) What Do You Say After You Say Hello? New York: Bantam Books.

Berne, E. (1975) Transactional Analysis in Psychotherapy: A systemic individual and social psychiatry. London: Souvenir Press.

Binswanger, L. (1958) The existential analysis school of thought. In: May, R., Angel, E., Ellenberger, J. (eds), Existence – A new dimension in psychiatry and psychology. New York: Clarion.

Binswanger, L. (1968) Being-in-the-World. New York: Harper Torchbooks.

Clarkson, P. and Fish, S. (1988) Rechilding: Creating a new past in the present as a support for the future. Transactional Analysis Journal 18(1): 51–59 (first published in Spanish translation, 1986).

Clarkson, P. and Gilbert, M. (1988) Berne's original model of ego states: Some theoretical considerations. Transactional Analysis Journal 18(1): 20–29 (first published in Spanish translation, 1986).

English, F. (1977) What shall I do tomorrow?: Reconceptualizing transactional analysis. In: Barnes, G. (ed.), Transactional Analysis after Eric Berne: Teachings and practices of three TA schools. New York: Harper's College Press, pp. 287–347.

Erickson, M.H. (1967) Advanced Techniques of Hypnosis and Therapy. New York: Grune & Stratton.

Erskine, R.G., Clarkson, P., Goulding, R.L., Groder, M.G. and Moiso, C. (1988) Ego state theory: Definitions, descriptions, and points of view. Transactional Analysis Journal 18(1): 6–14.

Fairbairn, W.R.D. (1952) Psychoanalytic Studies of the Personality. London: Tavistock.

Federn, P. (1977) Ego Psychology and the Psychoses. London: Maresfield Reprints.

Giorgi, A. (1970) Psychology as a Human Science: A phenomenologically based approach. New York: Harper & Row.

Goulding, M.M. and Goulding, R.L. (1979) Changing Lives through Redecision Therapy. New York: Brunner/Mazel.

Hall, J. (1989) Under Cover of Daylight. London: Heinemann Mandarin.

Hartmann, H. (1939a) Ich-Psychologie und Anpassungsproblem. International Zeitschrift für Psychoanalyse und Imago, XXIV. Translated in part in Rapaport (1951). Also published as Ego Psychology and the Problems of Adaptation. New York: International Universities Press.

Hartmann, H. (1939b) Psychoanalysis and the concept of health. International Journal of Psychoanalysis XX.

Hartmann, H. (1947) On rational and irrational action. In: Roheim, G. (ed.), Psychoanalysis and the Social Sciences, Vol I. New York: International Universities Press.

Holmes, J. and Lindley, R. (1989) The Values of Psychotherapy. Oxford: Oxford University Press.

Husserl, E. (1983) Ideas Pertaining to a Pure Phenomenology and to a Phenomenological Philosophy (F. Kersten, trans.). Lancaster: Nijhoff (original work published 1913).

James, M. (1974) Self-reparenting: Theory and process. Transactional Analysis Journal 4(3): 32–39.

James, M., and Jongeward, D. (1971) Born to Win: Transactional analysis with gestalt experiments. Reading, MA: Addison-Wesley.

Jaspers, K. (1963) General Psychopathology (J. Hoenig and M.W. Hamilton, trans.). Chicago: University of Chicago Press (original work published 1913).

Kohut, H. (1959) Introspection, empathy, and psychoanalysis: An examination of the relationship between mode of observation and theory. In: Ornstein, P.H. (ed.), The Search for the Self, Vol. 1. New York: International Universities Press, pp. 205–232.

Kohut, H. (1987) The Kohut Seminars on Self Psychology and Psychotherapy with Adolescents and Young Adults. New York: W.W. Norton.

Kris, E. (1952) Psychoanalytic Explorations in Art. Madison, CT: International Universities Press.

Langer, M.M. (1989) Merleau-Ponty's Phenomenology of Perception. London: Macmillan.

Loria, B.R. (1990) Epistemology and reification of metaphor in transactional analysis. Transactional Analysis Journal 20(3): 152–162.

Macdonald, A.M. (ed.) (1972) Chambers Twentieth Century Dictionary. London: Chambers.

May, R., Angel, E. and Ellenberger, H.F. (eds) (1958) Existence: A new dimension in psychiatry and psychology. New York: Simon & Schuster.

Merleau-Ponty, M. (1962) Phenomenology of Perception (C. Smith, trans.). London: Routledge & Kegan Paul.

Minkowski, E. (1970) Lived Time (N. Metzel, trans.). Evanston, IL: Northwestern University Press (original work published in 1933).

Misiak, H. and Sexton, V.S. (1973) Phenomenological, Existential, and Humanistic Psychologies: A historical survey. New York: Grune & Stratton.

Onions, C.T. (ed.) (1986) The Shorter Oxford English Dictionary. Oxford: Oxford University Press.

Penfield, W. (1952) Memory mechanisms. Archives of Neurology and Psychiatry 67: 178–198.

Rogers, C. (1951) Client-centered Therapy. Boston: Houghton Mifflin.

Runes, D.D. (ed.) (1966) Dictionary of Philosophy. Totawa, NJ: Littlefield, Adams & Co.

Ryle, G. (1954) Dilemmas: The Tarner lectures. Cambridge: Cambridge University Press.

Samuels, A. (1985) Jung and the Post-Jungians. London: Routledge & Kegan Paul.

Schiff, J.L., Schiff, A.W., Mellor K. et al. (1975) Cathexis Reader: Transactional analysis treatment of psychosis. New York: Harper & Row.

Shaffer, J.B.P. (1978) Humanistic Psychology. Englewood Cliffs, NJ: Prentice-Hall.

Spiegelberg, H. (1972) Phenomenology in Psychology and Psychiatry: A historical introduction. Evanston, IL: Northwestern University Press.

Spinelli, E. (1989) The Interpreted World: An introduction to phenomenological psychology. London: Sage.

Stewart, I. and Joines, V. (1987) TA Today. Nottingham: Lifespace.

Trautmann, R. and Erskine, R.G. (1981) Ego state analysis: A comparative view. Transactional Analysis Journal 11(2): 178–185.

Watkins, J.G. and Watkins, H.H. (1986) Hypnosis, multiple personality, and ego states as altered states of consciousness. In: Wolman, B.B. and Ullman, M. (eds), Handbook of States of Consciousness. New York: Van Nostrand Reinhold, pp. 133–158.

Weiss, E. (1950) Principles of Psychodynamics. New York: Grune & Stratton.

Zohar, D. (1990) The Quantum Self. London: Bloomsbury Publishing Ltd, p. 102.

Chapter 6
Reclamation of the Child II: fixated and accessible Child ego states

Federn's student Weiss (1950, p. 79) clearly acknowledges the 'residual infantile ego state of the adult person, which usually remains cathected but in any event is easily recathected'.

In addition to the examples noted above, in several places in *Transactional Analysis in Psychotherapy* (1975b), Berne referred to Child ego states that are not necessarily pathological and that often positively enhance Adult effectiveness. He used as an example the way in which therapeutic effectiveness is enhanced by the therapist's cathecting Child while his or her Adult remains in the executive (Berne, 1975b, p. 69). This is similar to Kohut's (1987) advocacy of a controlled regression in the psychotherapist to enhance empathy in the psychotherapy. Berne (1975b) advised a client not to get rid of his Child because 'There's a lot of good in him that could be brought out, and he's a good kid to have around' (Berne, 1975b, p. 175).

Phenomenologically, people spontaneously relive earlier ages in themselves which are not pathological fixations or warped or unhealthy, although they may temporarily interrupt Adult contact. However, because two ego states can coexist, and if Adult enables effective productivity of such archaic experiences, much joy or great art can be brought into being. Kohut (1987, p. 7) is also very explicit: 'The very fixation on old modes of development, if they become subjugated by a certain rich ramification of the total personality, can lead to results that are vastly superior in our evaluations'. One famous example from literature is Proust's (1913/1983) magnum opus, *Remembrance of Things Past,* where the protagonist relives times past triggered by the smell of a madeleine cake. He is not just remembering the smell, he's actually investing a past self with psychic energy (cathexis). Memory is not equivalent to a phenomenological ego state – it is the traces of the ever-changing I-moments that can or cannot be re-experienced. In cases of fixation, the experience is relived but the conscious memory is lacking. Where the ego state is accessible to memory, it may or may not be choicefully (facultatively) relived.

Most people report easy and apparently non-traumatic reliving of happy moments triggered by smells (e.g. sea breezes, a much-loved perfume, retsina wine). These moments do not contaminate Adult reality processing, but may momentarily enhance and/or deepen their present experience, as is apparent from the following excerpt from Weiss (1950, p. 81):

> The writer would point out a common occurrence which is additional evidence for the latent presence of early ego states. In a moment of great and immediate danger a person often experiences a rapid and extraordinarily vivid review of his lifetime, which is not merely recalled but is re-lived with the previously experienced affects. An analogous phenomenon also occurs in the grief reaction. After the loss of father or mother, or any figure of similar importance in one's early development, there is frequently a re-cathexis of an early ego state. The memory of the lost love object as he appeared, often many years previously, frequently seems to replace entirely the actual person as he was at the time of death, and the mourner's early emotions, thoughts, feelings, and affects are intensely re-experienced in the mourning work.

Here Weiss is describing normal phenomena, easily cathected, which are obviously not fixated *even though they are not ego states only relating to current reality*.

> A thought or a memory which is now conscious may become unconscious for a certain time and again become conscious at some later time. Freud called such mental data, which have a certain coherent organization, 'pre-conscious.' By this term he wanted to express the fact that these mental contents, which remain temporarily latent, can, with some exceptions, easily reach consciousness. The mental phenomena in question reveal the same level of organization, namely, they belong to the mental field immediately preceding the conscious one, independently of whether or not they can easily reach consciousness.
>
> Weiss (1950, p. 118)

> The pre-conscious is the mental organization immediately preceding the conscious one (*conscious*), and is the mental field over which the ego extends itself. . . . The preconscious shows many characteristics. In the first place we realize that its contents are integrated in time, and according to concepts of space and causality, as are the conscious ones. Besides, they are expressed mentally in words and are subject to reality testing.
>
> Weiss (1950, p. 119)

> From past experiences we are confident of being able to master possible situations with which we may be confronted, in an integrative manner, provided we have not been 'traumatized' by experiences of failure so that our ego economy is damaged.
>
> Weiss (1950, p. 121)

Weiss is here clarifying three regions of consciousness: unconscious (difficult to access), preconscious (accessible) and conscious (current).

Fixated Child ego states located in the unconscious are a subset of archaic ego states which may be preconscious or conscious and which may be accessed through 'malignant or benign regression' (Balint, 1989, p. 141). Kernberg (1981, p. 352), too, differentiates regression that does not accompany fixation – 'fixation and/or regression'. In the following report of a 20-year-old female student nurse under hypnotic age regression with Erickson (1967, p. 379), he described an archaic ego state that cathects a vividly re-experienced, earlier ego state which is not necessarily pathological.

> I could say 'Daddy'. My father was holding me. He seemed to be awfully tall. He was smiling. He had a funny looking tooth, a front tooth. His eyes were blue. His hair was curly. And it looked yellowish. Now I'm going home and tell my mother.

Erickson's patient checked with her mother, who corroborated the facts and indicated that her father had left the mother when the patient was 11 months old. This 11-month experience represents a single archaic Child ego state. Similarly, the little boy of Berne's (1975b) patient, the lawyer Mr Segundo, represents a single Child ego state. There are potentially millions of these because every person has a multitude of such past ego states available. When activated by random stimuli or by posthypnotic suggestions in the form of script messages or script injunctions given to the Child by parent figures, any of these ego states can interfere with effective Adult functioning by hampering appropriate use of the reality principle, which is suited to the here-and-now situation (Conway and Clarkson, 1987).

Clinical investigation of pathological regression usually reveals earlier childhood ego states that are triggered by similar or reminiscent stimuli set in the person's present environment. In dreams and psychosis, of course, this phenomenon can occur to a seriously disturbing degree. However, Federn (1977, p. 218) also did not consider this spontaneous activation of earlier ego states as necessarily pathological:

> Both acquired ego attitudes and past ego states are to a great extent repressed. Through their access to consciousness and to the preconsciousness they influence actual decisions. The influence of ego attitudes and ego states is *helpful or disturbing* [italics added], depending on their normality and fitness for present needs.

When he focused on pathology, Berne (1975b) described the Child ego state as a bent coin that may skew the rest of the pile of coins. However, there are also *unbent* coins, as his diagram shows. He states that ego units are created day by day without necessarily being traumatically fixated.

In the case of the traumatic neuroses, the Child is that confused ego state that was fixated on the day X of the month Y of the year Z in that patient's infancy. In the case of the psychoneuroses, it is the unhealthy ego state which recurred day after day under similar adverse conditions from month A to month B of the year C in the patient's infancy. In either case, the number of fixated pathological archaic ego states (or a series of ego states) in any one individual is very limited: one or two, and in rare cases perhaps three.

Berne (1975b, p. 54)

Thus, in healthy adults there are many more than three Child ego states or ego units of the past that are available, and the metaphor of the pile of coins clearly suggests that there are many Child ego states that are not fixated. According to both Federn and Weiss, these can be easily re-cathected as 'the actually experienced reality of one's mental and bodily ego with the contents of the lived-through period' (Weiss, 1950, p. 141). By 1958, Berne had emphasized that it was not his intention to get rid of the *Child*, but to straighten out the confusion in the archaic area. 'The Child in the individual is potentially capable of contributing to his personality exactly what a happy actual child is capable of contributing to family life' (Berne, 1977, p. 149).

There are situations in which an internal change has to be made, and there are situations in which an external change has to be made. When one uses developmental or maturational terms, one must not confuse the direction of development or maturation with the movement from abnormal to normal. The fact that the development proceeds in a certain way includes, to my mind, the possibility of using any of the earlier positions if the situation demands it. In short, it is the *variety* of responses. This is certainly true for the capacity to play, to regress, to let oneself go.

Kohut (1987, p. 217)

Horowitz (1979) states, however, that 'the inability to maintain a stable state may be a sign of character weakness'; he also says that 'flexibility in entering multiple states may be a sign of character strength' (Horowitz, 1979, p. 32). Horowitz goes on to say of Federn:

He found evidence that the ego states of earlier developmental periods remained throughout life as potentially recurrent in behavior and experience. These might emerge during pathological or normal regressions.

In summary, evidence from other authors, particularly Federn, Weiss, Kohut, Horowitz and Erickson, corroborates Berne's that, although some archaic ego states may be fixated, many are not. Although the Child can be creatively used, the conditions in which Berne consistently considered the manifestations of Child ego states to be pathological are those when the

Child interferes with integrated Adult functioning, i.e. when it is excluded or excluding, when it contaminates the Adult ego state or when it is constant or fixated.

Fixation

A review of what fixation means is in order. The term 'fixation', according to *The Dictionary of Psychology*, is used 'to designate the attachment, generally interpreted psychosexually, to an early stage of development, or object at such stage, with difficulty in forming new attachments, developing new interests, or establishing new adaptations' (Drever, 1952, p. 98).

When an archaic ego state (whether designated as *Child* or otherwise) interferes with forming new attachments or developing or establishing new adaptations in the current reality, it can certainly (by this definition) be said to be fixated, e.g. fixation can be said to have occurred where there is an unclosed gestalt remaining with the past object(s), resulting in unexpressed or repressed rage which continues to be enacted, usually out of awareness, to the detriment of Adult functioning in current reality. For another definition we could turn to *A Critical Dictionary of Psychoanalysis* (Rycroft, 1968, p. 52):

> **fixation**: The process by which a person becomes or remains ambivalently attached to an object, this object being one which was appropriate to an earlier stage of development. Fixation is therefore evidence of failure to progress satisfactorily through the stages of libidinal development. The concept assumes that the fixated person (a) has a tendency to engage in infantile, outmoded patterns of behaviour or to regress to such patterns under stress; (b) to choose compulsively objects on the basis of their resemblance to the one on which he is fixated; and (c) suffers impoverishment of available energy as a result of his investment in the past object.

This definition again clarifies that fixation is evidence of maldevelopment in the sequence of psychosexual development, which results in pathological functioning in relation to others (objects) in the present.

Some transactional analysis (TA) authors, such as James and Jongeward (1971), Goulding and Goulding (1979), and English (1977), encourage the cathexis of Child ego states with Adult in the executive under appropriate conditions, in accord with Berne's (1975a) emphasis on the contribution to vitality and happiness that the Child can make to the Adult personality. Other TA authors appear to interpret Berne's (1975b, p. 77) definition of Child ego state - 'relics of the individual's own childhood'- as always equivalent to fixation: 'the Child is the full person in fixation at some other developmental period in time' (Erskine in Erskine et al., 1988, p. 7). However, Goulding, in the same paper, has a different view: 'Anything that happened yesterday, in terms of the theoretical understanding of the Child, is in the Child ego state. . . . I see the Child as always capable of change' (p. 8). Moiso (Erskine et al., 1988) also allows for the fact that archeopsychic material can become available for neopsychic use, so childhood relics can be used in the service of here-and-now functioning.

Loria (1988, p. 44), when writing about the therapist's ego state, comments:

> On the other hand, the archaic fixated ego states of the therapist are not useful sources of therapeutic interventions. For this writer, using the Child ego state in providing therapy is inappropriate, despite the popular belief that the Parent and Child ego states are used under Adult ego state control.

I agree with Loria that archaic fixated ego states are not useful sources of therapeutic interventions. By the definitions outlined in this chapter, pathological fixated archaic ego states are not under Adult ego state control. However, according to Berne and many other authors and clinicians (including Groder in Erskine et al., 1988), *unfixated* archaic ego states under the direction of Adult ego state control may be useful, healthy and enhancing, particularly for psychotherapists.

> The therapist's Child, working intuitively and subconsciously, rather than deliberately and consciously like his Adult, was able to perceive accurately the instinctual connections of the gesture, and its origin.
>
> Berne (1975b, p. 69)

The popular belief to which Loria refers seems to be based on a disagreement with major sections of Berne and other clinicians, and possibly misunderstandings of the terms and phenomenological context that this author is attempting to refer to source. Thereby, it is hoped to provide an inclusive, integrative, but clarified bridge between what can be seen as falsely opposing polarities in theory and practice, creating unnecessary confusion for trainees and clients alike.

Writing on psychopathology, Berne (1975b, p. 46) refers to a person who was on the one hand 'devoid of the charm, spontaneity, and fun which are characteristic of the healthy child, and on the other he was unable to take sides with the conviction or indignation which is found in healthy parents'. His Adult was defensively excluding his Child in order to remain functional, even though this exclusion occasionally broke down. (This formulation again indicates that a healthy individual would not defensively exclude the Child.)

Exclusion is manifested by a stereotyped, predictable attitude which is steadfastly maintained as long as possible in the face of any threatening situation. The constant Parent, the constant Adult, and the constant Child all result primarily from *defensive exclusion* [italics added] of the two complementary aspects in each case.

Berne (1975b, p. 44)

In Stewart and Joines (1987), exclusion is defined as 'the shutting out by the individual of one or more ego states' (p. 329). The shutting out of an ego state in the sense of exclusion is that it is unconscious and not *optional or facultative*, in Federn's terms. It is not available to be experienced consciously and it is not under the direction of the executive or Adult ego.

The ego unit or ego state that is excluded is therefore fixated in the technical sense. It can be said that such shut-out ego states are excluded and thus not available/accessible to be used in conjunction with the integrated ego for child-like motivation or parental convictions.

When Berne (1975b) discusses regression analysis, he writes that the psychotherapist's position is one of a split cathexis between Child and Adult ego states which 'requires the utmost concentration on his (Adult) part to keep both ego states active simultaneously' (p. 227). Berne here describes how he used one of his own archaic Child ego states in the psychotherapy observed by his Adult ego state – with both ego states simultaneously cathected.

This is another example from Berne, where a Child ego state of the psychotherapist can be cathected (accessible, not fixated) in the service of the client's psychotherapy. If it *were* fixated, in the sense of being defensively kept unconscious or interfering with current relationships, it would not be under Adult direction and would potentially be anti-therapeutic.

The notion of fixation is usually understood within the framework of a general approach presupposing an ordered development of the libido (fixation at a stage). It may also be viewed . . . as a name for the mode of inscription of ideational contents (experiences, imagos or phantasies) *which persist in the unconscious in unchanging fashion* [italics added] and to which the instinct remains bound.

Laplanche and Pontalis (1988, p. 162)

For an ego unit to meet this definition of fixation, it would therefore have to remain in the unconscious and persist there without change. Thus the conscious reliving of such an ego unit with here-and-now awareness would not qualify as an fixation according to this definition. Fixation is psychoanalytically understood to have a specific relationship to repression. 'Fixation is the basis of *repression* and may even be treated as the first stage of repression in a broad sense' (Laplanche and Pontalis, 1988, p. 163).

We have reason to assume that there is a *primal repression*, a first phase of repression, which consists in the psychical (ideational) representative of the instinct being denied entrance into the conscious. With this a *fixation* is established; the representative in question persists unaltered from then onwards and the instinct remains attached to it.

Freud (1915/1957, p. 147)

Repression or orthriogenesis

It is now necessary to review the definitions of repression in order to differentiate between ego states that are temporarily, or even by choice, out of awareness (preconscious) and that could be readily cathected in the present, and those that are genuinely in the unconscious and thus not at the individual's autonomous disposal for use in a current active adult life. According to Laplanche and Pontalis (1988, p. 390), repression is 'strictly speaking, an operation whereby the subject attempts to repel, or to confine to the unconscious, representations (thoughts, images, memories) which are bound to an instinct'.

Usually repression is the most important defense against drives and memories which threaten to disturb the integration of the ego. It consists in the *permanent* [italics added] exclusion from consciousness (and thus from the ego) of a drive itself, of the representations of the drive's objects and goals, and of traumatic memories.

Weiss (1950, p. 125)

The problem is confinement to the unconscious with the key thrown away, not temporary assignment to it while retaining accessibility. 'Two types of material are repressed: the unorganized instinctual contents of the id, and those ego-contents which cannot without threat to integration, be kept within the realm of the *pre-conscious* field available to the present ego' (Weiss, 1950, p. 127).

The ego development from infantile states, through childhood, adolescence and maturity to senility, is for the most part a smooth and indiscernible process. The adult only vaguely remembers his puberty and childhood and scarcely his infancy. Freud found that repression of infantile sexuality and of typical infantile conflicts, which is discussed shortly, was responsible for this amnesia.

Yet, the greater part of oblivion is due not to repression, but to the vanishing during sleep of all ego-cathexis, and to the ego's re-awakening through orthriogenesis. Federn observed that the re-awakened ego does not contain many disagreeable or only irrelevant impressions of the day preceding sleep. Therefore, every day can begin with new readiness for joy and pain. In other words, the orthriogenic re-awakening is, in a certain measure, selective in regard to the impressions contained in each newly awakened ego-state, following the criteria of the pleasure principle.

Weiss (1950, p. 144)

Orthriogenesis can be understood to be a good example of Federn's phenomenology. In the Federnian approach, orthriogenesis is the process by which the ego re-occupies its boundaries in everyday life in normal awakening. He uses it sometimes interchangeably with the orthodox term 'cathexis' (Spiegelberg, 1972). Weiss (1950) points out that orthriogenesis is the term introduced by Federn 'in analogy to the ontogenetic recapitulation in phylogeny' (p. 80). This refers to the way in which the development recapitulates the developmental stages of the species.

For Federn, as for Freud, it was common knowledge that the earlier developmental levels of the individual and the species remain in the body, the physiology, the neurology and the memory of adult individuals. For Minkowski, Merleau-Ponty, and Federn and Berne in particular, the ego was a *body ego*, retaining within it all the earlier egos – the body–mind wholes concomitant with chunks of time or naturally occurring psychological epochs. Humans retain branchial clefts and tailbone vestiges, which remind us of our animal ancestry.

Philogenetically older centres of the brain remain available to be released from recent cortical restraints in the modern adult and, according to Koestler (1989, p. 461), 'psychotherapy aims at undoing faulty integrations by inducing a temporary regression of the patient to an earlier level, in the hope that he will eventually reintegrate into a more stable pattern'. Most clinicians who have worked with individuals in spontaneous or planned age regression have observed bodily changes – the loss of age-appropriate coordination and the reinstatement of infantile reflexes – as well as emotional and cognitive changes.

Regression, whether malignant or benign, defensive or otherwise, is discussed more fully elsewhere (Clarkson and Fish, 1986/1988). In fact, were regression to previous intact ego states with their full bodily involvement not possible, psychotherapists could never connect with the phenomenological Child (whether 2 or 42 years of age) – as Berne (1975b) said, to bring the active Child ego state 'permanently at the disposal of the patient and the therapist' where it can be helped to cathart (abreact), to work through and be nurtured 'until it unfolds like a flower' (p. 226).

The repression of ego states is one of the most important findings of Federn. It can be experimentally proven that ego states of earlier ages do not disappear but are only repressed. In hypnosis, a former ego state containing the corresponding emotional dispositions, memories, and urges can be reawakened in the individual. In Federn's opinion, the unconscious portion of the ego consists of the stratification of the repressed ego states. Double and multiple personalities, as well as somnambulism, ensue when different ego states are alternately reawakened.

Weiss in Federn (1977, pp. 14-15)

Later John Watkins, who was also a student of Federn and who developed an ego state psychotherapy independently of Berne, pursued this extensively in theory and clinical practice with multiple personalities (Watkins and Watkins, 1986).

Both acquired ego attitudes and past ego states are to a great extent repressed. Through their access to consciousness and to the preconsciousness they influence actual decisions. The influence of ego attitudes and ego states is helpful or disturbing, depending upon their normality and fitness for present needs. . . . The permanence of previous ego states extends Freud's concept of ego fixation to the field of *normal psychology* [italics added]. Because of its influence on symptom and resistance formation, pathological fixation was recognized earlier than this normal process. But the concept of pathological ego fixation presupposes the concept of *a succession of ego states* [italics added].

Federn (1977, p. 218)

Another idea which needs some slight clarification is that of repression and forgetting. The persistence of every engram, once acquired, was accepted by Freud as a basic truth. Millions of engrams would interfere with every actual and normal reaction if they were accessible to consciousness. Their continuous retention by unconsciousness and their discontinuous, however controlled, delay through the preconscious, appear to be necessary for the normal thinking process. Yet there remains the problem of whether repression is always needed to make engrams lose their cathexis and to block their availability. By considering and watching the succeeding day-by-day ego states one recognizes the effect of the interruption of ego cathexis through the all night sleep. Every morning, when the ego is recathected through the process of orthriogenesis, many engrams acquired during the previous days are found to be no longer cathected. Only those new engrams which were related to important events, intellectual interests, or which for an emotional personal reason were included in the ego unit maintain their cathexis from previous days. The emotional reason may be a pleasurable or painful ego reaction. Many more engrams lose their ephemeral importance when yesterday's joy or pain no longer prevails. These engrams enter unconsciousness without repression through the screening influence of sleep itself.

Federn (1977, pp. 218-219)

Here Federn accounts for the disappearance of ego units into unconsciousness that is a normal (not defensive) process of forgetting or screening. Berne (1975b) repeats this idea (showing how closely he is following Federn's concepts and understandings) when he states: 'Each day's experiences, an ego unit, may be compared to the rough cast of a coin, which is polished during the night' (p. 52). Federn (1977, p. 219) stresses furthermore:

> Repression is reserved only for those painful or conflictual engrams and ego reactions which cannot be handled by sleep. It is provoked by the anxiety signals of the ego and is effected by complete withdrawal of cathexis from all connecting associations. This is in accordance with Freud's keen description of the relationship of anxiety and repression. Screening by sleep does not require the interference of anxiety. Yet, when repressed ego states re-enter consciousness or when repression to previous ego states sets in (as in hypnosis with concomitant age regression) then all engrams, repressed as well as screened, regain availability and influence.

It is thus safe to conclude that Berne assumed a similar understanding of repression in his readers, i.e. that it is reserved only for those painful or conflictual ego states that are not normally handled by forgetting and screening, thereby allowing for the potential existence of many more ego states that have not been repressed.

> Examples of repressed ego states are also found in dreams and hypnosis. For the most part one dismisses one's dream immediately upon awakening because the ego-state during dreaming is quite different from that of the re-awakened ego. If the dream is incompatible with present reality, it is not only dismissed, but even repressed . . . a regression to very early ego-states can be obtained by hypnotic suggestion. Breuer's basic findings in this field have been recently re-established by some American investigators (Wolberg, Brenman, Gill, Erickson and others). All this shows that previous forgotten ego states have not faded, but that they have been potentially preserved; otherwise they could not be re-awakened. Also the phenomenon of double or even multiple personality proves the existence of repressed ego states.
>
> Weiss (1950, p. 143)

> This haunting of the present by a particular past experience is possible because we all carry our past with us insofar as its structures have become 'sedimented' in our habitual body. There is thus an 'organic repression' which is part of our human condition and which constitutes so to speak 'an inborn complex'.
>
> Langer (1989, p. 33)

This bears a close correspondence to Federn's articulation above. Finally, the voice of Merleau-Ponty (1962, p. 83) brings together many of these strands in their particular relationship to time:

> For repression, to which psycho-analysis refers, consists in the subject's entering upon a certain course of action – a love affair, a career, a piece of work – in his encountering on this course some barrier, and, since he has the strength neither to surmount the obstacle nor to abandon the enterprise, he remains imprisoned in

the attempt and uses up his strength indefinitely renewing it in spirit. Time in its passage does not carry away with it these impossible projects; it does not close up on traumatic experience; the subject remains open to the same impossible future, if not in his explicit thoughts, at any rate in his actual being. One present among all presents thus acquires an exceptional value; it displaces the others and deprives them of their value as authentic presents. We continue to be the person who once entered on this adolescent affair, or the one who once lived in this parental universe. New perceptions, new emotions even, replace the old ones, but this process of renewal touches only the content of our experience and not its structure. Impersonal time continues its course, but personal time is arrested.

So a repressed ego state is a fixated one when it continues to interrupt current functioning or relationships, and otherwise healthy or healing ego states are screened or forgotten.

The Child ego state in psychotherapy

This chapter focuses on psychotherapy, emphasizing Child ego states, whether first experienced yesterday in a traumatic road accident or in a period of neglect during the mother's postnatal depression. Influencing Parent ego states may, of course, affect Child ego states or become active independently (Berne, 1966, 1975b), but it is the Child in its visceral, biological, phenomenological reality who makes script decisions and can therefore re-decide (Goulding and Goulding, 1979).

Such Child ego states, whether called historical, phenomenological or archeopsychic, can be deliberately accessed or can occur through spontaneous regression in psychotherapy. This is how Berne found them in his consulting room.

When a previously buried archaic ego state is revived in its full vividness in the waking state, it is then permanently at the disposal of the patient and the therapist for detailed examination. Not only do 'abreaction' and 'working through' take place, but the ego state can be treated like an actual child. It can be nurtured carefully, even tenderly, until it unfolds like a flower, revealing all the complexities of its internal structure. It can be turned over and over in the hand, so to speak, until previously unobserved features come into full perception. Such an active ego state is not regarded in the manner of Kubie as a memory, but as an experience in its own right, more like Penfield's temporal phenomenon.

Berne (1975b, p. 226)

Again, temporality as a fundamental phenomenon of human experience is both matrix and living fibre in life, psychotherapy, phenomenological philosophy and physics. Zohar (1990, p. 127) writes:

Through the process of quantum memory, where the wave patterns created by past experiences merge in the brain's quantum system with wave patterns created by present experience, my past is always with me. It exists not as a 'memory', a finished and closed fact which I can recall, but as a living presence which partially defines what I am now. The wave patterns of the past are taken up and woven into now, relived afresh at each moment as something which has been but also as something which is now being. Through quantum memory, the past is alive, open and in dialogue with the present. As in any true dialogue, this means that not only does the past influence the present but also that the present impinges on the past, giving it new life and new meaning, at times transforming it utterly.

It is the current author's conviction that TA in the 1990s can benefit from such modern quantum approaches to physics, which are in such close correspondence with the original phenomenological, philosophical and intellectual ground of this discipline, e.g. in addition to objective time, Minkowski (1933/1970) wanted phenomenology to help people 'reconquer our right over lived time' (p. 3).

Surely this is the task of psychotherapy. Divisions and factionalism in TA with singular received truths can thus be replaced by the celebration of multiple relative perspectives. These may even be contradictory from singular vantage points, but their complementarity may be obvious when seen from an inclusive metaperspective which validates differences in different contexts with different overlaps for different purposes (Clarkson, 1987).

Berne sometimes emphasized Child ego states as fixations, whereas with others he emphasized their creative, joyous, continuing presence in the Adult. These perspectives are *both* valid, and have therapeutic leverage depending on how the individual psychotherapist wishes to use them. Certainly people have been transformed by working with psychotherapists who use only the functional model of ego states, those who use mixed models and others who hold any of a number of differing beliefs about Child ego states.

In this respect it is salutary to recall Jung's (1928) admonition: 'Learn your theories as well you can, but put them aside when you touch the miracle of the living soul. Not theories but your own creative individuality alone must decide' (p. 361). Jung (1934/1954, p. 169) was probably the first psychologist to call us to honour 'the child in the adult'.

It is in this spirit that this author concludes this investigation into Child ego states by suggesting three different ways of conceptualizing and assessing psychological disturbance (roughly corresponding with the emergence of these three different foci of treatment approaches in transactional analysis):

1) through affective and cognitive interference in the functioning of the integrated ego (confusion model); 2) through the existence of internal conflict between different parts of the ego (conflict model); 3) through developmental deficits and inadequate parenting (deficit model).

Clarkson and Gilbert (1988, p. 27)

Seinfeld (1990) – discovered by me after writing the above – also distinguishes as *complementary* psychotherapeutic approaches treating the 'structural deficit (of positive self and object representations) and conflict (the bad object situation)' (p. 12). The latter resembles re-parenting and re-childing, and the former resembles re-decision approaches to treatment.

Originally, Berne saw decontamination and de-confusion as preceding psychoanalysis proper, but, as the contributions of Goulding and Goulding, Schiff and others have shown, a complete armory has been assembled in TA, resembling the shift in psychoanalysis from drive theory to ego psychology and object relations to self-psychology. (This is further discussed in Clarkson, 1992.)

In terms of the focus on Child ego states in this chapter, reconstructive psychotherapy involves Adult decontamination with accessing of archaic ego states and enabling: (1) their deconfusion, through regression analysis, for example; (2) their conflict resolution between different Child ego states and/or Parent ego states through redecisions; or (3) their provision of new experiences on previous planes of experience at the archaic levels of deficit or trauma through re-parenting or re-childing procedures.

> We now return from the examination of the affects in relation to narcissism to the behavior of the patient when in analysis former ego states emerge. It is normal that more or less strong affects arise at these occasions; sometimes they take time to become manifest and intense, at other times they erupt so suddenly that they take hold of the rest of the ego more or less intensively, totally or partially, only to fade away again or to be disposed of in some other manner. The ego participates in each such dramatic occurrence, either joyfully or with suffering, and defending itself with libido cathexes which either continue to exist in an unsatisfied state or are satisfied and come to rest.
>
> Federn (1977, pp. 341-342)

De-contamination and de-confusion

Child ego states of earlier developmental levels are accessed in psychotherapy in order to do decontamination through Berne's (1966) basic techniques and/or de-confusion, e.g. through regression analysis. When earlier ego states are accessed, fixations are lifted so that contact with the present is both conscious and disconnected.

Conscious memory often absolves it from having to be compulsively (however partially) relived as discussed in the section on fixation in my previous paper entitled *A Definition of Ego States.*

> By taking up a present, I draw together and transform my past, altering its significance, freeing and detaching myself from it . . . it is a matter of reliving this or that as significant, and this the patient succeeds in doing only by seeing his past in the perspective of his co-existence with the doctor. The complex is not

dissolved by a non-instrumental freedom, but rather displaced by a new pulsation of time with its own supports and motives.

Merleau-Ponty (1962, p. 455)

As Cornell (1988) pointed out, although early childhood is significant in terms of script development, experiences at much later ages may potentially be just as, or even more, influential as in such cases as adult hospitalizations, accidents, the death of a child and rape.

> Psychotherapists are very familiar with the process of quantum memory, though most might be surprised upon first being told that! The physics by which the wave functions of our various past sub-selves can overlap with, and hence get taken up into, our present self is the physics by which psychotherapists get their patients to relive past experiences in the 'now', thus robbing them of their isolation and their sting and wedding them to the present. This moment of psychoanalytic 'insight', during which the past *is*, now, and both past and present are transformed, is quite different from a simple, intellectual remembering of past events.
>
> Zohar (1990, p. 105)

Conflict resolution

> In ascribing to the ego the control of regression in terms of shifts in the cathexis of ego functions, which can be related to or pitted against each other in various ways, we gain a frame of reference that might in the present tentative state of our knowledge prove useful in various ways.
>
> Kris (1952, p. 313)

In impasse resolution resulting in script re-decisions, earlier Child ego states are accessed in order to resolve conflicts (between different Child ego states, or between Child ego states and Parent ego states) (Goulding and Goulding, 1979). 'Ego-state therapy is the utilization of family and group treatment techniques for the resolution of conflicts between the different ego states that constitute a "family of self" within a single individual' (Watkins and Watkins, 1986, p. 149).

Deficit replenishment

The third kind of treatment approach focuses on structural psychological deficits, which may be the result of an inadequate environmental response during trauma or the persistent absence of an empathic caretaker (mirroring self-object) (Kohut, 1984) during childhood or significant later periods.

Deficit replenishment takes a myriad forms, from radical re-parenting (Schiff et al., 1975) to transmuting internalization (Kohut, 1984) to providing the recognition to the infant in the Adult that Balint (1989) proposes. All of these therapeutic approaches can be seen to involve the creation of new historical or new Child ego states, specifically to provide, e.g. in areas of specific structural deficits, positive self- and object representations.

Deficit, whether as permission for catharsis or the provision of a corrective experience (of nurture or control, mirroring or optimal frustration), can be done through re-parenting (Schiff, 1975), self-re-parenting (James, 1974), or self-re-childing procedures which use a functional model (James and Savary, 1977).

Re-parenting is going back to earlier Child ego states and providing a new object relationship – not re-archaicing them, but finding previous developmental levels of fixation, undoing them, and providing new or corrective experiences where these are lacking or needed.

Re-childing within a structural or phenomenological model of ego states is more fully discussed by Clarkson and Fish (1988), which should be read in conjunction with Clarkson and Gilbert (1988). Briefly, re-childing is defined as 'the creation of new ego states on psychophysiologically developmentally earlier sub-strata' (Clarkson and Fish, 1988, p. 52). 'Thus the new Child ego state is *both* archaic and new; it is new in its creation today, and it is the archaic relic of tomorrow. It is also archaic because it is formed on an earlier developmental psychophysiological substratum.'

Newly created ego states in the present are different from newly created ego states on much earlier (archaic) developmental levels, as has been discussed in the section on orthriogenesis in an earlier paper by this author in this series, *A Definition of Ego States*. According to Koestler (1989, p. 461), psychotherapists 'try to make the patient revert to unconscious and infantile planes of experience, and to regenerate, as it were, into a more or less new-born person. Thus psychotherapy may be called an experiment in artificially induced regeneration'. It is the transactional equivalent of Balint's (1989, p. 146) 'true new beginning . . . ending in a real new discovery' accomplished through 'the benign form of regression'.

> Since the basic fault, as long as it is active, determines the forms of object relations available to any individual, a necessary task of the treatment is to inactivate the basic fault by creating conditions in which it can heal off. To achieve this, the patient must be allowed to regress either to the setting, that is, to the particular form of object relationship which caused the original deficiency state, or even to some stage before it. . . . Only after that can the patient 'begin anew', that is, develop new patterns of object relations to replace those given up.
>
> Balint (1989, p. 166)

Such new beginnings on 'earlier levels' (Koestler, 1989, p. 462) are possible because phenomenologically time is not unidirectionally linear and, in Samuels' (1985, p. 145) restrained phraseology, experientially 'the rules of time may not always apply'. Phenomenologically, *logical* is a different (even complementary) universe of discourse from *psychological*.

Re-childing does not have to be done in psychotherapy. As pointed out by Winnicott (1960) earlier, people can do it for themselves when the environment is more conducive to health and growth. It can also occur spontaneously as in the creation of healthy functioning new Child ego states, e.g. a grown man buying himself a teddy bear or a train set when he never had one as a little boy. This is phenomenologically true both to the observer and to the person himself in the validity of this experience at the moment. He is buying it for the residual child in himself – still there, still capable of assimilating new experiences at archaic or previous developmental levels or old ego states, still acting as motivation for a greater fullness of life.

Earlier ego units (epochs) are not full because time in the human psyche is pliable. As the popular lapel buttons say (no doubt reflecting some wisdom from the collective unconscious): 'It's never too late to have a happy childhood!'

In re-childing the emphasis is not on the psychotherapist as Parent so much as on the use of self and spontaneously occurring peer situations in order to access earlier ego states. Re-childing does not replace past ego states; it creates new experiences in past psychological places – the past cannot be changed, but as a result of the marvellous elasticity of time we can create alternative pasts.

Erickson (in Rossi, 1979) showed this most convincingly with the February man, where a new childhood history was created for a woman, which she could use to support her current functioning and henceforth access as an alternative to her own, actually true, painful past.

Re-childing cannot, in fact, be done without the presence of another, but this presence may be imaginary (conscious, preconscious or unconscious) or making the good object stay on purpose (Seinfeld, 1990). The actions of the other may be active, as in radical re-parenting, re-birthing or happily leading your own life while trainees map theirs off yours.

Psychotherapist and clients witness the creation of alternative childhoods (Shapiro, 1988) or alternative past experiences that can be voluntarily accessed by the Adult ego instead of the earlier depleted, underdeveloped or traumatized states. A client reports after a re-birthing experience that culminated in an alternative birthday: 'I can energize the old experience or this one which has given me trust in the world.'

Reinforcement

There is a fourth way that may intentionally or unintentionally occur inside or outside psychotherapy using earlier healthy ego states. In psychotherapy, it is not unusual to find or to use an earlier happy Child ego state (e.g. reliving the experience of being warmly held and comforted) in helping a person to find internal supports for integrated Adult functioning (Clarkson and Fish, 1988). Groder adduces a poignant example of this (Erskine et al., 1988, p. 10).

Neurolinguistic programming (Lankton, 1980) refers to a similar process of accessing resourceful earlier sensory/memory states in order to support or 'anchor' (p. 156) new healing experiences, e.g. this way of accessing or cathecting useful historical Child ego states can be used to support redecisions.

'Regression analysis is a deliberate attempt to shift the study of the Child from an inferential basis to a phenomenological one' (Berne, 1975b, p. 227). As has been shown, regression is a function of the integrative ego for Balint (1989) and for others, as well as Fairbairn (1952, p. 205):

> She was reunited to her grandfather in phantasy and played gaily with him in the elysian fields. Repressed emotional experiences of a libidinal nature thus broke through the trammels of years; and she re-discovered what she came to describe as her 'infantile self', which had remained for long repressed in her unconscious.

The above are all methods of healing and/or reclaiming the Child.

> Put in quantum terms, the wave function of a relived past moment overlaps with the wave function of now, and the two unite to form a new way forward. The person gains perspective and becomes more coherent. Thus through quantum memory we take up the past and make it ours in the present. We reincarnate the past (all our past selves), giving it new life in a new form. . . . By reliving past moments the quantum self is creative on two fronts – on the one hand it reincarnates the past, giving it renewed life and meaning; on the other it recreates itself at every moment.
>
> Zohar (1990, p. 105)

In most cases of script change there is an other – a relationship – even if it is only represented by the provision of the time and milieu for doing so. There is a difference between whether the others (such as the therapists) are doing it to us in re-parenting or whether we are recreating ourselves through the grace of their witness or participation.

Through Bergson's *élan vital* (1913) and its contribution to creative evolution, there is a similar emphasis in Berne on the natural healing growth force of *Physis* (Berne, 1966, 1973, 1975a). This is the creative evolutionary force that helps us to see and find creative solutions to yesterday's problems in order to free us for tomorrow with all its challenges, pain and joy.

Berne (1966) defines *Physis* as 'The growth force of nature, which makes organisms evolve into higher forms, embryos develop into adults, sick people get better, and healthy people strive to attain their ideals' (pp. 369-370). He diagrams such aspiration toward *the future* as arising from the Child (Berne, 1973, p. 128).

Conclusion

Chapters 5 and 6 have reviewed TA as a *phenomenological* psychology according to Berne's stated intention, and recapitulated understandings of ego and ego states by emphasizing the reality of ego states understood within an epistemology based on the philosophy and method of phenomenology. The central role of subjective time in psychological life is supplemented by understandings from modern physics.

Definitions of structural (or phenomenological) Child ego states were retrieved from Berne as well as other major TA theorists, and showed from both literature and subjective experience that there are at least two varieties of such Child ego states - fixated or accessible. Although the functional model of ego states was specifically excluded from this discussion, making a conceptually and theoretically coherent integration as offered in this chapter has advantages for whichever model of ego states is used.

Psychoanalytic definitions of fixation were re-examined and repression as a defence mechanism is differentiated from the evolutionary healthy process of orthriogenesis. A reminder of the nature of the Adult ego state, particularly in terms of its executive function, was followed by consideration of Child ego states in healthy functioning and in creativity.

A summary concludes by showing how Child ego states are accessed in psychotherapy in order to focus on confusion, conflict or deficit models of assessment and treatment of *the Child* which is fuelled by *Physis*.

References

Balint, M. (1989) The Basic Fault: Therapeutic aspects of regression. London: Routledge.

Bergson, H. (1913) Time and Free Will. (F.L. Pogson, trans.). New York: Macmillan.

Berne, E. (1966) Principles of Group Treatment. New York: Grove Press.

Berne, E. (1973) What Do You Say After You Say Hello? New York: Bantam Books.

Berne, E. (1975a) The Structure and Dynamics of Organizations and Groups. New York: Grove Press.

Berne, E. (1975b) Transactional Analysis in Psychotherapy. London: Souvenir Press.

Berne, E. (1977) Intuition and Ego States. San Francisco, CA: TA Press.

Clarkson, P. (1987) Meta-perspectives on diagnosis (waves or particles?). ITA News 18: 6-11.

Clarkson, P. (1992) Transactional Analysis Psychotherapy: An integrated approach. London: Routledge.

Clarkson, P. and Fish, S. (1988) Rechilding: Creating a new past in the present as a support for the future. Transactional Analysis Journal 18(1): 51-59 (first published in Spanish translation, 1986).

Clarkson, P. and Gilbert, M. (1988) Berne's original model of ego states: Some theoretical considerations. Transactional Analysis Journal 18(1): 20-29 (first published in Spanish translation, 1986).

Conway, A. and Clarkson, P. (1987) Everyday hypnotic inductions. Transactional Analysis Journal 17(2): 17-23.

Cornell, W.F. (1988) Life script theory: A critical review from a developmental perspective. Transactional Analysis Journal 18: 270-282.

Drever, J. (1952) The Dictionary of Psychology. Harmondsworth, Middx: Penguin.

English, F. (1977) What shall I do tomorrow?: Reconceptualizing transactional analysis. In: Barnes, G. (ed.), Transactional Analysis after Eric Berne: Teachings and practices of three TA schools. New York: Harper's College Press, pp. 287-347.

Erickson, M.H. (1967) Advanced Techniques of Hypnosis and Therapy. New York: Grune & Stratton.

Erskine, R.G., Clarkson, P., Goulding, R.L., Groder, M.G. and Moiso, C. (1988) Ego state theory: Definitions, descriptions, and points of view. Transactional Analysis Journal 18(1): 6-14.

Fairbairn, W.R.D. (1952) Psychoanalytic Studies of the Personality. London: Tavistock.

Federn, P. (1977) Ego Psychology and the Psychoses. London: Maresfield Reprints.

Freud, S. (1957) Repression. In: Strachey, J. (ed., trans.), The standard edition of the complete psychological works of Sigmund Freud, Vol. 11. London: Hogarth Press, pp. 141-158 (J. Strachey, trans.; original work published 1915).

Goulding, M.M. and Goulding, R.L. (1979) Changing Lives through Redecision Therapy. New York: Brunner/Mazel.

Horowitz, M.J. (1979) States of Mind: Analysis of change in psychotherapy. New York: Plenum Medical.

James, M. (1974) Self-reparenting: Theory and process. Transactional Analysis Journal 4(3): 32-39.

James, M. and Jongeward, D. (1971) Born to Win: Transactional Analysis with gestalt experiments. Reading, MA: Addison-Wesley.

James, M. and Savary, L. (1977) A New Self: Self-therapy with transactional analysis. Reading, MA: Addison-Wesley.

Jung, C.G. (1928) Analytical psychology and education. In: Contributions to Analytical Psychology (H.G. Baynes and F.C. Baynes, trans.). London: Trench Trubner, pp. 313-382.

Kernberg, O.F. (1981) The development of intrapsychic structures in the light of borderline personality organization. In: Greenspan, S.I. and Pollock, G.H. (eds), The Course of Life: Psychoanalytic contributions toward understanding personality development, Vol. III. Adulthood and the aging process. Adelphi, MD: National Institute of Mental Health, pp. 349-366.

Koestler, A. (1989) The Act of Creation. London: Arkana.

Kohut, H. (1984) How Does Analysis Cure? Chicago: University of Chicago Press.

Kohut, H. (1987) The Kohut Seminars on Self Psychology and Psychotherapy with Adolescents and Young Adults. New York: W.W. Norton.

Kris, E. (1952) Psychoanalytic Explorations in Art. Madison, CT: International Universities Press.

Langer, M.M. (1989) Merleau-Ponty's Phenomenology of Perception. London: Macmillan.

Lankton, S.R. (1980) Practical Magic: A translation of basic neuro-linguistic programming into clinical psychotherapy. CA: Meta Publications.

Laplanche, J. and Pontalis, J.B. (1988) The Language of Psycho-analysis. (D. Nicholson-Smith, trans.). London: Karnac.

Loria, B.R. (1988) The parent ego state: Theoretical foundations and alterations. Transactional Analysis Journal 18(1): 39–46.

Merleau-Ponty, M. (1962) Phenomenology of Perception (C. Smith, trans.). London: Routledge & Kegan Paul.

Minkowski, E. (1970) Lived Time (N. Metzel, trans.). Evanston, IL: Northwestern University Press (original work published in 1933).

Onions, C.T. (ed.) (1973) The Shorter Oxford English Dictionary. Oxford: Oxford University Press.

Proust, A. (1983) Remembrance of Things Past (C.K. Scott Moncrieff and T. Kilmartin, trans.). Harmondsworth, Middlesex: Penguin (original work published 1913).

Rossi, E.L. (ed.) (1979) The Collected Papers of Milton H. Erickson on Hypnosis, Vols. I–IV. New York: Irvington Publishers.

Rycroft, C. (1968) The Critical Dictionary of Psychoanalysis. Harmondsworth, Middlesex: Penguin.

Samuels, A. (1985) Jung and the Post-Jungians. London: Routledge & Kegan Paul.

Schiff, J.L., in collaboration with Schiff, A.W., Mellor K., Schiff, E. et al. (1975). Cathexis Reader: Transactional analysis treatment of psychosis. New York: Harper & Row.

Seinfeld, J. (1990) The Bad Object: Handling the negative therapeutic reaction in psychotherapy. NJ: Jason Aronson.

Shapiro, M.K. (1988) Second Childhood: Hypno-play therapy with age-regressed adults. New York: W.W. Norton & Co.

Spiegelberg, H. (1972) Phenomenology in Psychology and Psychiatry: A historical introduction. Evanston, IL: Northwestern University Press.

Stewart, I. and Joines, V. (1987) TA Today. Nottingham: Lifespace.

Watkins, J.G. and Watkins, H.H. (1986) Hypnosis, multiple personality, and ego states as altered states of consciousness. In: Wolman, B.B. and Ullman, M. (eds), Handbook of States of Consciousness. New York: Van Nostrand Reinhold, pp. 133–158.

Weiss, E. (1950) Principles of Psychodynamics. New York: Grune & Stratton.

Winnicott, D.W. (1960) The Maturational Processes and the Facilitating Environment. London: Hogarth Press.

Winnicott, D.W. (1975) Through Paediatrics to Psycho-analysis. London: Hogarth Press and the Institute of Psycho-Analysis.

Zohar, D. (1990) The Quantum Self. London: Bloomsbury.

Chapter 7
Variations on I and Thou

This chapter considers that there are five identifiable, interweaving, but potentially distinct, kinds of therapeutic relationship to be found in gestalt theory and practice. These are the working alliance, the 'unfinished' (or transference/countertransference) relationship, the reparative (and/or developmental) relationship, the I-you (or dialogic) relationship and the transpersonal relationship. Each and all of these modalities are available for constructive use in gestalt clinical work and its supervision to give nuance to theoretical understanding, to refine conscientious research and to contribute to the development of our discipline.

Laura Perls was profoundly influenced by a personal meeting with Martin Buber and has said that the true essence of gestalt therapy was the relationship formed between the therapist and the client (Hycner, 1985). Relationship can be defined as 'the state of being related; a condition or character based upon this kinship' (Onions, 1973, p. 1786). Relationship is the first condition of being human. It circumscribes two or more individuals and creates a bond in the space between them that is more than the sum of the parts. It is so obvious that it is frequently taken for granted, and so mysterious that many of the world's greatest psychologists, novelists and philosophers have made it a lifetime's preoccupying passion. Research has shown that statistically you are more likely to be killed by a relation than by a stranger. Results of studies also consistently show that the choice of a particular psychotherapeutic method appears to have much less discernible influence on the effectiveness of psychotherapy than the relationship between the therapist and the client (Norcross, 1986). Gestaltists, such as Polster and Polster (1973) and the existential psychotherapist May (1969), have also focused extensively on the existential nature of therapeutic relationship. The I-thou relationship has been given serious attention in gestalt psychotherapy. Another perspective may claim that I-you incorporates other relationship modes. It doesn't matter *how* we think about it; it matters *that* we think about it. [I agree with the Buber translator, Kaufmann, that I–thou more accurately represents the person-to-person intention and the lack of formality rendered in German *Du* which is not captured in English by the more formal thou (Kaufmann in Buber, 1970, p. 14).]

Some commentators believe that psychotherapy will disappear if people 'take care of each other' (Smail, 1987) and some feel that it *should* disappear because of the abuses inherent in the very activity of psychotherapy. Masson (1989), in his book *Against Therapy*, profoundly questions and criticizes *all* approaches to psychotherapy and demonstrates with a series of appalling examples how psychotherapists from Freud to Rosen have sexually used or abused their patients. Perls certainly did. Masson's criticisms represent a very important polarity to be considered by any practising psychotherapist and deserve to be taken very seriously. This is particularly important for gestalt therapists for whom authentic relationship is so vital because interpersonal intimacy is often confused with sexual intimacy in many cultures.

Five kinds of therapeutic relationship

There is no single, simple, dividing line between the infinitely different ways of being with 'an other' in growthful or healing encounter. There are many different ways of thinking about and experiencing the nature of the therapeutic relationship. At any time one aspect of relationship may be in particular focus, but other modes of therapeutic relationship may also be present in the background of being.

A qualitative research project spanning some 20 years and some 1000 texts led to the differentiating framework of five kinds of therapeutic relationship potentially available for constructive use in psychotherapy (Clarkson, 2003b).

Illustrations from gestalt theory and practice formed the primary matrix for its development (Clarkson, 1989) and the first presentation of this work was as a keynote talk at a UK national gestalt conference (subsequently published as Clarkson, 2003a). In the following section the five kinds of therapeutic relationships (the working alliance, the unfinished [transferential] relationship, the reparative/developmental relationship, the I–thou relationship and the transpersonal relationship) are made temporary figures for our attention in order to contribute to the enhancement of therapy, training and supervision in gestalt.

The working alliance

The working alliance is probably the most essential relationship modality that is operative in psychotherapy. Without such an agreement psychotherapy is limited in its goals and restricted in its scope. This working alliance is represented by the client's or patient's willingness to engage in the here and now of the psychotherapeutic relationship even when he or she is projecting the past. The client may fear terrible retribution if he or she shares his or her anger at the therapist because this was the way that it used to happen in the childhood home. In part, the working alliance refers to the awareness level of the client, e.g. the client may be projecting a lot of old material on to the therapist even though, in reality, the therapist does not fit that projection – the client can remain (or is willing to become) aware that this current therapist person may *feel like* the old one, but based on his or her own past experience of the current therapeutic relationship, the therapist does not physically abuse him or her (as dad used to do) when he or she is angry. The working alliance can be translated as therapist and client sharing a similar existential project: a mutual engagement, whether dangerous or delicious, with a common figure of interest – the client's desire.

When past relationship patterns or archaic unfinished business intrude on a client's awareness field, it may push the authentically real here-and-now relationship with the therapist out of awareness for moments or even extended periods of time. Dealing with these unresolved gestalten as they impede, distort or limit current potential for authentic relationship can be seen as the very stuff of therapy. To actualize this, however, a shared working relationship needs to be maintained. Which aspect of the encounter is brought into figure, or focus, depends on the nature of the psycho-therapeutic task at a particular time with each patient.

The working alliance is the crucial and necessary relationship for effective therapy. It certainly is the necessary cooperation that even a physician requires in order to work effectively with patients, be it simply at the level that the patient takes the medication as prescribed. Anecdotal evidence and research (Francis et al., 1969; Becker and Maiman, 1975) have shown that this working alliance is frequently missing in general medical practice.

> The therapeutic alliance is the powerful joining of forces that energizes and supports the long, difficult, and frequently painful work of life-changing psychotherapy. The conception of the therapist here is not of a disinterested observer-technician but of a fully alive human companion for the client. In this regard my view is in marked contrast to the traditional notion of the psychotherapist as a skilled but objective director of therapeutic processes.
>
> Bugental (1987, p. 49)

The unfinished relationship

The 'unfinished relationship' is another way in which gestalt therapists may name the phenomenon that psychoanalysts refer to as 'transference' in order to deal with it differently.

> Now of course we know that relating is always a mixture of contact and transference, but we deal phenomenologically and dialogically with transference. We recognise it, neither forbid it nor encourage it. *We know and use alternatives to interpretation of the transference* [italics added].
>
> Yontef (1988, p. 23)

Many gestalt psychotherapists have had extensive psychoanalytic training and experience and use the transference relationship as a living and growthful matrix for therapy. Even those without such training have appreciated the dynamic of people attempting to 'finish' experiences with childhood figures in current adult relationships as being one of the most compelling sources of frustration and unhappiness. Both the philosophy and technology of the gestalt approach can be used to engage the person more fully in authentic contact with self and other in the here and now.

Freud went so far, at one point, as to suggest that the analyst model himself on the surgeon, put aside his human sympathy and adopt an attitude of emotional coldness (Freud, 1912b, p. 115). At times Freud advocated that the analyst refrain from intruding his personality into treatment, and introduced the simile of the 'mirror' for the analysand (Freud, 1912b, p. 118). This position is a stereotype of analysis and anathema to gestalt.

Actually, the populist interpretation of Freud's work may not be an accurate picture of Freud. Like Perls he was, and is, subject to much misunderstanding. Perhaps Freud emphasized certain of the 'unnatural' aspects of psychoanalytic technique because they were so foreign and artificial to the usual doctor–patient relationship and the customary psychotherapy of his day. He *did not exclude* other forms of therapeutic relating, e.g. at the time when he was recommending emotional coldness and a mirror-like attitude, Freud (1912a, p. 105) states:

> Thus the solution of the puzzle is that transference to the doctor is suitable for resistance to the treatment only in so far as it is a negative transference or a positive transference of repressed erotic impulses. If we 'remove' the transference by making it conscious, we are detaching only these two components of the emotional act from the person or the doctor; the other component, which is admissible to consciousness and unobjectionable, persists and is the vehicle of success in psycho-analysis exactly as it is in other methods of treatment.

The reparative relationship

The reparative relationship is another relationship mode that can occasionally be differentiated from the others. This is the intentional provision by the psychotherapist of a corrective/reparative or replenishing parental or educational or spiritual relationship (or action). This would apply where the original fixed gestalt was incomplete and therefore fixed as a result of conditions such as abuse or overprotection. It can also be seen as the relationship in the therapeutic encounter that provides the atmosphere wherein the client is able to connect with the innate process of growth and self-support. Gestalt theory and practice usually emphasize the therapist's task as the reinstatement of growth. However, there are many examples of gestalt therapy being experienced as reparative of earlier relationship damage as is shown, for example, in the following excerpt from Polster (1985, p. 6) discussing a young colleague's work with a client:

> For reasons I thought were good, what she [the gestalt therapist] did was spend considerable time giving her patient instructions in communicating with her friends; simple things like helping her to realize when she had not completed a sentence and so on. She was marvellously kindly in teaching her how to talk to these people. Her conversational, instructive mode is what she thought might not be Gestalt therapy. She thought it wasn't present oriented; she didn't use the empty chair to have her actually talk to her friends; she didn't ask anything about the patient's awareness. Her work did represent a faithfulness to the *contact* between her and her patient, a very sensitive contact in which she was very giving; giving exactly what she believed this particular patient, at this particular moment, needed most or was most called for by the dynamics of their interaction.

The therapist was *giving* the patient what was needed at that moment – what was interpreted as 'needed' in the context of a reparative developmental process. Korb et al. (1989) write: 'When working with clients who are committed to completing the maturational process, the Gestalt therapist sometimes works as an educator as well as a therapist . . . [sometimes] provides necessary and appropriate support' (pp. 114 and 118). This dimension of the therapeutic relationship refers to those aspects of relationship that may have been absent or traumatic for the client at particular periods of his or her past (as child or adult) and that are supplied by the psychotherapist – even to the 'safety provided' (Ciornai, 1995, p. 8). This is usually done on request by, or with agreement from, the patient during the psychotherapy through 'teaching patients how to become more aware, make better contact, achieve grounding, undo fixed Gestalts and increase chronically missing support' (Melnick, 1995, personal communication). Often it is the *unavoidable* corrective experience together with a patient's subjective experience that, for the first time in his or her life, someone values, listens, confirms, includes, concentrates, pays attention, is fully present for him or her.

Ferenczi (1926), one of Freud's early followers, also attempted to give people what they needed for their growth or development early in the history of psychoanalysis. He departed from neutrality and impassivity in favour of giving nursery care, friendly hugs or management of regression to very sick patients, including one whom he saw any time, day or night, and took with him on his holidays. Sechehaye (1951) worked in a similar fashion, holding and feeding her patient and crying over her. Fromm-Reichman (1974) too interacted with her patients in ways that are direct, interventionist and active, e.g. when a psychotic patient soiled her clothes with faeces, she simply wore a white coat next time – to protect herself, while at the same time giving the patient the room for her expressiveness in the reality of the relationship. Ferenczi held that there needed to be a contrast between the original trauma in infancy and the analytic situation, so that remembering rather than re-traumatizing the patient can be facilitated.

Here follows a brief transcript of a moment in gestalt therapy where the client asks the therapist to provide permission and affection, which was missing for him as a child, as he relives being that child in the *present relationship* with the psychotherapist:

- I want to be energetic about it . . . it's been with me for some time.
- Help me to see where it goes, more into sensation . . . I want to run at something.
- Do you want to run at the couch against the wall?
- Feeling lips puckering up, making a fist – what a size that is.
- Hm, hm.
- Make a noise to go with it.
- What's going on?
- I'm wondering whether I stood up to you or not? I don't want to see you crumble.
- You need to be able to resist me.
- Is it OK that I got angry?
- It's fine, it's good.
- I'm feeling a bit small now.
- In what way small?
- Like a little boy – I need you to tell me it's all right.
- It's fine. It's great that you got angry. You're a capable man.
- Do you still love me?

- Yes, I do.
- I found it a bit scary, but great.
- I liked being with you while you were doing that.

The advocacy relationship proposed by Miller (1981, 1986), which has been adapted by a number of gestalt therapists, can be seen to be the provision of a developmental process in a child's life that should have been provided by a parent or other significant caretakers. In many cases the psychotherapist ultimately provides this. In view of the regressive nature of this kind of work and the likely length of time involved in working with people who have been severely damaged, the professional and ethical responsibilities of the psychotherapists are also concomitantly greater.

The I–you relationship

The therapeutic relationship modality that shows most continuity with the healing relationships of ordinary life is what Buber (1970) called the I-you relationship to differentiate it from the I-it relationship. It is very probably those ordinary relationships that human beings have experienced as particularly healing over the ages.

With Freud's discovery of the importance of the transference relationship came deep suspicion of the real relationship - the therapeutic relationship most similar to ordinary human relationships. Object relations theorists have offered psychotherapy profoundly useful concepts and theoretical understandings. However, the I-you relationship, which is the core of gestalt, is *the opposite* of an object relationship. For Buber (1970, p. 55), the other is *a person*, not an object.

> Whoever says You does not have something for his object. For wherever there is something there is also another something; every It borders on other Its; It is only by virtue of bordering on others. But where You is said there is no something. You has no borders. Whoever says You does not have something; he has nothing. But he stands in relation.

The emotional involvement in this relationship between psychotherapist and patient is that between *person and person* in the existential dilemma where both stand in a kind of mutuality to each other. It is a kind of mutuality because the psychotherapist is also in role.

> Healing, like educating, requires that one lives in confrontation and is yet removed. . . . Every I-You relationship in a situation defined by the attempt of one partner to act on the other one so as to accomplish some goal depends on a mutuality that is condemned never to be complete.
>
> Buber (1970, p. 179)

However, in the immediacy of the existential encounter, the mutuality is almost complete and the Self of the psychotherapist becomes the instrument through which the healing evolves. Such self-disclosure needs to be done with extreme care and in its most abusive form is an excuse for inauthentic eruptions or leakage of the therapist's need for display, hostility or seductiveness. Genuine, well-judged use of the I–you relationship is probably one of the most difficult forms of therapeutic relating. Doubtless this was the reason behind the early psychoanalysts regarding it with extreme suspicion. Many personal encounters have been destructive under the guise of the I–you relationship. It probably requires the most skill, the most self-knowledge and the greatest care because its potential for careless or destructive use is so great. However, it is the one form that gestalt therapists in particular use and celebrate, perhaps more than any other. It is also exemplified in papers in the *Gestalt Journal* devoted to this subject (Korb, 1988; Hycner, 1990). 'There can be no psychoanalysis without an existential bond between the analyst and the analysand' writes Boss (1963).

> This means that to imagine there can be analysis without countertransference, without involvement and response on the part of the analyst, is an illusion. The analyst can deny but cannot avoid having an emotional relationship with the analysand: even the objectifying attitude of indifference is a mode of emotional relating.
>
> Friedman (1985, pp. 79-80)

The I–you relationship is characterized by a *here-and-now existential encounter* between the two people. It involves mutual participation in the process and the recognition that each is changed by the other. The real person of the psychotherapist can never be totally excluded from an interactional matrix of therapy. Existential psychotherapy (Boss, 1963; Binswanger 1968; May, 1969) specifically includes the I–you genuine encounter as a major therapeutic modality, and it has always been a central, if not the central, concern in gestalt therapy.

> The basic word I-You (Thou) can be spoken only with one's whole being. The concentration and fusion into a whole being can never be accomplished by me, can never be accomplished without me. . . . No purpose intervenes between I and You, no greed and no anticipation. . . . Every means is an obstacle. Only where all means have disintegrated encounters occur. . . . The actual and fulfilled present exists only insofar as presentness, encounter and relation exist. Only as the You becomes present does presence come into being.
>
> Buber (1970, pp. 62-63)

What is therapeutic, when it is achieved, is 'the moment of real meeting', according to Guntrip (1961). This experience is transforming for both psychotherapist and patient because it is not what happened before (i.e. unfinished business from the past) but what has never happened before, a genuine experience of relationship centred in the here and now.

Of course, the humanistically oriented psychotherapies, such as gestalt, which emphasize relationship based on here-and-now *contact* and phenomenological focusing, as opposed to a relationship based on transference and interpretation, have greatly amplified the value and use of the person-to-person encounter in psychotherapy. This has been our gift to psychotherapy in general – perhaps more than any other.

> The details of technique vary, but the strategy is always to keep a steady, gentle pressure toward the direct and responsible I–thou orientation, keeping the focus of awareness on the difficulties the patients experience in doing this, and helping them find their own ways through these difficulties.
>
> Fagan and Shepherd (1971, p. 117)

According to Malcolm (1981), honesty and spontaneity can correct the patient's transference misperceptions and make the psychotherapist's responses unpredictable and therefore less likely to be manipulated by the patient. Such authenticity on the psychotherapist's part may mean that the therapeutic relationship changes the therapist as much as the patient. Both Jourard (1971) and Jung (1966) held this as a central truth in all healing endeavours. Searles (1975) also believed that the patient has a powerful innate striving to heal the therapist (as he or she may have desired to heal the parents), which can and does contribute to greater individuation and growth for the psychotherapist as they are *both* transformed in the therapeutic dialogue. This is, of course, consistent with the gestalt notion of self-actualization bound up with the organism/environment field unity.

In the best cases the person-to-person relationship is usually honoured by truthfulness or authenticity – not at the expense of the client but in the spirit of mutuality. According to Buber (1970) the genuine psychotherapist can accomplish the true task of regenerating the stunted growth of a personal centre only by entering as 'a partner into a person-to-person relationship, but never through the observation and investigation of an object' (p. 179). Significantly, however, this does not mean injudicious honesty or belabouring clients with personal details, sorrows or frustrations that do not belong to them and with which the therapist had better work out in his or her own psychotherapy. Buber (1970, p. 179) further acknowledges the limited nature of the psychotherapeutic person-to-person relationship:

> Every I-You relationship in a situation defined by the attempt of one partner to act on the other one so as to accomplish some goal depends on a mutuality that is condemned never to become complete.

The transpersonal relationship

The transpersonal relationship is the spiritual dimension of relationship in psychotherapy. There is surprisingly little documented about the transpersonal relationship in psychotherapy. Buber mentions the concept of grace as the ultimate factor that operates in the person-to-person encounter and that may make the difference of whether or not a patient gets better.

Je le pensay, et Dieu le guarit [we treat them, but it is God who cures them].
Agnew (1963, p. 75)

Or, according to Perls et al. (1951, p. 248), *natura sanat non medicus –* nature heals. Naranjo (1982) writes about it. It is about a kind of sacredness in the therapeutic relationship that I am appreciating more and more as the *élan vital* (or life force, physis), as I engage with my life or enter client situations (Clarkson, 1991, 1993). 'We are in a numinous state of contact and confluence that is life-giving and healing for us both' (Korb, 1988, p. 101). Zinker (1977, p. 3) calls it the 'expression of the presence of God in my hands, eyes, brain, in all of me'.

The nature of this transpersonal dimension is therefore quite difficult to describe, because it is both rare and not easily accessible to the kind of descriptions that can be used in discussing the other forms of therapeutic relationships. 'The *numinosum* is either a quality belonging to a visible object or the influence of an invisible presence that causes a peculiar alteration of consciousness' (Jung, 1969, p. 7). It is also possible that there may be a certain amount of embarrassment in psychotherapists who have to admit that, after all the years of training and personal analysis and supervision, ultimately we still don't know precisely what it is that we are doing or whether it makes any difference at all. This is the kind of statement that one can only be sure of being understood correctly by experienced psychotherapists who have been faced repeatedly with incomprehensible and unpredictable outcomes – the person of whom you despaired suddenly and sometimes apparently inexplicably gets well, thrives and actualizes beyond all expectation. At the other polarity, the client for whom the psychotherapist had made an optimistic prognosis reaches plateaux from which in effect he or she never moves and the therapy is abandoned with a lingering sense of potential glimpsed, but never to be reached.

The transpersonal relationship is often characterized by its *lack* of person-to-person connectedness. It is as if the ego of even the personal unconscious of the therapist is 'emptied out' of the therapeutic space, leaving the room for something numinous to emerge in the 'between' of the relationship. This space can then become the *temenos* or 'the *vas bene clausum* inside which the transmutation takes place' (Adler, 1979, p. 21). It implies the presence of a letting go of skills, of knowledge, of experience, of preconceptions, even of the desire to heal. It is essentially allowing passivity, receptiveness, for which preparation is always inadequate because it cannot be made to happen; it can be encouraged only in the same way that the inspirational muse of creativity cannot be forced, but needs to have the ground prepared or seized in the serendipitous moment of readiness. What can be prepared are the conditions conducive to the spontaneous or spiritual act.

The essence of the communication is in the heart of the shared silence of being together in a dimension that is impossible to articulate exactly, too delicate to analyse and yet too pervasively present in gestalt psychotherapy to ignore.

> When the full implications of Gestalt therapy are lived through, from the perspective of the I-thou relation, then I think it is impossible to divorce transcendence - and therefore spirituality - from one's view of the nature of persons, and from the therapy process . . . and perhaps (Gestalt therapy) can re-enter the world of mutuality, with the potential and transcendence that exists when two individuals, fully responsible, allow their innermost selves to meet.
>
> Jacobs (1978, pp. 132-133)

True to gestalt's paradoxical theory of change, we may need to relinquish the desire for our clients to be different or even wanting them to want to change because the therapist needs this in order to feel worthwhile. The atmosphere is more a trance-like meditation, the quality that is conveyed by the 'being with' of master therapists with patients who are in acute psychosis (such as Gendlin, 1967) who affirm the spiritual dimension in psychotherapy. It is of course quite possible that psychotherapists may be deluding themselves in ways that may be dangerous for themselves and their clients if they mistakenly, prematurely or naïvely focus on the transpersonal and, for example, overlook or distort unfinished projections of transferential or personal phenomena.

> I believe that the spirit and the spiritual has been present in Gestalt therapeutic process from the beginning. Perhaps now we may affirm it and articulate some aspects with a degree of cogency and clarity.
>
> Korb (1988, p. 104).

The gestalt notion of the ego-less Self in contact with the other resembles the archetype of the Self that Jung refers to as the person's inherent and psychic disposition to experience centredness and meaning in life, sometimes conceived of as the God within ourselves. Buber was essentially concerned with the close association of the relation to God with the relation to one's fellow men, with the I-thou that issues from the encounter with the *other in relationship*. This dimension in the psychotherapeutic relationship cannot be proved and can hardly be described. 'Nothing remains to me in the end but an appeal to the testimony of your own mysteries' (Buber, 1970, p. 174).

Conclusion

In summary, the working alliance concerns the love of the work; the I-thou/person-to-person relationship concerns the love of the other; the unfinished (transference/countertransference) relationship concerns the love of the truth (the authentic); the reparative/developmental relationship concerns love for the unfinished issues in the person, more in line with process rather than structure; the transpersonal relationship concerns the love of God, whatever we may conceive it to be.

A gestalt approach to psychotherapy training, experience and supervision requires the ability to distinguish between different forms of therapeutic relationship and to assess and evaluate the usefulness of each at different stages of therapy or for individuals with different characteristic ways of relating so that there is not a slipshod vacillation prompted by the therapist's own unfinished business. It is equally important that gestalt therapists do not participate in or collude with abuse by not confronting it in their clients, themselves or their colleagues.

> In the past decade Gestalt therapy has been true to its existential heritage by increasing attention to human relations, as increasing respect for the phenomenology of the patient, and beginning to deal with issues of continuity. This more mature existential attitude has been the basis for a more sophisticated clinical methodology and a framework for assimilating new psychoanalytic insights.
>
> Yontef (1987, p. 51)

This maturing of gestalt theory and practices brings with it increased responsibility as well as increased range and expanded understandings. Freedom does not mean that we forgo discipline. Courage in actively embracing the fullest range of potentials of gestalt, the self or the transcendent needs to be accompanied by the severest form of testing and forged anew with each client from moment to moment. Of course, this can never truly be described, because, as soon as the word is uttered or the thought captured on paper, its most authentic moment of truth has already escaped.

This chapter has briefly described five kinds of therapeutic relationship available as potential avenues for constructive use in gestalt therapy, and indicated some characteristics of each in an effort to clarify, specify and differentiate more acutely in theory and practice the nature and intentions of the multiplicity of therapeutic relationships available and used by gestaltists throughout the world. We weave a rich tapestry when we enter into relationship with another. I also do not believe that any amount of serious study, comparison with other approaches, questioning or scrutiny of our own experience can ever destroy the spontaneous liveliness of the encounter and the infinitely varied treasures of the gestalt itself.

References

Adler, G. (1979) Dynamics of the Self. London: Coventure.

Agnew, L.R.C. (1963) Paré's oeuvres. Journal of the History of Medicine XVIII: 75–77.

Becker, M.H. and Maiman, L.A. (1975) Sociobehavioural determinants of compliance with health and medical care recommendations. Medical Care 13: 10–24.

Binswanger, L. (1968) Being-in-the-World. New York: Harper Torchbooks.

Boss, M. (1963) Psychoanalysis and Daseinsanalysis (L.B. Lefebre, trans.). New York: Basic Books.

Buber, M. (1970) I and Thou (W. Kaufmann, trans.). Edinburgh: T & T Clark.

Bugental, J.F.T. (1987) The Art of the Psychotherapist. New York: W.W. Norton & Co.

Ciornai, S. (1995) The importance of the background in Gestalt therapy. Gestalt Journal XVII(2): 7–34.

Clarkson, P. (1989) Gestalt Counselling in Action. London: Sage.

Clarkson, P. (1991) Individuality and commonality in Gestalt. British Gestalt Journal 1: 28–37.

Clarkson, P. (1993) On Psychotherapy. London: Whurr.

Clarkson, P. (2003a) The Therapeutic Relationship, 2nd edn. London: Whurr.

Clarkson, P. (2003b) Researching the 'therapeutic relationship' in psychoanalysis, counselling psychology and psychotherapy. In: The Therapeutic Relationship, 2nd edn. London: Whurr, pp. 329–354.

Fagan, J. and Shepherd, I.L. (eds) (1971) Gestalt Therapy Now: Theory techniques applications. New York: Harper & Row.

Ferenczi, S. (1926) Further Contributions to the Theory and Technique of Psycho-Analysis. London: Maresfield Reprints (reprinted 1980).

Francis, V., Korsch, B.N. and Morris, J.J. (1969) Gaps in doctor–patient communication: Patients' response to medical advice. New England Journal of Medicine 280: 535–540.

Freud, S. (1912a) The Dynamics of Transference, standard edn, Vol. 12. London: Hogarth Press, pp. 97–108.

Freud, S. (1912b) Recommendations to Physicians Practising Psycho-analysis, standard edn, Vol. 12. London: Hogarth Press, pp. 109–120.

Friedman, M. (1985) The Healing Dialogue in Psychotherapy. New York: Jason Aronson.

Fromm-Reichman, F. (1974) Principles of Intensive Psychotherapy. Chicago: University of Chicago Press.

Gendlin, E. (1967) Subverbal communication and therapist expressivity: Trends in client-centred therapy with schizophrenics. In: Rogers, C.R. and Stevens, B. (eds), Person to Person: The problem of being human. Lafayette, CA: Real People Press.

Guntrip, H. (1961) Personality Structure and Human Interaction: The developing synthesis of psychodynamic theory. London: Hogarth Press and the Institute of Psycho-analysis, (1982).

Hycner, R. (1985) Dialogical Gestalt therapy: An initial proposal. Gestalt Journal 8(1): 23-49.

Hycner, R. (1990) The I-thou relationship and Gestalt therapy. Gestalt Journal 13(1): 41-54.

Jacobs, L. (1978) I-thou relation in Gestalt therapy. Unpublished doctoral dissertation. California School of Professional Psychology, Los Angeles.

Jourard, S.M. (1971) The Transparent Self. New York: Van Nostrand Reinhold.

Jung, C.G. (1966) The Collected Works, 16, 2nd edn. London: Routledge & Kegan Paul.

Jung, C.G. (1969) The Collected Works, 11, 2nd edn. London: Routledge & Kegan Paul.

Korb, M. (1988) The numinous ground: I-thou in Gestalt work. Gestalt Journal 11(1): 97-106.

Korb, M.P., Gorrell, J. and Van De Riet, V. (1989) Gestalt Therapy: Practice and theory, 2nd edn. New York: Pergamon Press.

Malcolm, J. (1981) Psychoanalysis: The impossible profession. New York: Knopf.

Masson, J. (1989) Against Therapy. London: Collins.

May, R. (1969) Love and Will. London: Collins.

Miller, A. (1981) Thou Shalt Not Be Aware: Society's betrayal of the child (H. Hannum and H. Hannum, trans.). London: Pluto Press.

Miller, A. (1986) The Drama of Being a Child: And the search for the true self (R. Ward, trans.). London: Virago Press.

Naranjo, C. (1982) Gestalt conference talk 1981. Gestalt Journal 5(1): 3-19.

Norcross, J.C. (ed.) (1986) Handbook of Eclectic Psychotherapy. New York: Brunner/Mazel.

Onions, C.E. (ed.) (1973) The Shorter Oxford English Dictionary. Oxford: Clarendon Press, Oxford.

Perls, F., Hefferline, R. and Goodman, P. (1951) Gestalt Therapy. New York: Julian Press.

Polster, E. (1985) Imprisoned in the present. Gestalt Journal 8(1): 5-22.

Polster, E. and Polster, M. (1973) Gestalt Therapy Integrated. New York: Random House.

Searles, H. (1975) The patient as therapist to his analyst. In: Langs, R. (ed.), Classics in Psycho-analytic Technique. New York: Jason Aronson.

Sechehaye, M. (1951) Reality Lost and Regained: Autobiography of a schizophrenic girl (G. Urbin-Rabson, trans.). New York: Grune & Stratton.

Smail, D.J. (1987) Taking Care: An alternative to therapy. London: J.M. Dent.

Yontef, G. (1987) Gestalt therapy 1986: A polemic. Gestalt Journal 10(1): 41-68.

Yontef, G. (1988) Assimilating diagnostic and psychoanalytic perspectives into Gestalt therapy. Gestalt Journal 11(1): 5-32.

Zinker, J. (1977) Creative Process in Gestalt Therapy. New York: Vintage Books.

Chapter 8
The Life Review Aid and the Needed Therapeutic Relationship: Freud's Rat Man and your clients

The most important question for the psychotherapist is: What does this unique person with this background at this moment need from me? The next most important question is: How can I differentiate what the client really *needs*, other than simply providing untherapeutic or even damaging gratification? (Balint, 1989.)

To facilitate imagination, creativity and critical reflection on theory, here follows an aid that can be used by the client or the clinician (or both together) to review life. Obviously it can also be used to anticipate therapeutic directions in terms of providing the needed relationship a plan for the future – in so far as one can. It is meant to be used imaginatively and creatively – perhaps with other symbols or drawings or a scripted life drama which can be told, re-told or enacted in a group, perhaps even identifying subpersonalities at the time of their emergence. It is meant for adaptation and modification by individual people to aid them in their lives and therapy.

It is obviously a supremely subjective instrument, *meant to be used in the context of a therapeutic relationship*. An essential and important feature of this aid is that it focuses not only on the negatives, but also on the positives of a person's life. The latter are too frequently neglected in psychotherapy theory and practice. Yet, without resilience, a strong constitution and accidental good experiences, probably few of us would be alive. In fact, positive psychology (Seligman, 2002) works from the capacities and competencies of people, instead of, as happens only too often, focusing almost exclusively on their problems, their difficulties and their impasses.

So the *Life Review Aid* concerns unhappy, painful or Saturnian experiences such as trauma, strain and stressors, and also happy, fulfilling or Jupiterian experiences such as the discovery and celebration of capacities, the existence of good enough relationships, as well as the role of luck – or good fortune – which represents the sudden intrusion of blessings or undeserved fortunate events that touch most lives at some time.

Talents and capacities (e.g. doing well at school, being an athlete, artistic ability) are represented by exclamation marks (!), *good-enough relationships* (with a nanny, parent, teacher) by a series of stars (*) and *other fortunate events* (such as finding a soul-mate, being blessed with healthy children, recovery from a coronary) by a horseshoe (Ω).

Trauma (e.g. illness, a sibling's suicide, parental divorce) is represented by a triangle (Δ) (for danger), *strain* (e.g. an alcoholic parent, undiagnosed dyslexia at school, having a skin disease) by a series of slashes (\\\) and *other stressors* (such as natural disasters, lack of social security, an impoverished environment) by crosses (×).

The *severity or beneficence of life's experiences* can be assessed only by what it means (or meant) to the person concerned. It is a phenomenological rating that is of interest and use. Pain cannot be compared. What is devastating to one person (e.g. being black in British society) may be just a minor problem for another; what is tremendously advantageous to one (e.g. inherited wealth) may be a major stressor for another.

So, in filling in such an aid, be sure to differentiate – a parent's death may be one triangle for one person and three for another. Rejection by school friends may be fortunate for one child who used it to develop his artistic abilities (rating three exclamation marks), but catastrophic for another who lost all confidence and lived on to become, in his own eyes, little else other than one of life's sad victims (rating three triangles, for example). Before too long you may also notice that terrible events deserving of triangles are only too often accompanied by horseshoes. (It is a peculiar attribute of existence that quite often great good fortune comes from, or accompanies, great misfortune.)

In this aid I have used *Erikson's famous developmental stages*. This is not because I believe that it is the best by any means, but because it is one of the best-known of such attempts by white theoreticians to plot the predictable stages of a human life. Most students are already familiar with it in any case, and it is useful to see how time of life, for example, interacts with trauma and strain (and the reparative relationship) differently, depending on the age of the person concerned (the developmentally needed relationship), e.g. the trauma of a parent's death is differently experienced at 6 weeks, 1 year, 4 years, 11 years, 18 or 40 years of age. A rape at 80 years is differently experienced from sexual abuse at 5. But how? So, this is an attempt to bring that factor into the clinician's thinking for consideration and refinement.

Any other narrative or format (including completely idiosyncratic ones) can be equally – or more – helpfully substituted for it. In the same way, the distribution into segments of weeks, months or years can, and should, be adapted to suit the individual concerned. The divisions of time that I have suggested are just there as an *aid-mémoire*. First follows an example of the form that has not been filled in to familiarize users with the conceptualization. Then, as I am trying to minimize references, it is followed by a necessarily imaginative example roughly drawn from the famous 'Rat Man' case study of Freud because most people will already be familiar with it.

Example of Freud's Rat Man patient (Ernst) (Figure 8.2)

The Rat Man wanted/needed Freud to be a kind and wise father figure who would not beat him for his sexual fantasies and desires. Freud explained the rules of his treatment (working alliance), but he also offered to do whatever was in his power to guess the full meaning of any clues his patient gave him. He thus made it easier for him to recall hearing about the dreadful rat torture. Some commentators have judged that Freud was being too helpful (overuse of the reparative relationship) in this way.

When the Rat Man reproached himself, Freud suggested that, at the level of the unconscious, the Rat Man has wished his father dead. Freud provided the Rat Man with much intellectual feeding and facilitated a dialogue, which allowed the Rat Man to relive the traumatic incident with the officer. Instead of hurting or rejecting him, he gave him ideas and insights which helped him to understand himself.

Freud clearly displayed patience, understanding and compassion, like that of 'a good parent, and served to foster the rematuration of Ernst after his fixation points had been loosened. Freud countered Ernst's confused thinking with precise formulations, provided him with new object- and self-images, and served as a dependable model, correcting the undependability of the models he had had in his early childhood' (Kestenberg in Schoenewolf, 1990, p. 80).

There are some important points where Freud attempted *reparative interventions* that went wrong. On one occasion he asked Ernst to bring in a photograph of his lady friend, which Ernst understood as Freud trying to interfere with his sexual life, as his father had done. Ernst wanted to quit the treatment because of this.

On another occasion. Freud gave Ernst some herring to eat during the session. Ernst felt that Freud cheated him because he lost analytic time over this.

In the third instance, Freud lent him a book which he thought would be useful, but Ernst was still too suspicious of Freud's motives rather than accepting the intentional provision of reparative or developmentally needed relational opportunities.

The transference was possibly too active for these reparative interventions to be effective.

Overall, the very fact that Freud allowed Ernst to criticize and verbally abuse him without beating him (like his father had done) is in itself of course a profoundly reparative experience. Ernst could not criticize his father while he was alive without being/feeling in danger of the most horrendous punishment, yet he could do this with Freud.

These examples alert us to the dangers of attempting such reparative interventions at times when our clients may be experiencing the transference very intensely, and thus not being able to use the corrective emotional experience.

Regarding the transference, Ernst projected on to Freud (among other notions) that Freud was like his father, believing that Freud would punish Ernst in the same horrendous ways that he felt or feared his father would punish him.

There has been some speculation that Freud's own countertransference contributed to some of the difficulties he encountered in this analysis. Perhaps, for example, a *concordant proactive countertransference* stemming from the moment when the 8-year-old Freud urinated on the floor of his parents' bedroom and his father shouted. 'This boy will come to nothing'. (We should not discount the possibility that this was facilitative in some way, because it could have allowed Freud to have a thorough empathetic understanding of what such a pronouncement of a father might mean to his son. A *complementary proactive countertransference* of Freud might have been involved in terms of interpretations that Ernst, like some other patients, wanted to marry Freud's daughter.)

Finally, just to round off the commentary on this case study, it should be noted that Freud spelt out the *working agreement* at the beginning of their first session and at many other times: 'to say everything that came into his head, even if it was unpleasant to him or seemed unimportant or irrelevant or senseless' (Schoenewolf, 1990, p. 159).

It is not clear if Freud used any deliberate *self-disclosure*. Yet there was an accidental disclosure of Freud's family life when his patient caught sight of his daughter on the stairs. But why herring?

There is no mention that I can see of dealing with the *transpersonal* relationship. However, Ernst had spoken of punishments in the next world, and Freud thought that his religious ideas were contributory to his thinking problems.

T. Ormay (personal communication) stresses that Freud did have interest in the transpersonal but he did not clearly separate it from what he called the ontogenetic, e.g. he often talks about 'the mother' or 'the father' instead of specifying the patient's parents. This kind of ambiguity comes naturally to German-speaking people because, in that language, the general form is more

		Significant psychosocial positives		
Age (years)	Erikson's stage	Talents and capacities	Good-enough relationships	Other fortunate events
		!	********	Ω
96–100+				
86–95	Integrity vs Despair			
76–85				
66–75				
51–65				
40–50	Generativity vs Stagnation			
33–39				
25–32				
20–24	Intimacy vs Isolation			
17/18/19	Identity vs Identity Confusion			
15/16				
13/14				
11/12	Industry vs Inferiority			
10				
9				
8				
7	Initiative vs Guilt			
6				
5				
4				
3	Autonomy vs Shame and Doubt			
2				
18 months				
1				
6 months	Trust vs Mistrust			
3 months				
6 weeks				
Birth				
Pre-birth				
		Severity of psychosocial stressors		
		Δ	\\\\\\\\\\\\	×
		Trauma	Strain	Other stressors
© P. Clarkson, PHYSIS, 2000. See text for symbols.				

Figure 8.1 The clinician's aid for identifying needed relationships (or a person's aid in life review and planning for the future). Please note that the life review aid should be read from the bottom upwards.

Age (years)	Erikson's stage	Significant psychosocial positives		
		Talents and capacities !	Good-enough relationships *********	Other fortunate events Ω
33–39		Died at 36 in World War I		
25–32		\\\\\ Fears that Freud would beat him like his father did for his verbal abuse – but ΩΩ he does not; he hears him out and understands		
		ΩΩ Starts psychoanalysis with Freud at 30 years		
		Δ Obsession to repay mistaken debt		
		ΔΔΔ Cruel captain's story about the rat torture		
		ΔΔ Unrequited love for older woman		
		\\\\\ Strained relations with officer at 29 years		
		*** Good relationship with male friend who gives him reassurance that he was not a criminal		
		!! Gained law degree		
		! First sexual intercourse at 26 years		
20–24	Intimacy vs Isolation	\\\ Indecision between own choice and mother's choice of wealthy marriage results in Δ illness		
		ΔΔ His father died when Rat Man was 21 years		
		Δ Missed being with his father at father's death		
		\\\\\\ Father's opposition to his hoped-for marriage to a poor woman would disappear if father died		
		Lady friend rejected marriage proposal, followed by revenge fantasies		
17/18/ 19	Identity vs Identity Confusion	Δ Wanted to cut his own throat because lady friend cancelled appointment		
		\\\\\\\ jealousy led to !!! weight-loss campaign		
15/16		ΔΔ Male friend rejects him		
13/14		*** Good relationship with a man who told him he was a genius		
11/12	Industry vs Inferiority	Δ* Thought that if his father died he would win the little girl he loved		
10				
9				
8		\\\\\\ Infected with intestinal worms		
7	Initiative vs Guilt			
6		\\\\\ Complains to mother about erections		
5		! Fingered the genitals of his governess		
4?		Δ Stunned younger brother with toy gun		
3	Autonomy vs Shame and Doubt	ΔΔΔ Older sister died and patient bit someone, for which angry father beat him very severely		
2		! Saw older sister (who died following year) sitting on potty		
18 months				
1 year				
6 months	Trust vs Mistrust			
3 months				
6 weeks				
Birth		Born 1878. \\\\\\\\ Mother rich; father low rank army man		
Pre-birth				
		Severity of psychosocial stressors		
		Δ	\\\\\\\\\\\\	×
		Trauma	Strain	Other stressors
© P. Clarkson, PHYSIS, 2000. See text for symbols.				

Figure 8.2 Example of Freud's Rat Man patient (Ernst).

often used and also because all nouns are written with an initial capital letter. It is like when in English somebody jokingly refers to his parents as 'the mater' or 'the ancients'. Up till about 1910 or when Freud published *Totem and Taboo*, he was obviously interested in the transpersonal, or the 'phylogenetic' as he called it. But when he and Jung separated, the experience was traumatic for both of them. Freud lost interest in the transpersonal and Jung lost interest in childhood. After some 15 years Freud returned to the transpersonal in his notes for an encyclopaedia.

The developmentally needed or reparative relationship

> . . . a patient came in in a very aggressive mood and said: I *must* smash something! What about your sham mink pot?' I had no time to think; I said: 'I'll just about kill you if you smash my pot!' She was shocked, and we were both silent for some minutes. Then I said: 'I think you thought I really might kill you'. I then reminded her of an earlier happening when she had heard my volatile daily help having a row with the laundryman. After listening to them, she had asked: 'What are you thinking?' I've often seen you look like that, and I didn't know what it meant.' I said I was just thinking that I would like to bang their two heads together and throw them down the stairs. We both laughed, and the tension eased. Then I showed her it was possible to have such thoughts and feelings, but not to *act* on them. This was a new idea to her; she was a very impulsive person. Finally I showed her the sham mink pot, which (although not sham Ming) was antique, and beautiful, and had a value for me. This led to her understanding that I would protect what I valued; and that even if, at times, I had *felt* I could kill her, nevertheless I had not *done* so; that I valued her, and would protect her from my own aggression. She learnt a great deal about reality and the difference between psychic and factual reality in that session.
>
> Little (1986, p. 286)

This chapter on the developmentally needed or reparative relationship puts into context the interest in this kind of therapeutic relationship, compares definitions and descriptions, and considers how the clinician can identify and think diagnostically about the 'corrective therapeutic experience' or its variants. It overviews the influence of expectations of both psychotherapist and patient, consider the factors important in establishing it as well as failures, its management, opportunities for breakthrough and criteria for evaluating effectiveness.

Context

The developmentally needed or reparative relationship is the intentional provision by the psychotherapist of a corrective/reparative or replenishing parental relationship (or action) where the original parenting was deficient, abusive or over-protective.

The developmentally needed or reparative relationship is one of the five potentialities for relationship in psychotherapeutic work. It is possible to think about developmentally needed or reparative work in the psyche, self or ego because of the phenomenon of regression: the psychological possibility of cathecting parts of the psyche at earlier epochs of time. Some practitioners will roundly eschew its relevance, possibility or usefulness. Some classic orthodox psychoanalysts even view this set of ideas with suspicion, distaste and denial. It has become fashionable in traditional analytic circles to use the term 'corrective emotional experience' to denounce any alternative framework as 'not psycho-analysis'. Detrick and Detrick (1989, p. 101) note that 'The corrective emotional experience is a valuable method and concept that has been distorted by traditionalists to denote supportive and cathartic methods without insight'.

Others deliberately use and enhance its existence and growth, e.g. as Samuels (1985) noted, both eminent psychoanalysts such as Balint and Kris are closely connected with 'the idea that regression in analysis may be helpful and useful, and can be worked with' (p. 10).

Yet, although others publicly reject it, their patients usually experience the analysis or treatment as reparative. As research (e.g. as surveyed by Lambert in Norcross and Goldfried, 1992) has shown, patients and practitioners do not always ascribe change or improvement to the same factors. Some colleagues talk about it among friends, but omit it in discussion with colleagues or supervisors. To some it seems absurd that the therapeutic relationship should be kept void of reparative intention or outcome; to others this safeguards the notion that analysis and therefore insight is the primary objective of the work. The idea that the therapeutic relationship can be reparative seems to imply to some that the work of the analysis is undermined by gratification or 'support'; to others it seems clear that there can be no psychotherapy, indeed no psychoanalysis without some elements of reparation or healing – even if only through the provision of the presence of another person available to you at regular times.

Language and countertransference

It seems to me that, once again, words have attracted different meanings and connotations over time, and become influenced by political, socioeconomic and ideological considerations, which obscure the more basic commonalities and similarities between different perspectives, different narratives and the realities of practice behind closed doors. Differently oriented practitioners emphasize different aspects, and possibly nowhere are the gulfs and frontiers more jealously guarded than in this domain. This is perhaps the mysterious and dangerous, subterranean and primitive psychological world of dependency – possibly because it concerns the nature of addiction, the hunger for love and affection, the yearning for control, structure, security – 'Someone who knows what is right or true for me, someone to take care of me'.

For the psychologist, it may constellate terrors drawn from his or her own unmet needs for dependency, for power, for gratitude, for care. All the possibilities of destructive use of countertransference and projective identification or hypnotic inductions come into play as much as, if not more than, in other modes of the therapeutic relationship. It is possible that much of the anxiety about this reparative area in clinical work is phobic or counterphobic, derived from discomfort or perhaps too much comfort with this particular kind of relating. Unfortunately, along with this go ambivalent and contradictory attitudes between theory and practice, as well as between what is said and what is actually done.

A colleague reported that she had only really understood psychotherapy after she had spent several years in a very orthodox Kleinian analysis with one of the leading Kleinian training analysts in a particular country. The analyst had been extremely conscientious in withholding any resemblance of any other kind of therapeutic relationship except that of the transference. He made an interpretation only once every few weeks and focused primarily on envy and the death instinct. I asked her 'What was your most significant psychotherapeutic experience in that analysis?' After considerable thought she said, 'There was a day when it was very rainy and I slipped on the marble floor of his entrance hall. He came over towards me to help me up, saying "My dear girl, my dear girl". It made such an impression on me I shall never forget the loving affection in his eyes, his voice, and his hands as he helped me up.' We can question whether this was person to person or an accidental but pivotal re-parenting and reparative experience.

The chasm between different approaches is rarely as wide as in their avowed use of the reparative or developmentally needed relationship. We are looking at a range that encompasses primal cathartic work (e.g. Janov, 1973) and bioenergetics, on the one hand, through to the regressive therapeutic experiences of Kingsley Hall when Laing was there (or the Cathexis experience in the USA), to the 'holding environment' of Winnicott or the provision of life management skills via Masterson (1985), the empathic nurturing relationship with Kohut (1984), the provision of mutative metaphors to Broadmoor prisoners by Cox and Theilgaard (1987), and the advocacy of Miller (1986), on the other.

Suffice it to say, for the sake of this piece here, that this is a topic that should be approached with due respect for its difficulty and the many ways in which practitioners avoid it, fear it, reject it, overindulge it – much as they struggle with the fact that some form of reparation is probably inevitable in all effective psychotherapies or psychoanalyses. As we all know, avoiding something does not necessarily make it go away.

The view of the person

I think that the major division between those who unapologetically but carefully provide a developmental or reparative relationship and those who would claim publicly or in writing that they do not provide such a relationship in analysis or therapy may be the result of the more fundamental division about what is seen as the basic nature of human beings and the processes of change. Where the emphasis is on analysis alone, it is usually accompanied by written perspectives on human beings in terms of the drive or death-instinct version (Freud, 1920; Klein, 1984), whereas those who also embrace the possibilities of developmental or reparative relationship are more usually associated with concepts to do with healing, actualizing, growth and evolutionary tendencies (Rogers, 1951; Erickson, 1967; Kohut, 1984). We return later to this theme.

The viewpoints that cluster around seeing the human being as having a directional tendency to grow and to develop are contrasted with traditional orthodox psychoanalysis. Kohut, like Fairbairn, maintains that 'We are born as an assertive whole, as an affectionate whole, not as a bundle of isolated biological drives – pure aggression or pure sexual lust – that have to be gradually tamed' (in Graf, 1984, p. 74).

We have seen earlier how transference interpretations have been gradually supplemented by empathic operations in the psychoanalytic canon. Empathy as a method has of course flourished in existentially oriented approaches since the beginning of the twentieth century, as described in at least the following works: Jaspers (1963), Minkowski (1970), Moreno (1965). *Empathy is often thus used as a paired intervention with interpretation, as a basic facilitative condition in the healing encounter, or as countertransferential data from which to enter into, understand and be choiceful in responding to regressive phenomena.*

Definitions and descriptions

There is frequently a strong, and occasionally denied, reparative or developmentally needed aspect embedded or attendant upon other therapeutic relationships. We remember that Freud criticized his patients, gossiped, gave them advice, lent them money and got involved in their lives in many ways, which sounds quite contradictory to the conventional prescription to remain as a mirror, blank screen or surgeon. I think that it is impossible to explore this aspect without dealing with the concept of regression – another battleground or bridge for perspectives on human nature.

Regression

> Regression is a flight backwards in search of security and a chance of a new start. But regression becomes illness in the absence of any therapeutic person to regress with and to.
>
> Guntrip (in Goulding and Goulding, 1979, p. 86)

Regression and psychotherapy embrace an enormous body of psychological literature. Here we discuss some of the outstanding contributions, starting with Freud's (1968, p. 554) useful definition:

> Three kinds of regression are thus to be distinguished; a. *topographical* regression, in the sense of the schematic picture [of the physical apparatus]; b. *temporal* regression, in so far as what is in question is a harking back to older psychical structures; and c. *formal* regression, where primitive methods of expression and representation take the place of the usual ones. All these three kinds of regression are, however, one at bottom and occur together as a rule; for what is older in time is more primitive in form and in psychical topography lies nearer to the perceptual end.

Almost all psychotherapists, psychoanalysts, counsellors and psychologists, not to mention a variety of other helping professionals such as pastors and doctors, have come to know the occurrences and challenges of *regression* in those who came or were sent to them for help, if not also in themselves. Loosely understood, regression is a ubiquitous phenomenon, capable of great creative as well as great pathological potential. In Kohut's (see Elson, 1987, p. 16) words: 'the incapacity of the ego to maintain its ties to reality may . . . given certain circumstances, become an asset to the personality, and its absence may be a defect'. Many of the psychological or psychotherapeutic theories that are built on a developmental matrix would consider such regression essential to effective psychotherapy, to the retrieval and renewal of the trauma and injuries caused in the course of an individual's history. Winnicott (1975, p. 281) phrases it like this:

> One has to include in one's theory of the development of the human being the idea that it is normal and healthy for the individual to be able to defend the self against

specific environmental failure by a freezing of the failure situation. Along with this goes an unconscious assumption (which can become a conscious hope) that opportunity will occur at a later date for a renewed experience in which the failure situation will be able to be unfrozen and re-experienced, with the individual in a regressed state, in an environment that is making adequate adaptation. The theory is here being put forward of regression as part of a healing process, in fact, a normal phenomenon that can properly be studied in the healthy person.

Running the risk, as summaries often do, of omitting many qualifications, exceptions and disputational points, it can be said that in the psychological literature *regression* is primarily divided between *malignant* and *benign* types. These latter two are Balint's terms (1989, p. 141), which I have found eminently suitable. Clearly, 'the healing power of relationship' (1989, p. 159), which depends on therapeutically correct use of a developmentally needed reparative relationship (or interventions), should be carefully utilized in certain circumstances of benign regression.

Regression is frequently seen as a hindering mechanism of defence, a significant factor in pathogenesis, and a potentially recalcitrant form of resistance. In these cases, I take it that we are referring to malignant regressions – those that are not useful for psychotherapy, are chronic, dangerous to self and others and not amenable for use.

Regression and fixation

A Critical Dictionary of Psychoanalysis (Rycroft, 1968/1972, p. 52) provides a convenient definition:

> fixation: The process by which a person becomes or remains ambivalently attached to an object, this object being one which was appropriate to an earlier stage of development. Fixation is therefore evidence of failure to progress satisfactorily through the stages of libidinal development. The concept assumes that the fixated person (a) has a tendency to engage in infantile, outmoded patterns of behaviour or to regress to such patterns under stress; (b) to choose compulsively objects on the basis of their resemblance to the one on which he is fixated; and (c) suffers impoverishment of available energy as a result of his investment in the past object.

One obviously needs to distinguish regressive states that are acute, disturbing and disintegrating, regressive states that are temporarily hindering and regressive states that are fixated. Both Balint and Kernberg, among many others, differentiated accessible, healthy ego states (even though they may be in pain or fear) from fixated states. The concept of *fixation* assumes that the regression is chronic, compulsive and damaging to the individual.

Regression and the role of time

Whether the psyche is also conceptualized as in the temporal nature of psychotherapy, it seems to be a point of agreement across all schools and orientations as far as I know. Simply stated, it concerns recognition of the person's existence in time and a notion of being able to move backwards and forwards in time (linear) or even synchronistically (acausal). (In the latter case there is the recognition of simultaneity in time.) The developmentally needed or reparative relationship is particularly concerned with the conceptualization of the psyche, the self states, psychological epochs, 'earlier phases of development or earlier phases of experience' (Samuels, 1985, p. 145), ego states, schemas, and other ways in which the psyche's relationship to time has been construed. Koestler (1989, p. 461) summarized it as follows: 'Psychotherapy aims at undoing faulty integrations by inducing a temporary regression of the patient to an earlier level in the hope that he will eventually reintegrate into a more stable pattern'. Elsewhere I have discussed extensively the notion of temporality and psychotherapy, developing the argument that psychotherapy can essentially be seen as a productive manipulation of subjective phenomenological time experience.

The notion that the body retains traces of philogenetic as well as ontogenetic substrata, which remain available for regression throughout a person's life, is well established in biology, phenomenology and bioenergetics, for example. To choose but one writer on the subject, Merleau-Ponty (1962, p. 82) states that the body comprises both the 'habitual body' and the 'present body': '. . . our body comprises as it were two distinct layers, that of the customary body and that of the body at this moment. Langer (1989, p. 32), a major exponent of Merleau-Ponty, continues that the body:

> . . . draws together a comprehensive past which it puts at the disposal of each new present, thereby already laying down the general form of a future it anticipates. With its 'two layers' the body is the meeting place, so to speak, of past, present and future because it is the carrying forward of the past in the outlining of a future and the living of this bodily momentum as actual present.

I believe that it is because of this plasticity of time in the psyche that psychotherapy is possible at all. Notions of the reparative relationship are inevitably wedded to an acceptance of at least some of the outlines of what most psychologists and psychotherapists would understand by the notion of regression – although details may of course differ.

Regression and creativity

Regressive phenomena, whether conceptualized as pathological, sublimating or optimally healthy, are frequently considered as part of, if not partner to, creativity.

Maslow (1968), in speaking of the latter phases of self-actualizing creativity, also draws attention to the potentially voluntary nature of regression, its role in creativity and the necessary secondary process (or Adult) work involved. 'The voluntary regression into our depths is now terminated, the necessary passivity and receptivity of inspiration or of peak-experience must now give way to activity, control, and hard work' (p. 143). Maslow (1968) is but one of the many authors (including Rank, 1989) who specifically acknowledge the role of Child-like states or regression to earlier selves, historical object-relations experiences in service of creative productivity in adulthood. Kris (1952, p. 253), for example, studied regression in the service of the ego, particularly in relation to creativity:

> The psychic activities or functions devoted to the adaptation to reality are encompassed in the psychoanalytic concept of *ego*. Central to artistic – or indeed, any other – creativeness is a relaxation ('regression') of ego functions. The word 'fantasy' conveys just this disregard of external stringencies in its reference to the process and product of creative imagination. In fantasy and dream, in states of intoxication and fatigue, such functional regression is especially prominent; in particular, it characterizes the process of inspiration. But the regression in the case of aesthetic creation – in contrast to these other cases – is purposive and controlled.

The major difference between the transference relationship and the reparative relationship rests on differentiating when an act, word or absence will repeat and be replayed within the archaic drama ('My father never gave me any presents and through transference interpretations and empathic reflection I can begin to experience the pain and disappointment of that'; or whether the gift, the word, the advice that would 'begin to provide me with an experience of having a transitional object for the first time, experiencing understanding for the first time, internalizing a loving object for the first time'). The time-honoured advice against giving advice or gifts or even presents came from the frequently observable clinical experience of having provided something intended to be reparative which crashed on the ungiving rocks of the patient's transference – 'I knew that you were only giving me that object which I asked for over the summer break in order to fob me off, the way my parents often gave me "things" instead of their love'.

The new reality

> The disabilities of patients arose, Fairbairn (1958) held, not from the distortion of early experiences with objects, but 'from the effects of unsatisfactory and unsatisfying object-relationships experienced in early life and perpetuated in an exaggerated form in inner reality (p. 377). Therefore, only the actual relationship between analyst and patient as persons could constitute a new reality and thus an indispensable therapeutic factor. Only such a relationship could provide a means of correcting distorted internal relationships and also provide the patient with the opportunity, foreclosed in his childhood, 'to undergo a process of emotional development in the setting of an actual relationship with a reliable and beneficent parental figure' (p. 377). He maintained that although such an actual relationship is difficult to reconcile with a psychology of object relations and dynamic structure.
>
> Brandchaft (1989, p. 252)

In much of psychotherapeutic literature we see this concatenation of the old psychic reality which the patient brings and the new reality that is forged in the relationship between the therapist and the client in the consulting room. Of course there is understanding, thoughtfulness and discrimination in the service of the client's needs, but the new reality is inescapable – the simple re-creation of the old one almost always is damaging if not understood and untransformed, as Lowen (1969, p. 250) writes:

> A therapist responds to a patient's needs. He calms the anxious patient, reassures the frightened one, and sustains the faltering one. It can be said that in his supportive capacity he functions like a mother. However, he doesn't have the personal feeling for a patient that a mother has for her child. His response to the patient is realistic. He can reassure the frightened patient because in reality the fear is groundless. Should there be a real cause for fear, such reassurance would be disastrous. A mother, on the other hand, takes the burden of reality upon her own shoulders and spares her child. . . . As an ideal father, the therapist is the representative of outer reality, the reality of the world. In this capacity, he has to interpret the world for the patient, as a true father does for his own children. On the other hand, an ideal mother is the representative of inner reality, the reality of body and its feelings. The therapist, whether man or woman, must be familiar with both realities so that he can help the patient reconcile his conflicts. He must know when to be supportive and when to be critical.

In practice, of course, this kind of provision of a new relationship (however defined) will be modified, influenced and shaped by the practitioner's developmental theory and notions of appropriate parenting. These will be coloured by the practitioner's own upbringing and primary training and the countertransferential implications of class or economic status, skin colour and culture.

Sechehaye (1951, p. 17) writes:

> Whenever possible, I gave Renee whatever she desired. In the beginning, her interests were of the most primitive kind: food, physical development, all that which increased her intrinsic value, her strength, her physical beauty, her knowledge.

Kohut

> . . . intentionally giving or withholding, this process can become infinitely more accurate, reliable and helpful. The absence of much discussion and training, assessment and discrimination, sharing and experience in the accepted canonical literature belies the reality of what some of our clients feel. Kohut (1984) recognised that the corrective emotional experience to which Alexander (1933) and Alexander and French (1946) had described well before him, was relevant because the empathic failures of childhood need to be ameliorated in the psychoanalytic situation. Then maybe from time to time one can, recognizing an enormous need, give something that one knows is, for the time being, necessary. I have a nice phrase for it: I call it the 'reluctant compliance with the childhood wish'.

Kohut in Elson (1987, p. 39)

It may be reluctant, but the poignancy of some of the reported examples, such as the woman sucking his fingers, beggars a simplistic denial of the enormous reparative value of such generosity based on clinical assessment, acumen paired with humanity. It reminds me of Fromm-Reichman (1974) whose psychotic patient smeared her dress with faeces. The next time she saw this patient she wore a white coat so that the patient would not be hindered in doing what was needed for recovery (*Principles of Intensive Psychotherapy*). Other examples may be less dramatic, but they occur regularly, perhaps much more frequently than any of us would like to acknowledge. Naturally it will be affected by the developmental or historical needs of each client. Equally, it will be affected by the prism of developmental theory that the clinician holds – Stern or Mahler, Anna or Melanie Freud, Vaillant or Kohlberg, Goldstein or Piaget, Hillman or Anthony and Cohler, Liedloff or Spock, Confucius or Great White Bear – if the clinician is conscious of the existence and significance of this relationship and what the patient is taking, as well as what he or she may inadvertently receive from the relationship with us – whether or not it is allowed, recognized or acknowledged. Sometimes, this acknowledgement of the 'second chance' at normal childhood development is but obscurely phrased:

> The analyst's protracted and consistent endeavour to understand his patient leads to two results that are analogous to the outcome of normal childhood

development: (1) his occasional failures, constituting optimal frustrations, lead to the building up of self structure, while (2) his on the whole adequately maintained understanding leads to the patient's increasing realization that, contrary to his experiences in childhood, the sustaining echo of empathic resonance is indeed available in this world.

Kohut (1984, pp. 77-78)

Masterson

This sustaining provision of both the optimal frustrations and the empathic resonance, which is contrary to the patient's experiences in childhood, can be described as a form of re-parenting – a questionable and questioned term. Of course it rather depends on how you define and describe this activity. Masterson denies that he is doing a form of 're-parenting'. However, he writes thus:

> Is this a form of reparenting, i.e., meeting the patient's deprived infantile emotional needs in treatment? On the surface it would appear that that is exactly what is being done, but more careful study reveals that this is not the case. The issue turns upon the reality of the therapist and his actions versus how the patient experiences them. The therapist is not a parent; he is carefully introducing a therapeutic technique which meets patients' therapeutic needs. The patient, on the other hand, through the transference, particularly his fantasy that the therapist *is* that mother who approves and acknowledges his emerging self that he always wished for, would experience the activity as an effort to substitute or make up for that which he was deprived of in childhood. The difference, then, is between the reality of the therapist and his actions and how the patient perceives and experiences them. This distinction often does not become clear to the patient until the last or separation phase of treatment when the transference fantasy must be analyzed if the patient is to fully resolve his developmental arrest.

Masterson (1985, p. 63)

Other examples

In psychodrama (Greenson, 1965; Moreno, 1965; Holmes et al., 1994), there is the use of a concept called 'surplus reality' – the notion that through enactment new realities can be formed, which can change a protagonist's perception, attitudes and behaviour permanently – or at least provide them with new possibilities, an enhanced life repertoire and what I have called a 'conceivable self' (Clarkson, 1992, p. 196).

This idea that the human psyche cannot distinguish between real and vividly imagined experiences may in developed form underlie much of what clients experience as the remaking of their birth and a renewed opportunity to 'grow up' in more benign circumstances.

This growing up has been particularly eloquently expressed when patients write about their experiences of healing in psychotherapy as evinced in the stories of Mary Barnes, the Schiff children, Fromm-Reichman's patients and many others. One in the genre is that of Nakhla and Jackson (1993). This patient spent the first 18 months of her sessions in complete silence and then her communication was by means of mutilating herself with broken glass to the extent that she severed the tendons in her arm. In this book, analyst and patient describe how a regression led to the emergence of a separate self. Through physical contact, home visits, variable time duration of sessions, etc. Kalisch's report (1994, p. 46) sums up some of the ambivalences between psychoanalysis and the reparative relationship:

> I squirmed slightly at the way that Dr Nakhla felt he had to uneasily glance over his shoulder at his more orthodox psychoanalytical colleagues and justify these departures from detached analysis into a world of human meeting where he, like Grace, was not equipped with the knowledge of the rules beforehand.
>
> In sum, the book is an unusual demonstration of the power of therapeutic relationship in whatever approach the practitioner rests and shows how the analytic tradition, despite or even perhaps because of its many constraints, still has the ability to throw up people who are brave enough to go beyond it.

Diagnosis and identification

Identification

A vital part of responding appropriately to developmentally or reparatively needed therapeutic requirements of patients is the nurturance and development of the capacity correctly to identify the nature of the injury or the kind of developmental deficit. This will depend very largely on the clinician's familiarity with many different models of child development, different cultural practices in child-rearing and an awareness of the socio-ideological, the constructed nature of the notion of 'the child' and the imposition (or not) of linear developmental expectations on the natural unfolding of the human being. Eurocentric, patriarchal, white, able-bodied models of child development are of course not the only ones in existence, even though they may have clinical, theoretical and economic hegemony at this time. Some studies (Brandtstädter, 1990; Carugati, 1990; Gergen et al., 1990) have, for example, shown how parental expectations for children conform to such theoretical and (of course) therefore ideological patterning as they grow and develop. In particular, it is important also to take note of research in terms of invulnerability, competency and mastery – work that all suggests that the deterministic ideas that childhood significantly or profoundly influences adult pathology, limitation or creativity are challenged (Chess and Thomas, 1986, 1987).

Probably the most important aspect of working with this relationship vector is to differentiate between the other kinds of relationship (working alliance, transference/countertransference, person to person and transpersonal) and to be as sure and clear as possible that a reparative act, attitude, behaviour or relationship is both needed and likely to be effective at that time. It is particularly important to be aware, through one's own therapy and supervision, that needs for dependency or independency hassles are not being met through clients. In the same way, the fear of or the desire for intimacy may predispose a therapist towards either a transference/countertransference mode of working or a person-to-person form of therapeutic relationship, which would have more to do with the individual history proclivities and preferences of the therapist than with the needs of the client.

> . . . many severely ill patients have other needs which have to be met; if they are
> not met, analysis becomes impossible.
>
> Little (1986, p. 53)

Having established that it is indeed a new kind of relationship that is required – and not the bringing to awareness of an archaic relationship anymore – the task is to identify the nature, intensity, duration and variety of reparative or developmentally needed relationship that is required by the client.

The developmentally needed relationship

> Commonly encountered psychotherapeutic situations involve the patient who presents with a difficulty or symptom which seems to relate in an obvious way to a particular developmental period, rather than to one traumatic childhood event. No matter what comes up for consideration in a session, it always seems to relate back to that one period. That stuck place, sometimes referred to as a fixation point, is often a time when, for some reason, the developmental needs of the patient were not met, or not met sufficiently. The synonymous term, a developmental 'arrest', need not, as Sullivan (1954) notes, 'imply that things have become static, and that from thenceforth the person will be just the same as he was at the time that development was arrested' (p. 217). Rather, it is later on that we see 'the appearance of eccentricities of interpersonal relations' which betray 'signs of developmental experience which has been missed or sadly distorted' (Sullivan, 1954, p. 218). The fixation point can also be seen from a multi-leveled perspective. The person looking back, reinterpreting his or her history, might even identify the embryonic beginnings of such an 'arrest' before its definitive experience.
>
> Shapiro (1988, p. 57)

As pointed out above, all of the clinician's knowledge of developmental stages, critical periods, parenting, social needs of children and adolescents, bonding and attachment will be brought to bear in terms of what the client calls forth in the interaction with the clinician. The rapid blinking of a confused and frightened infant when a door bangs is different from the feel and the look of a 2 year old testing the limits of tolerance around missing sessions and coming late. It is different again from a 5 year old's fantasies about therapists' sexuality or love life and is again different from an 11 year old exploring the nature of satisfactions to be had from achievements, as again different from the hostile, denigrating attacks on a parent which often seem part of the natural, familial break that is the separation of adolescence. How we respond to these would form the touchstone of the psychotherapy. A 2 year old's rage for independence, control and separation simply needs a very different response from that of an adolescent. Clinicians experienced in identifying the different facets of their own developmental history and that of others will, combined with sensitive intuition and acute awareness, attune themselves to the therapeutic necessities evoked by the infants or children in the adult who comes to us for 'a second chance'.

Schwartz-Salant (1982, pp. 160, 161), working as a Jungian, writes that for certain people 'It is essential *not* to interpret this dynamic, at least at the outset and often not for some time after its appearance. Rather one must *become the parent* which means to relate as a parent to this child-quality of the patient. Being the parent does not mean giving advice. It represents a feeling state that is unconsciously communicated to the patient. It shows that the analyst is willing to get close in a kinship sense, to *see* and understand within that emotional framework. One incarnates the identity of the positive nurturing mother or father that the patient had so little of'.

The reparative relationship

Accurate effective and time-efficient provision of the reparative relationship can be enhanced to the extent that the clinician is able to identify the nature, severity and duration of the injury that has led to the deformation, deprivation or distortion experienced by the patient. The three major categories in this section seem to me to be: (1) trauma, (2) strain and (3) extra-familial limitations and catastrophes.

Trauma

The idea that psychological distress or impaired development is a result of trauma is solidly ensconced in counselling psychology and psychotherapy literature. Whether the trauma is considered to be purely imaginary (as in Freud's Seduction Theory) or real (for Fairbairn and Miller) is a debatable issue. Elsewhere I discuss levels of reality in psychotherapy, but for our purposes here I would say that the subjective reality of the patient is the heart of the matter and the province of the expertise of a clinician.

Strain

Then there is the category that some authors have identified as strain (Anthony and Cohler, 1987). This is the long-term, not necessarily traumatic, subclinical experience of pain, rejection, deprivation, neglect, pressure, coercion, seduction, and all the other many ways in which a child can be subjected to undue difficulties in growing up healthily, imaginatively and emotionally robust.

Extra-familial limitations and catastrophes

The first seems to me to be a necessary acknowledgement of the damage that is visited upon children or adults through accidents of genetics or nationality. A child born to a heroin-addicted mother who is suffering from HIV, a Hutu child spending his most vital formative years in starvation and flight from one refugee camp to another, the child who survives a mining disaster, the woman who loses a child in stillbirth, the long-term effects of pollution and radiation, the lasting scars of falling into the so-called 'underclass of society' through illness, social isolation, and economic and educational deprivation. Not all psychological problems are caused by childhood experiences. Not all emotional stress concerns individuals. The influence of history, geography, economics, philosophy and religion on individual responsibility, I believe, is vastly underestimated. Helping someone who has been tortured in a political prison does not require vastly different approaches from a therapist than other, less collective phenomena.

Expectations

For both the developmentally needed and the reparative relationship, I believe there is a natural desire to reach for, and repair, the original neglect, injury, or developmental deficit. I think this self-actualizing tendency (Goldstein, 1939) or the effects of the creative, healing and evolutionary life force Physis (Zeno in Murray, 1915), often prepare and keep clients in a state of anticipation or on a quest for the needed or reparative relationship, either in their ordinary lives or in their counselling/psychotherapeutic relationships. It is very similar to what Kohut called the 'natural developmental tendency' (1977).

Patient expectations

On the one hand, the person may expect that the psychotherapist will not be able to provide the developmentally needed or reparative relationship. Similar to what is taught on a number of psychotherapy courses, such relationships are frowned upon, avoided or at the very best interpreted in several approaches to psychotherapy. On the other hand, there is often a naïve wish for the psychotherapist to be on the person's side, doing for them what the original parents could not or would not do.

Such expectations that a therapist would believe one, support one and be willing to fight for one are also influenced by media exposure of the work of Miller as in the five-part Channel 4 TV series in Britain (Mackenzie, 1989), and the advocacy movement (compare the Institute for Self-analysis) may have led to some very false expectations (Meacham, 1992). Miller has taken eloquent issue with all psychoanalytic approaches that ignore the reality of a child's experience and do not see symptoms as a response to environmental injury. Miller (1985, p. 60) writes:

> In [Klein's] descriptions of the early stages of the child's emotional life, Klein presents us with the portrait of a wicked infant in which she fails to show the connections between the infant's violent feelings (such as hate, envy, and greed) and the unconscious of the parents, as well as the humiliation, mistreatment, and narcissistic wounds the latter inflict on the child.

As a result of theoretical differences and professional feuds, media exposés and the lack of information, clients may end up being extremely confused as to what is ethical, expectable or reprehensible practice in this area. It has historically always been a contentious part of counselling and psychotherapy, and it is no accident that Ferenczi, Balint, Sullivan and Fromm-Reichmann, even Federn, ended up in the sidestreams of psychoanalysis, rather than in its mainstream harbours.

Psychotherapist expectations

The expectations of the therapist can rule out, permit or encourage regression and developmentally needed or reparative experiences. As Miller points out, Klein's view of the child as wicked 'affects the analyst's attitude toward the patient, as can be observed, for example, in the cases presented by Segal. Whenever her patients have an exaggerated fear of the envy of those around them, she always sees this as a projection of their own feelings of envy onto others' (Miller, 1985, p. 60).

As discussed more extensively above, the way the clinician approaches a regressive phenomenon or the possibility of reparative potential will of course be determined by his or her skills, talents and prejudices, own experience of giving and receiving parenting and healing, supervision, and the content and process of his or her training around and towards these issues.

Family and/or institution

The influence of the family or the institution can also be decisive in affecting the outcome of regressive or reparative experiences. Some families can allow an 11-year-old child to make temporary regressive events for himself, such as if he starts wanting a bottle again when a young sibling is born. Institutions such as Kingsley Hall or the Cathexis Community in Birmingham can have rules and structures that support, control, encourage or limit regressions. The very construction of a room and availability of materials such as bottles, toys, paint, etc. can make it very clear to both patient and therapist what the expectations are in terms of regression and its potential for humiliation, rejection, analytic interpretation, meeting, replenishment or reparation.

Establishment of the developmentally needed/reparative relationship

In many cases, it is not really necessary to establish a developmentally needed or reparative relationship with a patient. People frequently, repetitively and profoundly regress to previous developmental stages or other traumatic events (such as flashbacks after rape or car accidents). It is my experience that, even if a clinician wanted to avoid working with individuals in regression, it would be an extraordinary achievement because most human beings come for help as a result of their failure to avoid regressing out of the here and now of their current adult reality. Even when building a scale relating to the fear of going into a room where a mother committed suicide (Evans et al., 1993), the cognitive or systemic therapist is dealing with regressive phenomena. And who is to say that slow encouragement by increasing the graded steps of anxiety with the supportive and confronting presence of the psychologist is not reparative, or exactly what was needed developmentally when that currently crippling phobia was a small anxiety based on a simple misunderstanding of the apportionment of blame or responsibility in a family divorce? So, whether or not the psychotherapist wishes to work with individuals in regression or in this particular form of relationship, the everyday contingencies of practice will probably require it. *Therefore, all psychotherapists need to have theoretical understanding, personal experience and supervised skills training in the identification*, and *transformative or emergency management of regressive states.* There are of course many approaches to psychotherapy that deliberately and intentionally welcome or invoke such states in order to accomplish the goals of the clients.

Regression

As we have seen, regressive phenomena occur in many life situations and frequently in psychotherapy. Regression, whether initiated by the psycho-analyst or by the client, can occur spontaneously, it can be facilitated or induced by the practitioner, it can specifically be contracted for or it may be recognized as the state of the individual who presents him- or herself in the session. Here follows the briefest of highlights under these headings.

Spontaneous

These are the occasions when clients come into the consulting room in a state of regression or when they spontaneously regress or go into shock in response to something that the therapist said or did (but which was not intended to evoke this response). The therapist has but little choice except to deal with it, and frankly any intervention to people in an extreme state of distress is likely to be reparative, if not also developmentally needed.

During the 9 months of her weekly 3-hour sessions, Evert often spontaneously fell into a trance state in which her wounded-child complex would manifest itself. She would become the kid and repeatedly experience intense psychological and physical terror. Bijkerk had to summon up her own physical and emotional strength to protect Evert's wounded inner child, whose emergence, expression, growth and transformation she supported and encouraged. Both Evert and Bijkerk write frankly about times of doubt and resistance concerning their therapeutic relationship. Yet, despite its risk and the strain and hurt that it caused, both persisted in the relationship (Avrech, 1989, p. 209).

Facilitated

This would imply those strategies and interventions that, although not specifically intended to provoke regression, may make it easier for a person to connect with these earlier layers of their self and thus to become more available for reparation or healing in the psychotherapy. Facilitation may be as simple as the provision of a safe and calm space for exploration. Equally it may be the provision of noisy instruments such as drums and messy media such as finger paint, which can enable certain archaic needs to be met. Sometimes the facilitation is as simple as a touch on the shoulder, sometimes it may be a metaphor, the permission to turn a somersault (Balint, 1989, p. 134) or the singing of a song (Symington, 1986, p. 202).

> A client came to psychotherapy whose friends would have described her as bright, attractive, assertive, confident, and successful, which she was in many respects. Her immediate spur to come into therapy was the breakdown of her marriage and her husband having an affair with another woman. She felt a deep pain and despair about this and a feeling of failure, as this had happened years before with a live-in lover.
>
> The psychotherapist reached behind this gilded mask to the empty, arid, emotional landscape and provided physical closeness in terms of being available to this independent 32-year-old woman's Child whenever she needed a lap to huddle in or an arm to cling to. 'Welcome in from the desert', the psychotherapist said. The woman understood what she meant and her Child felt deeply seen. This 'greening of the desert' was necessary to build a sturdy enough sense of self to tolerate the extent of the actual deprivation, a structure that was not reliably in place in the persona of the person, for all its seeming competence.

The task for the psychotherapist is to calibrate when there is enough ego strength or sense of core self (Stern, 1985), unconditional sense of worth (Rogers, 1977) or incorporated nurturing (Kohut, 1968/1989) to sustain the client through the re-experiencing of the actual deficit and what would be an overindulgent smothering and further abuse.

The turning point with this particular client was when she began to report dreams in which both her friends and her psychotherapist were loving to her, and she felt loved just as she was. The psychotherapist took this as an indicator that she had taken in and felt nourished at a very fundamental level, and that she had enough to hold her through tracing the lack in her own childhood and the subsequent 'lack' in her psychotherapist. The psychotherapist was no longer unequivocally available for physical contact. She would invite the client to think about what was happening, and deliberately delay instant gratification in order to work through the resultant tantrums, acting out and the underlying rage and despair. If the client had collapsed, the psychotherapist would have known that there was work to be done or the shift was too great.

Induced

Several approaches to counselling psychology and psychotherapy specifically train their practitioners in the induction of regressive states in order to facilitate the availability of the individual patient for the reparative or developmentally needed experience as the case may be. An outstanding example of this, of course, is the work of many hypnotherapists, neurolinguistic programming (NLP) practitioners and psychotherapists ranging from Janov-style rebirthers (1973; see also Minett, 1994) to the gentle Biosynthesis work of David Boadella or the hyperventilated catharsis of Grof.

> The goal of age regression is completion, most commonly through revivification of memory followed by appropriate psychotherapeutic intervention. On the one hand, age regression can attempt the completion of a circumscribed, perhaps traumatic event, usually located in the distant past; as will be discussed in later chapters, this event can have occurred during the preverbal as well as the verbal stage of development. Or, via age regression, especially when linked with hypno-play therapy, one can attempt the completion - perhaps the total construction - of a developmental stage.
>
> Shapiro (1988, p. 47)

Erickson was a past master at the spontaneous and speedy induction of regressive states which, by most accounts, enabled him to achieve dramatic and permanent 'cures' for a large variety of human pains and symptoms. The example that for me most graphically illustrates this is of the February Man, where a new childhood history was created under hypnosis for a woman, which she could use to support her current functioning and henceforth access as an alternative to her own, actually true, painful past:

> What happens, however, when the patient has been severely deprived in some basic life experiences? Can the therapist supply them vicariously in some way? Sensitive therapists have long recognized their role as surrogate parents who do, in fact, help their patients experience life patterns and relationships that have been missed. . . . We will present some of the senior author's approaches to supplying a patient with a personal relationship in a manner that anchors her within a more secure inner reality around which she can create a new identity for herself. This is the case of a young woman who so lacked the experience of being mothered that she gravely doubted her own ability to be one. Through a series of age regressions the senior author visited her in the guise of the February Man: A kindly granduncle type who became a secure friend and confidant. A series of such experiences enabled her to develop a new sense of confidence and identity about herself that led her eventually to a rewarding experience of motherhood with her own children.
>
> Erickson and Rossi (1979, p. 525)

A full and valuable discussion of Erickson's work in hypnosis is given by Erickson and Rossi (1979).

Recognized

This category concerns the facility to recognize when patients become regressed before or during a session. This is not always easy because many people can be said to live their lives in extended periods of age regression.

Kohut (1981) discussed his work with a woman who was strongly suicidal:

> In one session she was so badly off that I thought, 'How would you feel if I let you hold my fingers for a little while?' I am not recommending it, but I was desperate, so I gave her two fingers to hold. I immediately made a genetic interpretation to myself. It was of the toothless gums of a very young child, clamping down on an empty nipple. . . . I reacted to it even then as an analyst to myself. . . . I wouldn't say that it turned the tide, but it overcame a very difficult impasse at a dangerous moment. [The analysis went on for years and was reasonably successful.]
>
> Kohut (1981)

> In this interaction, Kohut experienced desperation, caring and compassion. He found a beautifully symbolic gesture that enabled him to express something of what he was feeling. Yet, in his statement, he was apologetic about this act, about giving her his fingers to hold. Even more astonishing - and sad - is his interpretation to himself that he was giving her a dry nipple. He seemed unaware that by having given something of himself - his own deep and persistent feelings - he gave her the nourishing human caring and compassion which she so desperately needed. Having been open with his feelings with her was most therapeutic. Yet, he appeared to be unaware that this act was the most healing thing he could have done.
>
> Rogers (1987, p. 183)

Contracted

This is a form of age regression where clients overtly (as in transactional analysis) or covertly (as in Kleinian analysis), consciously and in awareness undertake to allow themselves to regress or 'go back to their traumatic events' in order to cathart the emotions or behaviours associated with the trauma (as in Daldrup et al., 1988) or to re-decide decisions that they made in moments of extreme stress, pain or rage (Goulding and Goulding, 1978). An example of the former is:

P: You know, I really can. It's very clear. I remember being 10 years old and I was crouching under the dining room table.
T: Why were you there?
P: My father was angry again and he was tearing up the living room. He was smashing things and looking wild.
T: Be in that scene for a moment. Be under the table. Allow yourself to know what you are feeling and what you are saying to yourself in your head. Say it to your father.

P: I am terrified and I'm saying that I'll never allow myself to get that way. I'll never be like you.

T: Now say that directly to your father.

P: I'll *never* allow myself to rant and rave. I'll never be like *you*!

T: It sounds as if you believe that to get angry is to get crazy.

P: Yeah. (pause) If I get angry I'm convinced I'll go crazy. I'll be like my father!

T: Are you willing to experiment by letting out a small piece of anger and seeing what happens?

P: That's scary!

T: I know. You might start by dealing with something about which you have only moderate anger.

Daldrup et al. (1988, p. 75)

In my opinion, the most beneficial form of working with regression is when the person intentionally and specifically contracts with the therapist to regress for a particular period of time, to monitor their own responsibility and experience, to be willing to cathect into the here-and-now Adult on an agreed signal or at an agreed time. In my experience this puts the person fully in charge of their own process and usually helps them manage themselves, not only in the psychotherapy but also in their real life outside.

Many approaches to therapy use contracted regression, either in the overall sense – where the person has an overall understanding that regressive experiences will be welcome, confronted or used – or, specifically, for example, 'In this session I want to regress to the time when I was sexually abused, re-experience that pain, let it out of my body and re-decide to live'. Among many approaches I am choosing this piece from primal integration:

The relationship is a contractual one, between adults. Each party is responsible for their own actions, experiences and feelings. The boundaries set by the simple agreements we have about commitment, financial arrangements and time-keeping serve as reminders of the 'here and now' nature of this relationship.

Brown and Mowbray (1994, p. 21)

Management and maintenance

To establish and maintain a reparative relationship, we need at least the following factors:

- a solid working alliance in a long-term psychotherapeutic relationship
- temporary remission of the transference relationship – these two are mutually exclusive
- reasonable certainty in the psychotherapist that the client understands

enough of the cognitive process to make good use of the planned or anticipated experiment in relating.

Indications and contraindications in terms of treatment planning

We have to recognize that the same paradox that we find in other areas of life is there too in analysis – that the same thing can be both bad and good, that what is most valuable can also be dangerous and useless. This is as true of transference interpretation as it is of answering questions, expression of feeling, acting on impulse, etc., by the analyst. The great need is for flexibility (which is not weakness), reliability, and strength (which is not rigidity), and a willingness to use whatever resources are available.

                                                                Little (1986, p. 76)

Relationship between transference and developmental need

Developmental deficit

We can identify a category of pathology that is not confusion or conflict, but which can best be described as developmental deficit. This implicates a developmental – therefore causal and sequential – paradigm. It is based on the notion that specific deficits, injuries or distortions in the parenting or upbringing process can limit or damage an individual child differentially, depending on which particular critical phases the child is undergoing when the injury or interference takes place.

So a reparative and developmentally needed relationship will be construed on the basis of how the psychotherapies and the patient understand and prioritize the source and need for this kind of relationship. Depending on which one or more of these are identified, the therapist may bring to bear nutritional information, on the one hand, or, on the other, skill in diagnosing and dealing with post-traumatic stress disorder. The implementation of physiological catharsis such as Grof's breathwork or bioenergetic stress positions, or artistic expressive techniques such as sand play or puppetry, and/or a thorough knowledge and understanding of the major models of child development and appropriate parenting will form the foundation for this kind of work. The range, appropriateness and suitability of what a person needed then and what can be provided now within a therapeutic process will obviously depend on the skills, range of experiences and the quality of resources that the practitioner has assembled throughout his or her career. This last may include pastoral advice, arts materials, information about voice or movement classes, for example. Of course one does not hand out information, advice or resources, criticism or support without extreme care and attention to the patient's clinical requirements.

Deficit work, re-parenting and re-childing

Deficit replenishment takes a myriad forms, from radical re-parenting (Schiff et al., 1975) to transmuting internalization (Kohut, 1984) to providing the recognition to the infant in the Adult, which Balint (1989) proposes. All of these therapeutic approaches can be seen to involve the creation of new historical or new Child ego states specifically to provide, in areas of specific structural deficits, for example, positive self and object representations. Deficit, whether permission for catharsis or the provision of a corrective experience (of nurture or control, mirroring or optimal frustration), can be done through re-parenting (Schiff et al., 1975), self-re-parenting (James, 1974), or self-re-childing procedures that use a functional model (James and Savary, 1977). Re-parenting is going back to earlier Child ego states and providing a new object relationship – finding previous developmental levels of fixation, undoing them, and providing new or corrective experiences where these are lacking or needed.

There may be a deficit in a sense of emergent self/core self, e.g. a client who needs something actively to be provided in order to create a person with whom you can have a relationship. This could be facilitated by, for example, putting a withdrawn client into a group where they could witness an alternative 'family' environment while noise, activity, expression of feelings, conflict were expressed and managed with no-one being hurt, punished or isolated, gradually internalizing that this was an alternative to the repressive, unpredictable, terrorizing family regime in which she had grown up, and that perhaps she, too, could begin to interact in the ways she had been witnessing – she began to respond to other people – to give feedback, to practise different behaviours and to take confrontations from group members – particularly she witnessed other group members expressing the kinds of hopes, despair, rage, frustration and longing from which she had cut herself off and used this as a bridge to her own remembering and re-experiencing work.

Re-childing within a structural or phenomenological model of ego states is more fully discussed by Clarkson and Fish (1988), which should be read in conjunction with Clarkson and Gilbert (1988). Briefly, re-childing is defined as 'the creation of new ego states on psychophysiologically developmentally earlier sub-strata' (Clarkson and Fish, 1988, p. 52).

> In 1946 Franz Alexander, when describing the mechanism of psychoanalytic cure, introduced the concept of the 'corrective emotional experience'. The basic principle of treatment, he stated, is 'to expose the patient, under more favorable circumstances, to emotional situations which he could not handle in the past. The

patient, in order to be helped, must undergo a corrective emotional experience suitable to repair the traumatic influence of previous experience'.

Yalom (1975, p. 25)

Another problem in experiential psychotherapy can be a specific impasse. It occurs in situations where a good resolution is in principle possible, but would require an extreme experience of some kind that the client is unable or unwilling to face. Such psychological stumbling blocks vary considerably from individual to individual. It could be fear of facing psychological death ('ego death'), fear of losing control, or fear of insanity. Other times, the obstacle can be a reluctance to experience extreme physical pain, suffocation, or some other form of intense physical distress. It is common for the subject to recognize the problems involved as something that he or she knows from everyday life in the form of specific fears or uncomfortable symptoms. ('The last thing in the world I would do is to throw up'; 'The idea of having to face pain drives me crazy'; 'The most important thing for me is to be in control under all circumstances,' etc.) In situations of this kind, the therapist has the important task to identify the nature of the impasse and to help the client to overcome the psychological resistance that prevents him or her from facing it.

Grof (1988, p. 256)

The causes, origins and conditions of psychological damage constitute a vast and impressive library built up over thousands of years. It is not my intention to be comprehensive on this topic, because it is my belief that this is probably the most familiar to people in this field so I can rely on the reader's knowledge to fill in the gaps. I must just mention these aspects to highlight the functions, similarities and differences in dealing with the developmentally needed or reparative relationship in psychotherapy.

Gratification

Following on Freud's original admonishments to be abstinent or avoid getting gratification to the patient, there has been an understandable and conscientious avoidance and questioning of all analytic interventions that can be construed as gratifying. As must be clear from the many examples quoted in this section, so far in practice the exceptions rather outnumber the rule.

Anna Freud's oft-quoted patient who was allowed to ring up the analyst any time during the day or even the week-end is a convincing proof that acceptance and gratification of some regressive tendencies, or of acting-out, is not altogether incompatible with 'classical' technique; in other words, is not an irreversible parameter.

Balint (1989, p. 83)

Presence

It can hardly be argued that the sheer availability of a psychotherapist at a certain time and place is not reparative for most patients – particularly those for whom reliability, predictability and a holding environment is the kind of experience that they had never had before. (For others of course, this very provision can play into and reinforce an obsessive–compulsive kind of defensive structure against newness, spontaneity and the yielding of control. For those different experiences will consequently be reparative and the holding environment another re-traumatization or destructive learning experience.)

> Modell (1975) also recognizes the implicit gratification in the analyst's constancy, reliability, and perception of the patient's unique identity. Thus gratification can be seen as a necessary part of how the therapist offers him- or herself to the patient as the potentially good selfobject the patient has never had. The internalization of this good selfobject is necessary for the patient's arrested development to proceed, as Kohut and his co-workers found in treating their own patients.
>
> White and Weiner (1986, p. 41)

Intuition

Ferenczi (1980) thought that there is always a split whereby a part of the personality regresses to the pre-traumatic state which will thus become available in the analysis:

> If the original trauma consisted of over- or under-stimulation by the environment, with subsequent lack of understanding and indifference by the same people, then the aim of therapy must be: (a) to help the patient to regress to the traumatic situation, (b) to watch carefully what degree of tension the patient will be able to bear in this state, and (c) to see to it that the tension will remain at about that level by responding positively to the regressed patient's longings, cravings, or needs. A by-product of this research was the first intensive study of the doctor-patient relationship and the discovery of what nowadays is called the technique of counter-transference interpretations.
>
> Balint (1989, p. 126)

Receptivity

> Suddenly Joe was going, 'Mary, do you want me to put you to bed or do you want to stay here?'
>   Everything was going from me, I couldn't think.
>   'Er – er – want to stay here.' Ronnie was still there.

'Do you want to come downstairs to see me off?'

'Ugh, ugh.'

My body was turning away. Everything was getting black. The door shut. There was silence. I heard the noise of Joe's car. It was going away. There seemed nothing left. Nothing to live for, I went dead, sad, desolate. Tears came, silently. I was long alone, desolate. Then, in a tiny whisper, it seemed a struggle, to know it, to say it.

'Ronnie, please will you put me to bed?'

'You see, it's quite simple.' Ronnie was standing, we went downstairs to my room. 'Do you want the door open or shut?'

This was terrible, how to *know* which was 'right'. Ronnie helped me, opening and shutting the door. 'Shut.' It seemed I 'hadn't gone against'. The door was shut because I had wanted it shut. It was neither a reward nor a punishment. I was bad, sad, forlorn, because Joe had gone. But there was no 'Oh God, what *have* I done to cause the door to be shut.' Something was separate, me, the door, Ronnie. He was not cross with me. In the tiniest way there seemed an inkling of the truth, a glimmer of light. Things seemed strange and weak. But I was there, in bed. Lying still I went to sleep.

Barnes and Berke (1974, pp. 196–197)

Touch

As I mentioned in several places before, touch is a fraught issue within psychoanalysis and psychotherapy. Samuels describes refusing a woman's touch (1985); Thorne (1991) describes it in a questionably semi-sexual encounter and Kohut is described earlier. There are as many reported instances of the use of touch in counselling and psychotherapy perhaps as there are injunctions against it. The extent to which prescription and compliance diverge on this issue is perhaps an indication of the urgent necessity to review, re-vision and re-evaluate the movement and being moved, touching and being touched in all approaches to counselling and psychotherapy. Only by getting fully *in contact* with these issues will we be able to provide our trainees and our supervisees with the education, experience and expertise necessary to discriminate therapeutically in this dangerous and delightful zone.

That summer there was a big party at the house, many people came from other communities, the house was full of music and dancing. Peter was in his room. As the evening progressed he came downstairs and asked me if I would go up to his room. He had just moved to a new room, a big achievement for him, and had decorated it himself. He said he would very much like me to see it. Again, following the principle that had I been asked by any other resident I would have gone, I accepted his invitation. He let me into his room and invited me to sit down. I said I would, but only for five minutes. He wondered why and I said that I had come for the party; I was happy to see his room but I did not want to spend the evening there with him. I sat down, the room was very peaceful and pleasant.

Peter knelt down, put his head on my lap and arms around my waist; I felt calm and quite still, I had no desire to push him away. Time stood still for a few seconds. I was aware of the music downstairs. Peter's head started turning and a flutter of anxiety went quickly through me as I thought he might try to kiss me, but as soon as I saw his face I realized how wrong I was; it was the face of a toddler who had just been comforted by mum. He had an expression of innocence, completion and inner peace; I said the time had come for me to rejoin the party, and he slowly let go of me.

After that evening, Peter started taking part in household meetings; he stopped following me around, did not attempt to touch me and gradually the begging, longing, ever-starved look disappeared from his eyes.

Oakley in Cooper et al. (1989, p. 157)

Structure

Sometimes a client does not need, either in developmental or in reparative terms, further merging, empathy, understanding, support or encouragement. He or she may need challenge, control, criticism, structure or limits. Little (1986, p. 69) describes being tired of hearing her client's stories and telling her that she will not listen to them any more. When the client started on another story she said:

'I meant that. I'm not listening to any more of them.' She was silent, then giggled and said, 'It's *awful*. And it's *glorious*, to have you say something like that. Nobody has ever spoken to me like that before. I didn't know it could be like that. You've often told me about telling the children that I won't have them do things, but I simply didn't know how to do it.' And from then she began to be able both to accept 'no' for herself and to say it.

Self-object transferences

It becomes obvious, therefore, that from a therapeutic stand-point, interpretation is not enough, and it would appear to follow that the relationship existing between the patient and the analyst in the psychoanalytic situation serves purposes additional to that of providing a setting for the interpretation of transference phenomena.

Fairbairn (1958, p. 377)

Self-object transference can be empathized with, interpreted and responded to from a proactive or reactive countertransferential position.

The need for selfobject responses is not confined to the archaic selfobjects that are the normal requirements of the early years. Selfobject responses in a variety of forms are needed throughout the life span. Indeed, the need for selfobject responses is always present, waxing and waning with the ups and downs of the strength and vulnerability of the self.

Wolf (1988, p. 130)

There are many instances where the psychoanalyst or psychotherapist may provide those self-object transferential needs that an individual client may have need of in the analytic situation in order to have the resources to become effective in their extra-analytic life.

> To sum up, therefore: the patient transfers on to the analyst responsibility for emotional development in a failed area. One aspect of this process is that the patient needs to transfer on to the analyst his or her bad inner objects; the other aspect is that the patient requires an emotional capacity in the analyst in the particular area where there has been developmental failure.
>
> Symington (1986, p. 112)

An example of using Stern's notion of the development of the self

An experiment is suggested in which the client be allowed to explore the therapist's person, taking as much time as she needs and not 'looking after' the psychotherapist. The psychotherapist insists that she will take care of herself and stop the client, or move if she needs to. The client looks at the psychotherapist, who looks steadily back at the end of this process of coming to an agreement, whereupon the client bursts into tears and wants to hide her face, saying it is hard to see someone so steadily kindly towards her. The psychotherapist thus has some evidence of the client's struggle between the desire for new experience and some commitment to the old way. The psychotherapist comments in a rather casual way that the client can use the planned experiment in the most useful way for herself, thus distancing herself in advance from any desired outcome for the client.

The client has already made major commitments to a new way of being. She has decided about the quality of life she can sense would be available if she could only experience the ordinary in-betweenness of loving relating, and allow herself to be loved by others, *as well as love others*, and consciously cross-reference this to her presenting problems.

The client begins to explore the therapist's arm, then her attention is drawn to a dangling earring. The therapist says: 'Suppose you just explore, and I sit and don't say anything, just smile, or wink?' They look at each other for a time, then the psychotherapist pushes her own mouth up at the corners without a noise. The client laughs; the psychotherapist laughs. The psychotherapist hides her face and shows an eye, the client laughs and does the same, then buries her head in the therapist's lap. The game begins again as the client's eyes emerge from the therapist's lap – first one, then two. The psychotherapist covers her own eyes, then looks for client's eyes between her fingers, gives a little squeal of delight on finding two; and the client draws back startled, eyes flaring and hard. This may be an indication of some lack of ability in the emergent self to experience cross-modally.

The psychotherapist suspects a trauma at a very early stage in the development of the client's core self, when the consequences of her own actions were unpredictable because of the mother's inadequacy and unpredictability. That damage was also felt in the very organization of perceptual experience in the emergent self. The psychotherapist is aware of the client's inclination to pull away now into fear, thus re-traumatizing herself. The psychotherapist lowers her voice to a whisper and says: 'Now you really are at a choice point; you can carry on hiding, or you can do something different. The choice is always yours.' She keeps quite still to avoid any reinforcement of the old pattern, and this time she is more careful to match the levels of intensity and duration of contact in the cross-modalities, as she allows herself to be guided to a comfortable level of contact for the client. This shows in the client's little grunts of satisfaction, with which the psychotherapist also joins in.

Failures/opportunities for breakthrough

As many theorists and practitioners have pointed out throughout the history of psychotherapy and psychological counselling, it is important to fail our clients. It is in the working through of these failures that the potential for healing and autonomous growth can emerge. If the only thing that is provided in the consulting room is a technological instrument box or a reflecting screen, there is no potential for re-birth or another chance at growing up. It is not only inevitable, it is also necessary to fail our clients so that we do not create a false and entirely artificial, hermetically sealed incubator because, unless they develop some exposure and resistance to the vicissitudes of real life and its inevitable disappointments, disillusionments and disfigurements, they are unlikely to develop the kind of robustness, resilience and recalcitrance that may be necessary for the development of a sturdy self.

As I have stated in *The Therapeutic Relationship* (Clarkson, 2003), any intervention or any of the vectors of relationship discussed in this book as a result of self-awareness, theoretical background and clinical expertise and supervision. I would add a conscious incorporation of cultural dimensions and philosophical perspectives relevant to the issues and to the time. It is vital not to misinterpret, misunderstand or mismanage as individual issues those that are primarily concerned with cultural, collective, social or historical issues, e.g. the effect of a king's death on patients undergoing analysis (Fairbairn, 1952). (See also Samuels on the Political Psyche (1993) and Clarkson (1993, 1996) on the Bystander.)

It is vital to check on the other dimensions of the relationship before intervening energetically or passively in the idiom of the reparative or developmentally needed relationship. There is always the danger of misdiagnosis or missing of a predictable, non-productive or destructive transferential entanglement. Furthermore, there is the Scylla of crashing on the rocks of a catastrophic reaction and the Charybdis of getting stuck in a developmental theory freighted with historicity, ideology and conformity.

> As my therapist touched my feet I froze. I panicked as my field of vision narrowed and my breath became shallower. She encouraged me to stay with my breath and not verbalize – something was trying to break out. My body writhed, my tongue twisted, and I felt helpless and terrified. Then I looked towards the wall and saw the side of a cot, and with this came a blissful feeling of loving warmth and safety. Experiencing this depth of contact, trust and safety opened up a new space for me in which there was an instantaneous shift from terror to bliss. From this experience the insights flooded in. I saw that I had lived my life in defensive reactions to real human contact which was as intolerable for me as it was for my parents. My response was to split off from real contact and my feelings, project the intolerable parts, then defend myself from them with aggression and power play. I had abandoned my heart because the love I needed so much was terrifying. This left me feeling abandoned, unrecognized, depressed and psychologically unwell.
>
> Emerging from isolation into relationship with my therapist was fearful and dangerous for me. It was the quality of her skilled presence holding me in a safe place which enabled me to go beyond reactive defences and re-experience deep traumas.
>
> Donington (1994, pp. 66–67)

Permissions galore

The most important failures in this respect have to do with the premature or naïve provision of this enormously powerful type of relationship when the client is not in an optimum psychological state to utilize it or when it is used to gratify vicariously, or in a complementary way, the needs of the counsellor or psychotherapist. There has been, for example, an enormous romanticization of the role of advocacy in certain circles. Finally having accepted that the sexual abuse about which adult clients have often complained is based on real factual experience and not 'just fantasy', it became fashionable for a while for psychotherapists to take the side of the inner child and to become angry on its behalf with the abusing parent. Even though it was well meant in the wake of the enormous and eye-opening contribution of Miller (1985, 1986), it resulted all too often in clients becoming intrapsychically torn between their loyalty, often a romantic attachment, to the parent figure who abused them, and their connection with their psychotherapist who apparently took sides against the person from whom they had experienced the most profound feelings of love and physical acceptance.

Exiling introjects

The abused Child in the adult often still harbours a deep affection, or carries a torch, for the first lover of their life, even though this relationship was based on exploitation, abuse and even threat of physical violence: 'At least he loved me'. If the psychotherapist can remain open to the full complexity of feelings, the client may find themselves free enough to say, as one of my clients said to me, 'I know he did wrong, but I do not want you to hurt him or be angry with him. I want you to look after his child as well as mine, and not destroy what was beautiful, just because it wasn't right'.

Criteria for evaluating effectiveness

Balint (1959) was scrupulous in listing the points that he thought were characteristic of a 'new beginning':

> . . . [in] a first attempt at a clinical symptomatology of beneficial regression during analytic treatment. I intend to discuss in the following chapters how this list has changed in the light of my clinical experiences during the last thirty years.
> 1. During the increase of tension, that is before the gratification of the urge, most impressive and noisy symptoms appear; then a sudden change sets in, resulting in the feeling of a tranquil, quiet well-being which, if not carefully watched, may escape observation.
> 2. Intensity of gratification of the newly-begun activities never reaches end-pleasure levels.
> 3. All new beginnings happen in the transference, that is, in an object relationship, and lead to a changed relationship to the patient's objects of love and hate and, in consequence, to a considerable diminution of anxiety.
> 4. New beginnings also lead to character changes. Nowadays the same clinical observation would be described as a change in the ego. And, lastly, the most important:
> 5. New beginning means: (a) going back to something 'primitive', to a point before the faulty development started, which could be described as a regression, and (b), at the same time, discovering a new, better-suited, way which amounts to a progression. In my book *Thrills and Regressions* (1959) I called the sum-total of these two basic phenomena: regression for the sake of progression.
>
> Balint (1989, p. 132)

In a certain sense working within the transference relationship and working in the developmentally needed relationship are mutually exclusive. For any particular transaction, one or another of these will have to be privileged because one is a highlight or explication of a past pattern or relationship, and the other the introduction or exploration of a newly minted interpersonal experience. Usually, in order for a reparative or developmentally needed intervention/relationship to be effective, it is necessary for the transference to be permanently resolved or temporarily in remission. To be effective in either of these relationship modalities, it is crucial that the working alliance is intact and capable of sustaining the crisis of confidence, fear and potential satisfaction that attends a renewed resolution of life's developmental and existential crisis. The strength of the working alliance will determine the extent to which the person can take self-responsibility in psychological or practical emergencies. This will also be influenced of course by whether the client can generalize outside of the therapeutic relationship and/or whether the client can hold or contain the therapeutic *vas* as separate, distinct and potential for real life experiences. This fluctuation may be over a period of years, months or moments. A mistake, however, tends to feed back quite directly, quickly and vehemently in most circumstances. What is required of the clinician is that they are thoroughly comfortable with the theory and practice of reparative work both through their own experience and through their training and supervision, and that they have not been destructively or ignorantly drawn into disputes or debates that alienate the clinical participants from their phenomenological experiences – that all psychotherapies have reparative aspects whether or not the clinician takes responsibility for these.

Even if the practitioner is developmentally sophisticated or sensitized to the demands of a reparative relationship, they would need to take account of whether there is a bias influencing their client load or effectiveness in one direction rather than another.

Other criteria for evaluating effectiveness are: appropriateness, timeliness, intactness of the working alliance, neutralization of transference/countertransference dimension, generalizability and utility to other relationships, intrapsychic restructuring, increased adult effectiveness, enhanced stability under stress, establishment of intrapsychic nurturing (Kohut, 1968), freedom and spontaneity in current relationships, enhanced capacity for imagination and creativity.

Conclusion

The *developmentally needed/reparative relationship* can thus be differentiated as another kind of relationship that is potentially present and needed in psychotherapy. This is a traditional intervention in psychotherapy from Ferenczi (1980) to Fromm-Reichman (1974), Kohut (1977), and Schiff and Day (1970). Here the psychotherapist intentionally provides the corrective/reparative replenishing parental relationship (or action) in cases where the original parenting was deficient, abusive or over-protective.

References

Alexander, F. (1933) On Ferenczi's relaxation principle. International Journal of Psychoanalysis 14: 183–192.

Alexander, F. and French, T. (1946) Psychoanalytic Therapy: Principles and applications. New York: Ronald Press.

Anthony, E.J. and Cohler, B.J. (eds) (1987) The Invulnerable Child. New York: The Guilford Press.

Avrech, G. (1989) Book review of When You're Ready: A woman's healing from childhood physical and sexual abuse by her mother by Kathy Evert (1987). Psychological Perspectives 21: 209.

Balint, M. (1959) Thrills and Regressions. London: Hogarth Press.

Balint, M. (1989) The Basic Fault: Therapeutic aspects of regression. London: Routledge.

Barnes, M. and Berke, J. (1974) Mary Barnes: Two accounts of a journey through madness. Harmondsworth: Penguin.

Brandchaft, B. (1989) Klein, Balint and Fairbairn: A self-psychological perspective. In: Detrick, D.W. and Detrick, S.P. (eds), Self Psychology: Comparisons and contrasts. Hillsdale, NJ: The Analytic Press, pp. 231–258.

Brandtstädter, J. (1990) Development as a personal and cultural construction. In: Semin, G.S. and Gergen, K.J. (eds), Everyday Understanding: Social and scientific implications. London : Sage, pp. 83–107.

Brown, J. and Mowbray, R. (1994) Primal integration. In: Jones, D. (ed.), Innovative Therapy: A handbook. Buckingham: Open University Press, pp. 2–27.

Carugati, F.F. (1990) Everyday ideas: Theoretical models and social representations: The case of intelligence and its development. In: Semin, G.S. and Gergen, K.J. (eds), Everyday Understanding: Social and scientific implications. London: Sage, pp. 130–150.

Chess, S. and Thomas, A. (1986) Temperament in Clinical Practice. New York: Guilford Press.

Chess, S. and Thomas, A. (1987) Origins and Evolution of Behavior Disorders: From infancy to early adult life. Cambridge, MA: Harvard University Press.

Clarkson, P. (1992) Transactional Analysis Psychotherapy: An integrated approach. London: Routledge.

Clarkson, P. (1993) Bystander games. Transactional Analysis Journal 23: 158–172.

Clarkson, P. (1996) The Bystander: An end to innocence in human relationships? London: Whurr.

Clarkson, P. (2003) The Therapeutic Relationship, 2nd ed. London: Whurr.

Clarkson, P. and Fish, S. (1988) Rechilding: Creating a new past in the present as a support for the future. Transactional Analysis Journal 18(1): 51–59 (first published in Spanish translation, 1986).

Clarkson, P. and Gilbert, M. (1988) Berne's original model of ego states: Some theoretical considerations. Transactional Analysis Journal 18(1): 20–29 (first published in Spanish translation, 1986).

Cooper, R., Friedman, J., Gans, S. et al. (1989) Thresholds between Philosophy and Psychoanalysis: Papers from the Philadelphia Association. London: Free Association.

Cox, M. and Theilgaard, A. (1987) Mutative Metaphors in Psychotherapy: The Aeolian mode. London: Tavistock.

Daldrup, R.J., Beutler, L.E., Engle, D. and Greenberg, L.S. (1988) Focused Expressive Psychotherapy: Freeing the overcontrolled patient. London: Cassell.

Detrick, D.W. and Detrick S.P. (eds) (1989) Self Psychology: Comparisons and contrasts. Hillsdale, NJ: The Analytic Press, pp. 231–258.

Donington, L. (1994) Core process psychotherapy. In: Jones, D. (ed.), Innovative Therapy: A handbook. Buckingham: Open University Press, pp. 51–68.

Elson, M. (ed.) (1987) The Kohut Seminars on Self Psychology and Psychotherapy With Adolescents and Young Adults. New York: W.W. Norton.

Erickson, M.H. (1967) Advanced Techniques of Hypnosis and Therapy. New York: Grune & Stratton.

Erickson, M.H. and Rossi, E.L. (1979) The February man: Facilitating new identity in hypnotherapy. In: Rossi, E.L. (ed.), Innovative Hypnotherapy: The collective papers of Milton H. Erickson on hypnosis IV. New York: Irvington Publishers, pp. 525–542.

Evans, R., Sills, S. and Clarkson, P. (1993) Systemic integrative psychotherapy with a young bereaved girl. In: Clarkson, P. (ed.), On Psychotherapy. London: Whurr, pp. 111–123.

Fairbairn, W.R.D. (1952) Psychoanalytic Studies of the Personality. London: Tavistock.

Fairbairn, W.R.D. (1958) On the nature and aims of psychoanalytic treatment. International Journal of Psychoanalysis 39: 374–386.

Ferenczi, S. (1980) Further Contributions to the Theory and Technique of Psychoanalysis. London: Maresfield Reprints/Karnac Books (first published 1926).

Freud, A. (1968) Indications for child analysis and other papers 1945 to 1956. In: The Writings of Anna Freud, Vol. 4. New York: International Universities Press.

Freud, S. (1920) Beyond the Pleasure Principle, Standard Edition, vol. 19. London: Hogarth Press, pp. 1–64 (first published 1955).

Fromm-Reichman, F. (1974) Principles of Intensive Psychotherapy. Chicago: University of Chicago Press (first published 1950).

Gergen, K.J., Gloger-Tippelt, G. and Berkowitz, P. (1990) The Cultural Construction of the Developing Child. In: Semin, G.S., and Gergen, K.J. (eds), Everyday Understanding: Social and scientific implications. London: Sage, pp. 108–129.

Goldstein, K. (1939) The Organism. New York: American Book.

Goulding, M.M. and Goulding, R.L. (1978) The Power is in the Patient. San Francisco: TA Press.

Goulding, M.M. and Goulding, R.L. (1979) Changing Lives Through Redecision Therapy. New York: Brunner/Mazel.

Graf, C.L. (1984) Healthy narcissism and new-age individualism: A synthesis of the theories of Carl Rogers and Heinz Kohut, unpublished doctoral dissertation, State University of New York, Stony Brook.

Greenson, R.R. (1965) The working alliance and the transference neurosis. Psychoanalysis Quarterly 34: 155–181.

Grof, S. (1988) The Adventure of Self-Discovery. New York: State University of New York Press.

Holmes, P., Karp, M. and Watson, M. (eds) (1994) Psychodrama since Moreno. London: Routledge.

James, M. (1974) Self-reparenting: Theory and process. Transactional Analysis Journal 4(3): 32–39.

James, M. and Savary, L. (1977) A New Self: Self-therapy with transactional analysis. Reading, MA: Addison-Wesley.

Janov, A. (1973) The Primal Scream. London: Abacus.

Jaspers, K. (1963) General Psychopathology (J. Hoenig and M.W. Hamilton, trans.). Chicago: University of Chicago Press (first published 1913).

Kalisch, D. (1994) Review of 'Picking up the pieces – two accounts of a psychoanalytic journey'. Self and Society 22(3): 45–56.

Klein, M. (1984) Envy, Gratitude and Other Works. London: Hogarth Press and Institute for Psychoanalysis (first published 1957).

Koestler, A. (1989) The Act of Creation. London: Arkana (first published 1964).

Kohut, H. (1968) The psychoanalytic treatment of narcissistic personality disorders: Outline of a systematic approach. The Psychoanalytic Study of the Child 23: 86–113.

Kohut, H. (1977) The Restoration of the Self. New York: International Universities Press.

Kohut, H. (1981) Remarks on Empathy [film]. Filmed at Conference on Self-Psychology, 4 October, Los Angeles

Kohut, H. (1984) How Does Analysis Cure? Chicago: University of Chicago Press.

Kris, E. (1952) Psychoanalytic Explorations in Art. Madison, CT: International Universities Press.

Langer, M.M. (1989) Merleau-Ponty's Phenomenology of Perception. London: Macmillan.

Little, M. (1986) Toward Basic Unity: Transference neurosis and transference psychosis. London: Free Association.

Lowen, A. (1969) The Betrayal of the Body. New York: Collier-Macmillan.

Mackenzie, M. (1989) Prisoners of Childhood. Channel 4 television broadcast, 30 May and 6, 13 and 20 June.

Maslow, A.H. (1968) Toward a Psychology of Being, 2nd edn. New York: D. Van Nostrand (first published 1963).

Masterson, J.F. (1985) The Real Self: A developmental, self, and object relations approach. New York: Brunner/Mazel.

Meacham, A. (1992) Call Me Mom. Changes (August): 57–63.

Merleau-Ponty, M. (1962) The Phenomenology of Perception (Colin Smith, trans.). London: Routledge & Kegan Paul.

Miller, A. (1985) Thou Shalt not be Aware: Society's betrayal of the child (H. Hannum, trans.). London: Pluto (original work published 1981).

Miller, A. (1986) The Drama of Being a Child. London: Virago Press.

Minett, G. (1994) Breath and Spirit: Rebirthing as a Healing Technique. London: Aquarian Press.

Minkowski, E. (1970) Lived Time (N. Metzel, trans.). Evanston, IL: Northwestern University Press (first published 1933).

Modell, A.A. (1975) A Narcissistic defense against affect and the illusion of self-sufficiency. International Journal of Psychoanalysis 56: 275–282.

Moreno, J.L. (1965) Therapeutic vehicles and the concept of surplus reality. Group Psychotherapy XVIII: 213.

Murray, G. (1915) The Stoic Philosophy. London: Watts: Allen & Unwin.

Nakhla, F. and Jackson, G. (1993) Picking up the Pieces – Two accounts of a psychoanalytic journey. Yale: Yale University Press.

Norcross, J.C. and Goldfried, M.R. (eds) (1992) Handbook of Psychotherapy Integration. New York: Basic Books.

Rank, O. (1989) Art and Artist: Creative urge and personality development. New York: W.W. Norton (first published 1932).

Rogers, C.R. (1951) Client-Centered Therapy. Boston: Houghton Mifflin.

Rogers, C.R. (1977) On Personal Power. London: Constable.

Rogers, C.R. (1987) Rogers, Kohut and Erickson: A personal perspective on some similarities and differences. In: Zeig, J.K. (ed.), The Evolution of Psychotherapy. New York: Brunner/Mazel, pp.179–187.

Rycroft, C. (1972) A Critical Dictionary of Psychoanalysis. Harmondsworth: Penguin (first published 1968, 2nd edn 1979).

Samuels, A. (1985) Jung and the Post-Jungians. London: Routledge & Kegan Paul.

Samuels, A. (1993) The Political Psyche. London: Routledge.

Schiff, J.L. with Schiff, A.W., Mellor, K., Schiff, E. et al. (1975) Cathexis Reader: Transactional analysis treatment of psychosis. New York: Harper & Row.

Schiff, J.L. and Day, B. (1970) All My Children. New York: Pyramid Publications.

Schoenewolf, G. (1990) Turning Points in Analytic Therapy: The classic cases. Northvale, NJ: Jason Aronson.

Sechehaye, M. (1951) Symbolic Realization: A new method of psychotherapy applied to a case of schizophrenia. New York: International Universities Press.

Seligman, M.E.P. (2002) Positive psychology, positive prevention and positive therapy. In: Snyder, C.R. and Lopez, S.J. (ed) Handbook of Positive Psychology. Oxford: Oxford University Press, pp. 3-9.

Shapiro, M.K. (1988) Second Childhood: Hypno-play therapy with age-regressed adults. New York: W.W. Norton.

Stern, D. (1985) The Interpersonal World of the Infant. New York: Basic Books.

Sullivan, H.S. (1954) The Interpersonal Theory of Psychiatry. New York: Norton.

Symington, N. (1986) The Analytic Experience: Lectures from the Tavistock. London: Free Association.

Thorne, B. (1991) Person-Centred Counselling: Therapeutic and spiritual dimensions. London: Whurr.

White, M.T. and Weiner, M.B. (1986) The Theory and Practice of Self Psychology. New York: Brunner Mazel.

Winnicott, D.W. (1975) Metapsychological and clinical aspects of regression within the psycho-analytical set-up. In: Through Paediatrics to Psycho-analysis. London: Hogarth Press and the Institute of Psycho-Analysis, pp. 278–294.

Wolf, E.S. (1988) Treating the Self: Elements of clinical self psychology. New York: Guilford.

Yalom, I. (1975) The Theory and Practice of Group Psychotherapy. New York: Basic Books (first published 1931).

Chapter 9
In Search of Supervision's Soul: a research report on competencies for integrative supervision in action

With Marie Angelo

The research process

In telling stories of research, it may be helpful to remember that what we are doing is a special kind of searching – searching again, going over the ground, crafting our material in a particular way. As in all good stories, it is not only the end that counts; we need to know more about the story search itself so that we understand who is searching, what for, where and how. We consider each of these questions first, to set the research findings and discussion in context.

As researchers we have an eye attuned to relationship. The most influential factor in determining the effectiveness of psychotherapy is the relationship between client and therapist (Norcross and Goldfried, 1992). Clarkson's work discussed in *The Therapeutic Relationship* (1995) takes up this finding and explores the implications, not only in psychotherapy, but as an orienting perspective in all professional activities that make intentional use of relationship. The five-relationship model becomes an integrating perspective – as with the parts of a tree, bringing together the working alliance, and the distortions that occur in it through recycled or transferred relationships, the reparative or developmentally needed relationship, the dialogic, person-to-person relationship and the transpersonal relationship.

Our intent was to look for soul, perhaps a surprising search where supervision is concerned. All too frequently colleagues' responses to research on supervision were rather negative ('Oh, how boring . . .'), but mention 'soul', and the energy comes back ('yes, fascinating – but what is it?'). In his classic text *Re-Visioning Psychology*, post-Jungian James Hillman defines soul as the archetype or deepest metaphor of life. Soul is not a

165

substance but a perspective: 'an unknown component which makes meaning possible . . . is communicated in love . . . has a religious concern . . . refers to the deepening of events into experiences . . . the imaginative possibility in our natures . . .' (Hillman, 1975, p. x). Surely here we are getting close to the living concerns of supervision. We cannot force the perspective of soul, but we can be attentive to the way we create the conditions that invite such enlivening power into our relationships, and into our research. With soul informing our searches, the sometimes dried-out concepts take on a fresh juiciness, and our findings are filled with life – embodied. That was our hope for the study of supervision.

The focus for our search was among possibly the most 'dried-out' aspects – descriptions of competencies for supervision. As the literature on supervision and supervision training increases, competencies become more important. Comprehensive overviews, such as that of Carroll (1996), list more and more skills, models and check lists. There is the development of competency listings in specific domains as comprehensive skill profiles, such as NVQ units, elements, performance criteria, range statements, knowledge specification and evidence requirements. The result is an increasingly elaborate language of skill requirements set out as minimum standards, to which trainees must match themselves in order to become accredited. Our concern is that such listings frame and define the field, giving all kinds of explicit and implicit messages about what is important and what counts, not only by the overall content, but by what is invariably said first, what is prioritized, what is not said, what is taken as read. Our research aim becomes to search for, and perhaps make, some soul among the competencies.

From the range of possible methods of search, we selected three areas for investigation:

1. Competencies listed and published by training bodies (see Addendum).
2. Spontaneous listings made by supervisees (see Addendum for the simple proforma used).
3. Remembered stories of supervision written by supervisees.

There are of course many other ways of looking, and we should emphasize that this research was undertaken as a pilot investigation in the light of a wider project concerned with looking beyond simple model-making in integrative work, towards a more organically and experientially valid integrative supervision and psychotherapy.

Results

As a result of following this method, there were some interesting results:

- The content analysis of published competencies showed markedly differing proportions allocated to the different relationships. The copied, cut and re-grouped lists resulted in:
  - five pages on the working alliance
  - three pages on transferred relationships (with a large percentage coming, as expected, from psychodynamic sources)
  - three pages on the reparative/developmentally needed relationship
  - one page on the dialogic, person-to person relationship
  - zero pages on the transpersonal relationship.

- Supervisee listings were acquired from 22 therapists, all currently in supervision with a number of different supervisors, with several reflecting on a long career during which there has been experience of many supervisors. A wide range of competencies was listed, ranging from 4 to 24 items, many of which emphasized the personal and transpersonal. Being particularly interested in prioritizing, we looked more closely at what was listed first. We found that this 'primary' competency was just as likely to refer to the personal or transpersonal as to the working alliance, transferential and developmental competencies. Hence, although there were listings that prioritized 'clarity of boundaries', 'support', 'listening', 'sound theory', and 'diverse knowledge', there were also listings that prioritized 'awareness of own limitations', 'integrity; creating a climate of trust', 'someone who gets to know my work' and 'insight; creativity'.

- Once invited to write a 'story' of personal experience, the whole dynamic of the results changed, pointing out once more how thoroughly the medium and instructions shape what is given. In selecting and remembering a significant supervision experience, the focus was on searching for something important to the person rather than the more systematic conceptual search suggested by listing. As a result, supervisees tended to be much more direct about their needs, putting the body back (i.e. 'remembering') into some powerful supervision qualities. There was a definite emphasis on the personal, in both negative and positive memories. There was, for example, the distress of being discounted – 'I only got ten words out before [supervisor] interrupted with a full interpretation' – or the thrill of positive recognition – 'Eye meeting rather than eye contact'. There were, also, transformative experiences, because for this supervisee, looking back with deep appreciation, 'I felt loved, heard. There was a feeling of universality, of being linked together . . . a feeling of love and care, and at the same time an openness and eagerness to learn. I felt enlightened, I felt full of life, I felt united – there was a desire to get more of it. . . . Openness to seeing the world in multiple perspectives'. The possibilities seem summed up in this supervisee comment about group supervision: 'where people have the kind of freedom and the right climate for nurturing ideas and exploring them that allows them to make a leap from the concrete to the abstract. It is at such times that complex, surprising and wonderful links are made between what initially appeared to be disparate elements. I would call this weaving, like a rich tapestry. It also gives a greater sense of a more global awareness of an issue or situation.'

Discussion

With these stories we are beginning to find a sense of the dynamic qualities that really count for supervisees. We are not building a model through a static assembly of requirements, but picturing simultaneities, being more true to lived experience.

The models so frequently used and listed operate as implicated narratives of mechanisms. They tend to 'start at the bottom', build up, and have a kind of fundamentalism and literalism that then becomes confused with minimal skill level/competency. For such a model, as for the published competency listings, the working alliance is always the starting point, the cool concept of reductionism revealing its fervent and harsh imagery as we argue that 'what it all boils down to' are the fundamental, boundary-making pragmatics of the work. Like a re-statement of Maslow's triangle of human needs, we seem to have here 'the bottom line', carrying most load, most importance – an essential to be put in place before other levels can be attained. From this perspective, where time and attention rest in the foothills, the personal is far up the mountain side, and the transpersonal is almost unimaginably remote, way up there as a sliver of potential along with the peak experiences, and certainly nothing to do with 'basic' competencies.

The major flaw in this social darwinism approach to competencies is just that with which we have long since critiqued and relativized – Maslow's picture. Humans do not proceed up a neat hierarchy of needs, or of competencies. We are complex, discontinuous, simultaneous beings, and such picturings serve rather as unreflected expressions of our socially constructed assumptions and preferences. We take them literally at our peril, imagining that these sober charts are somehow more 'true' than colourful images such as the woven tapestry described above. We would surely be better served by a more playful, picaresque and flexible approach that reconciles theory with story. Certainly, without a working alliance there is no effective supervision, but without a person there is no effective supervision either, and from a relational–narrative view that looks to include all the range and variety of relationships, it is arguably more appropriate to prioritize the person-to person, dialogic relationship as the starting point for attention.

So let us picture competencies differently, beginning with the person. This shift of perspective moves to the living qualities of relationship for which solid hierarchical models of representation won't do. We need organic, living picturings and, as we are dealing here with the heart of the matter, we can adopt that playful approach, turn the images around and find our model embodied in the metaphors of the heart (following Hillman's approach in his beautifully crafted piece, *The Thought of the Heart*, but staying more closely to the living heart rather than its literary evocations).

Consider: a heart isn't static unless it is dead; it pulsates and beats rhythmically, its two chambers working in relationship, holding and containing the pressure of life, but also enabling it to flow and circulate, receptive and dynamic as the valves open and close. This points to a relationship between the holding/boundary making of the working alliance and the mysterious opening/flowing of Physis or life energy which is so characteristic of the transpersonal. Rather than see these as separated functions, this more organic, embodied way of working keeps us in touch with the rhythm of containing and opening – and its heart-felt purpose.

Competencies can then be identified relationally without stopping the heart and killing the Physis (a 'heart attack' we regularly perform in making our models). The embodied metaphor celebrates the heart as a place of integrated working in which each aspect is intimately and simultaneously connected as a whole.

The kind of competencies we then begin to talk about emphasizes different personal roles. The person-to-person relationship is characterized by the *collegial role*, working 'heart to heart', and carrying the qualities that supervisees talk of as embodied ethics, authentic presence, mutuality, humility and humour. The working alliance becomes the *maker or shaper role*, establishing the rhythmically moving chambers of the heart, and initiating attentiveness between the workers in their alliance to boundaries, contracting, administering and time structuring. In relation to this, the transpersonal holds and models the *co-creator role* of openness, spontaneity, an awareness of levels of energy and work in the pulse of the blood, of events deepening into experiences beyond ego boundaries, a spaciousness through which awe and mystery can pass on a tide of life. Simultaneously, the *protector role* displays competencies around the disturbing dynamics of transferred relationships, e.g. through sensitivity to atmospheres, attending to distortions and dangers of arrhythmia, arterial hardening, low or high pressures, releasing insights from parallel processes.

As the heart pumps and blood flows, the *connecting roles* operate more and more effectively, repairing and developing the body through the airy exchanges of gases, the filtering out of wastes, and nourishment of every cell. As with the many and complex functions of the blood, the beating of the supervisory heart serves a number of connective functions. In helping the supervisee connect up with his or her own competency, the supervisor, at various times, and as appropriate, plays the roles of trainer, facilitator and educator. These are related but different roles, each aligning with a different level of discourse (Clarkson, 1995; Clarkson and Angelo, 1998). Hence, the training role of supervision helps the supervisee in a reparative manner to connect up with knowledge, credibility and resources, and to find 'names and images' for their experiences. The facilitating role is supportive and directive, helping the supervisee developmentally to connect up with the past, in terms of both the personal and the cultural, the two forming a web of interconnections that 'tell the stories' of the times. The educative role goes deeper into this process, as the root of the word demonstrates (from '*educare*', to call forth from within) because insights into narrative and the ways stories are made help the supervisee connect up with his or her own authoring ability, seeing beyond literalism into new imaginative possibilities. In this we move close to the transpersonal and the experiences of co-creating the new.

In our follow-up to this small pilot study, we hope to continue re-visioning and embodying supervisory competency in these personal, metaphorical ways. By differentiating supervision through 'heart–thought' relationships, we can understand the frameworks and criteria we create for our courses as dynamic picturings that operate as a fractal or cosmos of a living integrated system. Rather than 'concrete' grids and tick-box systems, they become vessels for soul, like those spoken of so eloquently by the great Neoplatonic philosopher Plotinus when he taught us that:

> though this Soul is everywhere tractable, its presence will be secured all the more readily when an appropriate receptacle is elaborated, a place especially capable of receiving some portion or phase of it, something reproducing it and serving like a mirror to catch an image of it.
>
> Enneads (4.3.11)

References

Borders, L.D. and Leddick, G.R. (1987) Handbook of Counseling Supervision, Alexandria, VA: Association for Counselor Education and Supervision. (Reprinted as Appendix 4 in Feltham and Dryden, 1994.)

Carroll, M. (1996) Counselling Supervision: Theory, skills and practice, London: Cassell.

Clarkson, P. (1995) The Therapeutic Relationship. London: Whurr.

Clarkson, P. and Angelo, M. (1998) Organisational counselling psychology: using myths and narratives as research and intervention in psychological consultancy to organisations. In: Clarkson, P. (ed.), Counselling Psychology: Integrating theory, research and supervised practice. London: Routledge.

Feltham, C. and Dryden, W. (1994) Developing Counsellor Supervision. London: Sage, pp. 140–145

Hillman, J. (1975) Re-Visioning Psychology. London: Harper & Row.

Holloway, E. (1995) Clinical Supervision: A systems approach. Thousand Oaks, CA: Sage, pp. 183–188.

Norcross, J.C. and Goldfried, M.R. (1992) Handbook of Psychotherapy Integration. New York: Basic Books.

Plotinus (1956) Enneads (Stephen MacKenna, trans.). London: Faber & Faber.

Rodenhauser, P. (1996) On the future of psychotherapy supervision in psychiatry. Academic Psychiatry 20: 82–91 (reprinted as an Appendix in Rodenhauser, 1997).

Rodenhauser, P. (1997) Psychotherapy supervision: prerequisites and problems in the process. In: Watkins, C.E. (ed.), Handbook of Psychotherapy Supervision. New York: John Wiley, pp. 527–548.

Addendum

Competency listings sources

These were collated from the major text, the Advice, Guidance, Counselling and Psychotherapy Lead Body, First Release Standards (which may be changed to meet NCVQ and SCOTVEC accreditation requirements).

Additional competencies were found listed by The Association for Counselor Education and Supervision Standards for Counselor Supervision, adopted by the American Association for Counseling and Development, 1989, reprinted as an Appendix in Holloway (1995).

The psychodynamic approach was able to be included through the listed Proficiencies for Psychodynamic Psychotherapy Supervisors, from Rodenhauser (1996).

Competencies of Supervisors from Borders and Leddick (1987).

Proforma for participants in the research study

(Photocopied on to separate sheets and given by hand by the two researchers.)

As part of an ongoing research project concerning Supervisor Competencies, we would appreciate it if you would please make a list of the competencies you look for in a supervisor. No names are being used and all information will be treated with respect and used to help understand more about the content and process of supervision in our fields. (Once supervisees have completed the list, in their own time, they were asked if they would complete a second stage, involving their response to the following.)

Please record a particular significant supervision session:

1. What made the experience so significant?
2. How would you describe the kind of experience you were having with supervision at that time?
3. The transpersonal relationship – can you say something about it?

(This last question was included after a rather telling comment from a participant in an early try-out of the questions to the effect that, 'I didn't realize that it was OK to write about such things'. We realized that in this secularized culture some positive discrimination was needed to give the transpersonal its voice, and this aspect has now been incorporated as part of the follow-up research.)

Chapter 10
The Beginning of Gestalt

> Life is achieved by resolving the tension in responsive feeling and creative
> activity, in which having is not eliminated but is assimilated to being, in which
> one and another become I and Thou; in which science is integrated with
> metaphysics; in which autonomy (managing my own affairs) is transcended in
> liberty, which is participation; in which my body and the world with which it is
> consubstantial and which enlarges and multiplies its powers is the place in which
> I bear witness to Being . . .
>
> Marcel (1952, p. 66)

Beginning the beginning

It has too often been said that gestalt therapy suffers from a lack of theory. At
the same time it has established itself in experiential and clinical applications
throughout the world. The author has personally taught gestalt in Italy,
Russia, North America, Scandinavia, Ireland, England and South Africa, and
students from many more countries, including Japan and Jamaica, have
studied gestalt with her in London. She has encountered two polarities in
dealing with this issue of lack of theory.

One way is to bring in – through importation, introjection or integration –
concepts, ideas and theories from other fields and other disciplines. These
are often far removed from both the philosophical and the cultural core of
gestalt, thus, in the author's opinion, impugning the integrity of the gestalt
approach. This tendency is exemplified in what someone has called the
'gestalt and' syndrome – gestalt and bodywork, gestalt and aromatherapy,
gestalt and object relations. However, as she wrote in Clarkson (1989), the
author has very serious doubts about the procedure described above as a
way of enhancing gestalt. It seems to be like providing an artificial limb for a
person who does not need one – as if gestaltists do not have or cannot
develop theory and methodology sufficient from what already exists in
gestalt. Somehow by a psychoanalytic child development add-on or a

psychodiagnostic DSM (*Diagnostic and Statistical Manual of Mental Disorders*, 4th edn – American Psychiatric Association, 1994) injection, gestalt would be 'saved'. I believe current tendencies in gestalt have reached their enantiodromic opposite. A new moment could envisage a return to the most ancient as well as a turn to the most new, not as an empty repetition compulsion but as an intentional action of re-creation.

The author thinks that there are a very large number of books, sources, theories and approaches that share the central philosophical and methodological tenets of gestalt. These need to be recognized as gestalt textbooks, because they belong inside the cadre of gestalt more than anywhere else. She is thinking, for example, of the work of the phenomenologists Merleau-Ponty (1962/1970), Marcel (1952) and Minkowski (1933/1970). An extensive discussion of these must wait for another time. However, the continuity of a tradition of 2500 years spans gestalt thinking from the beginning of time in the Western tradition, to the current frontiers of the scientific enquiry of our current world. Between them they seem to constitute a whole contact cycle from the ancient pre-Socratic texts of Heraclitus up to the modern interpreters of quantum physics and chaos theory, such as Capra (1978), Zohar (1990), Bohm (1980/1983), Gleick (1989), and Briggs and Peat (1989). They do not seem to be a wig to cover a full head of hair, but the articulation of the implicated order of gestalt itself, an improvization on Paganini which brings out more of the true beauty of the theme without destroying the integrity of the work of art.

The author happens to believe that gestalt is the psychological and therapeutic theory that will survive the necessary paradigm shifts of the twentieth century. It is the psychotherapy intrinsically most compatible and potentially comfortable with the discoveries flowing from quantum physics and chaos theory. Having its roots in the first mists of occidental philosophy, gestalt has already proved endurance. Remember that Perls said he had 'discovered gestalt, not invented it'. Gestalt will not survive if it runs like a yapping lapdog after the skirts of the psychoanalysis that Perls had found so wanting, or if it twists itself into a travesty of what is easiest to sell to managed care.

The author believes that the radical revisions and assumptions of the paradox-embracing, post-modern climate with which we are confronted on the conceptual, cultural and experiential horizons of our time are indeed most compatible with gestalt as a psychotherapeutic and organizational approach.

There will be others who talk of the end; the author wants to talk of beginning.

The beginning of gestalt: the drive to wholeness

The author's beginning was in South Africa. She was born there in the shadow of the mountains surrounding Pretoria to parents whose forefathers and foremothers had fled the religious persecutions of counter-reformation Europe. Her parents called General Smuts 'Oom Jannie' (Uncle Jannie) – a term of endearment for the last prime minister before apartheid, a philosopher king and warrior, an intellectual and spiritual giant, and the architect of what became the United Nations.

Smuts was the founder of the philosophy of Holism; his major book is called *Holism and Evolution* (Smuts, 1926/1987). Holism permeated the intellectual and spiritual atmosphere of that time and that place. Fritz and Laura Perls, of course, had fled to this area of South Africa when the German people turned against the Jews. Perls gave as the subtitle of his first book, *Ego, Hunger and Aggression*, the words: 'The Beginning of Gestalt Therapy' (1969). (This was with some hindsight, of course, in the Random House edition, after gestalt had already begun to gain acceptance as a psychotherapeutic method.) It was not just an elaboration of psychoanalysis, it was also an attack and rejection of its most valued tenets. Primacy and pre-eminence were accorded to Holism.

> The final net result is that this is a whole-making universe, that it is the fundamental character of this universe to be active in the production of wholes, of ever more complete and advanced wholes, and that the Evolution of the universe, inorganic and organic, is nothing but the record of this whole-making activity in its progressive development.
>
> Smuts (1926/1987, p. 326)

Fritz and Laura brought psychoanalysis with them and it co-mingled with Smuts' holism in their thought and practice. So much so, that the first section in their book, covering philosophical foundations, is called: 'Holism and Psycho-analysis'.

Perls then added the second section to expound his belief in the centrality of mental aggression in psychic life and he called this 'mental metabolism'. They called the method of psychotherapy that they had developed 'concentration therapy'.

Now we know that this was to become gestalt therapy – the Therapy of Wholes – the first and perhaps only holistic therapy. Perls took it for granted that everybody who read him had also read Smuts; this is another factor contributing to difficulties in understanding Perls' book.

When Perls, Hefferline and Goodman wrote that 'Concentration is the symptom par excellence of a sound holism' (1951, p. 63), they meant that through this concentration method now called gestalt, power can be withdrawn from destructive purposes against people and cities and be used for growth and development instead – as Smuts had originally meant.

Of course, as we go from Smuts to Perls, Hefferline and Goodman we find that the holism we have discussed is a process of creative synthesis. The wholes are not static, but evolutionary, creative and in a continual state of Heraclitean flux. Perls, Hefferline and Goodman (1951, p. 350) appeared to have understood this when they wrote: 'But in fact every successive stage is a new whole, operating as a whole, with its own mode of life; it is *its* mode of life, as a concrete whole, that it wants to complete; it is not concerned with seeking "equilibrium in general"'.

For many years the author has been tracing the notion that everything is a whole to Heraclitus (e.g. Clarkson, 1991b). In her 1993 paper '2,500 years of Gestalt: from Heraclitus to the Big Bang', she accepts Heraclitus as the original father of gestalt, there being many of his ideas and images intact and alive in the gestalt corpus. Heraclitus was a Greek philosopher of Ephesus who lived 'about 536–470 BC' (Runes, 1966, p. 124). Throughout the Heraclitean canon we find many and varied statements and restatements of the idea that everything is essentially a whole or a gestalt. To take only one example (Heraclitus in Guerrière, 1980, pp. 94–95):

connections
wholes and not wholes (= parts)
convergent divergent
consonant dissonant
out of all a one
and out of a one all.

Beginning at the beginning: the beginning as the summoning of creative and pro-social contact

The unifying force of all life phenomena that are suggested by Heraclitus is *physis*. The river water symbolizes the one *physis*, or life force. *Physis* was first named by the pre-Socratic Greeks as a generalized creative force of Nature (Guerrière, 1980). It was conceived of as the *healing factor in illness, the energetic motive for growth and evolution*, and *the driving force of creativity in the individual and collective psyche* (Clarkson, 1991a, 1996b). Physis can be understood to be the life force, or *élan vital*, which is the term Perls and his colleagues used:

> Now normally the *élan vital*, the life force, energizes by sensing, by listening, by scouting, by describing the world – how is the world there. Now this life force apparently first mobilizes the center if you have a center. And the center of the personality is what used to be called the soul: the emotions, the feelings, the spirit.

Perls (1969, p. 63)

Notice that for Perls too the life force 'energizes' and 'describes' from the 'centre'. In Perls, Hefferline and Goodman the importance of stressing creativity as the central activity of the healthy or holistic ego can of course be traced directly to the work of Otto Rank. In fact, Goodman, himself an artist, described Rank's (1932/1989) major work *Art and Artist* as being 'beyond praise'.

When the author asked Isadore Fromm about the difficulty so many gestaltists throughout the world report in understanding Perls, Hefferline and Goodman, he explained that it was because they had not read Otto Rank. Without an understanding of Rank's project, this major gestalt work remains obscure. As little as Perls thought that someone would not know about Smuts' holism, similarly Goodman did not envisage that generations of gestaltists would grapple with his text in ignorance of Rank's revolutionary break with Freud about the springs and nature of creativity. Anyone who blandly advocates a return to psychoanalysis to 'give gestalt more theory' has therefore completely missed the point that gestalt wanted to make.

Rank (1936) made a radical departure from the Freudian conception of the nature of the ego, id and superego because it did not sufficiently explain creative individuals or the creative personality. He developed the idea of the will as being the representative of the primal creative power, the striving force that can be found in creative individuals – similar to the concentration of awareness in gestalt.

> The psychological understanding of the creative type and of its miscarriage in the neurotic teaches us, therefore, to value the ego, not only as a wrestling ground of (id) impulses and (superego) repressions, but also as conscious bearer of a striving force, i.e. as the autonomous representative of the will and ethical obligation in terms of a self constituted ideal.
>
> Rank (1936, p. 5)

Freud sees creativity as sublimation; Rank (1989) sees it as central. In fact neurosis is a kind of creativity, but essentially the failure of creativity – the 'universal creative instinct in nature, which can produce mineral crystals and primitive ornament alike' (Rank, 1989, p. 94) and 'the primal creative urge of the individual to raise himself from creature to creator' (Rank, 1989, p. 219).

To create means:

- to begin
- to make a fuss
- to be aggressive.

Creativity is an act of aggression, *a reaching out* into the void not only to create a work of art but also to create or co-create a relationship with another. Creativity implies relationship (Zinker, 1978). All relationship implies co-creation – in science as much as in love (Clarkson, 1996a; Ribeiro, 1997). This is of course the quite contrary (and much less known) stereotypical polarity of Perls' gestalt prayer – again, a fact so well known, so deeply understood that they thought the opposite might need to be stressed.

> We have been at pains to show that in the organism before it can be called a personality at all, and in the formation of the personality, the social factors are essential. . . . The underlying social nature of the organism and the forming of personality – fostering and dependency, communication, imitation and learning, love-choices and companionship, passions of sympathy and antipathy, mutual aid and certain rivalries – all this is extremely conservative, resistible, but ineradicable. And it is meaningless to think of an organism possessing drives which are 'antisocial' in this sense, opposed to his social nature. . . .
>
> Perls, Hefferline and Goodman (1951, p. 333)

Of course being is not without strife and conflict. Heraclitus said that 'War is the father of all' (Kahn, 1987, p. 67). Indeed the creative aggression of the individual towards life is closely mirrored in the relationship between the creative individual and the collective (Rosenblatt, 1995).

> We are pro-social relationship-seeking beings, yet this is also paradoxically impossible without the productive achievement of outstanding individuals, who then become the pioneers and victims of this collective immortality, whether they will it or not.
>
> Rank (1989, p. 421)

> It has to do therefore, with a conflictual separation of the individual from the mass, undertaken and continued at every step of development into the new, and this I should like to designate as the never-completed birth of individuality. For the whole consequence of evolution from blind impulse through conscious will, to self-conscious knowledge, seems still somehow to correspond to a continued result of births, rebirths, and new births, which reach from the birth of the child from the mother, beyond the birth of the individual from the mass, to the birth of the creative work of the individual, and finally to the birth of knowledge from the work.
>
> Rank (1936, p. 12)

Beginning at the end: the cycle is the experiential reconciliation of permanence and regeneration

This mirroring of the creative and de-structuring interplay within the forces of life and death in the universe and within the individual – between the individual and the group – finds a metaphor in the notion of the *fractal* (Clarkson, 1991a). The fractal – a concept from chaos theory – is an immensely fruitful metaphor to draw upon within gestalt today. The word 'fractal' was coined by Mandelbrot (1974) to describe this phenomenon of a repeating pattern – the whole repeated in every fragment, and thus spiralling off each other towards creative evolution.

One of the many corollaries of appreciating the cyclic nature of phenomena is the perception of the void – the abyss space. It may be fertile or futile, according to Perls, but it is always a recurrent station in the perpetual cyclic motion. It is from the void that the new emerges; it was in the deepest darkness that Moses found God, and it is when we most truly let ourselves go into the emptiness that fullness can begin to arise. The recent scientific thrill of discovering evidence that our known world emerged with a 'Big Bang' from the void (e.g. Davies, 1992) echoes the human experience of a sudden insight, a figure/ground shift, a turnaround or *enantiodromia* that obliterates one phenomenological world and brings another into being.

Like death, it is inescapable and yet human beings so often try to avoid it. It is my conviction that if we only had time to teach the human race one set of skills before we self-destruct, it would not be the linear skills of making better products, but rather the cyclic skills of navigating the endless changes in our lives and in our worlds. Furthermore, I consider that the most important ability contained therein is the understanding of the void, along with the skills to transform our abyssmal void experiences into new beginnings again and again and again. I think these are the most valuable lessons now for our planet and particularly for our large systems and nations such as Russia, South Africa, Europe, and the many organizations facing progressively unpredictable and increasingly chaotic futures (Clarkson, 1995b).

Always beginning

To summarize, Perls, Hefferline and Goodman (1951) identified four major emphases in their work:

- To pay attention to experience, to become aware, to concentrate on the actual situation
- To preserve the integrity, the interrelationship of sociocultural, historical and animal/physical factors
- To experiment
- To promote creativity.

They intended gestalt to heal the splits and divisions of the person, science and psychotherapy among the items listed in Table 10.1.

Table 10.1 Healing the body–mind split

Body	Mind	To restore grace and joy
Self	External world	To question the political and interpersonal threat of a science built on such an 'absurdity'
Emotional (subjective)	Real (objective)	To show that the 'real' is intrinsically an involvement or 'engagement'
Infantile	Mature	To heal the preoccupation with the past in order to adjust to an adult reality that is 'not worth adjusting to' and to esteem childhood traits that vitalize adults
Biological	Cultural	So that education can take over the functions of psychotherapy; and to situate us in social context, and in the culture
Poetry	Prose	To restore the failure of communication that happens when poetry and the plastic arts become isolated and obscure
Spontaneous	Deliberate	To retrieve the 'unsought' and 'inspired' as a quality of all experience, not special states or individuals
Personal	Social	To restore community life its satisfactions, the inseparability of self and other
Love	Aggression	To disesteem 'a reactive passionless mildness, when only a release of aggression and willingness to destroy the old situations can restore erotic contact'
Unconscious	Conscious	To restore the esteem for the reality of dream, hallucination, play and art, and to retreat from an overestimation of the 'reality-value' of deliberate speech, thought and introspection

That is all very well, but what does it *mean* for everyday life, for clinical practice, for the profession of gestalt psychotherapy (Clarkson, 1995a, 1996c) (Table 10.2)?

Heraclitus said (and so did Perls) that we never step into the river twice and the sun is new every day. I think it should be so for gestalt.

> Upon those who are (in the process of) stepping
> into the same rivers
> different and again different waters flow.
>
> Heraclitus in Guerrière (1980, p. 104)

Table 10.2 Healing the body–mind split

What it does not mean	*What it could mean*
An identification with a diagnostic label: so that trainees are heard to say 'I don't know how to think about myself without my diagnostic label'	Acknowledging that the diagnostic label may contain more information about the diagnoser than the diagnosed
That qualified people assess the work of novices in ways that increase a perceived distance between themselves and the less experienced practitioners	Welcoming newcomers and enacting the 'generosity of the gifted and the abundant' in sharing learning with them as well as learning from their experience
The wholesale unthinking introjection of psychoanalytic terms or procedures into gestalt practice	Intellectual and academic work to create or discover terms that are idiomatically and uniquely gestalt, from the natural gestalt tradition and gestalt sources
A denial of the fact that the dialogic relationship is also an experiment and that it sets up a false competition	An acknowledgement and enactment that gestalt is about experiment in the first place – including relationship
An elevation of obedience to consensus-driven 'rules' – particularly in codes of ethics	Valorizing responsibility and freedom to choose – philosophical notions that used to be at the heart of gestalt
The use of an examination system that serves the status quo and the standardization and bureaucratization of 'what is gestalt?'	The use of an examination system functioning as a rite of passage, which includes members who may challenge or grow or overthrow 'what their elders thought gestalt was'
That trainees become scared and inhibited in their learning processes	The celebration of curiosity and joy in learning and unlearning for oneself
Adoption of a spurious substitute (usually from psychoanalysis) or apology for the fact that gestalt does not have a developmental theory	An abiding appreciation for the fact that in the major canons developmental theory was seen as infantilizing, reductionistic, and often unnecessary and unhelpful for clients and trainees
The imposition of the values of a small group in defining what gestalt is or is not, without exploration, academic credibility, evidence or consultation	Welcoming the diversity, creativity and spontaneity of the undiscovered, the inspired, the playful and the exceptional
An ignorance or rejection of the wealth of quantitative and qualitative research efforts that have gone before and a problematizing of questioning, enquiry and open-mindedness	A thorough and creditable grounding in those traditions that may involve a re-socialization out of the 'conventional paradigms that may have been unquestioningly introjected or to which there was a reluctant submission'

Change or evolution occurs for Heraclitus in a cyclic, patterned rhythm. '*The cycle* is the compact experiential reconciliation of permanence and degeneration. Man exists the cycle or the whole' (Heraclitus in Guerrière, 1980, p. 89). It is clear from this quotation that Heraclitus appreciated the necessity to hold within our experiential reality the notion that structuring and de-structuring are inevitably connected in a *cyclic* configuration. This cycle encapsulates in a metaphorically archetypal form the very nature of the whole of human existence as it exists in a state of ever-recurrent flux. What was right yesterday may just be the wrong solution for today's problems, and so on *ad infinitum*.

The cycle of gestalt formation and destruction has, since Heraclitus, therefore remained an intrinsic codification of the cyclic nature of the change of human evolutionary wholes. Contrary to some of the ideas in psychoanalysis, which emphasizes homoeostasis alone, gestalt acknowledges the need for the living being to create disequilibrium, to strive towards evolutionary or creative change as well, and recognizes the de-structuring activity as a necessary part of creative adjustment or creative transformation. And this must apply to our theory as well (Woldt and Ingersoll, 1991). Individuals, training and theory of gestalt will always go through cycles. In that lies our redemption and the way to be creatively always beginning again and again and again.

This requires an attitude of *ever new* – particularly towards the familiar. Remember, too, that both Rank and Goodman were poets. Here is a poem fragment from 800 years ago, made by the father of the Sufi movement (Rumi, 1990), to illustrate the universality of gestalt:

> Tell me, is there any blessing
> that someone's not excluded from?
> What do donkeys and cows have to do with fancy desserts?
> Every soul needs different nourishment,
> but be aware if your food is accidental
> and habitual, or if it's something
> that feeds your real nature.
> It may be, like those who eat clay, that human beings
> have forgotten what their original food is.
> They may be feeding their diseases.
> Tasting that is done without silverware,
> and without a throat. It comes down
> from the heart of the Life Force. This other
> is just dust kicked up from the carpet.
> But we can receive nourishment
> from everyone we meet. Any association
> is food. Planet comes near planet,
> and both are affected.

Man comes together with woman,
and there's a new baby! Iron meets stone,
sparks. Rain enters the ground, and sweet herbs appear.
When green things and people converge,
there'll be laughter and dancing,
and that makes good and generous things begin.
As we move about in the open, our appetites sharpen.
Flushed faces come from the sun. That rose-red
is the most beautiful colour on earth.
Through such runnings-together, the potential world
becomes actual. Live in that place of pure being.
Don't worry about having ten days of famousness here.
Revolve with me about the sun that is always new and never sets.
Work cannot be separated from the worker.

References

American Psychiatric Association (1994) *Diagnostic and Statistical Manual of Mental Disorders*, 4th edn. Washington, DC: APA.

Bohm, D. (1983) Wholeness and the Implicate Order. London: Ark Paperbacks (original work published 1980).

Briggs, J. and Peat, F.D. (1989) Turbulent Mirror. New York: Harper & Row.

Capra, F. (1978) The Turning Point: Science, Society and the Rising Culture. Toronto: Bantam.

Clarkson, P. (1989) Gestalt Counselling in Action. London: Sage.

Clarkson (1991a) Individuality and commonality in Gestalt. British Gestalt Journal 1(1): 28–37.

Clarkson, P. (1991b) New perspectives in supervision. Address delivered at the conference of the British Society for Supervision Research.

Clarkson, P. (1995a) The Soul of Gestalt – Gestalt as Qualitative Research. Workshop paper delivered at UK Gestalt Conference, Cambridge (manuscript available from PHYSIS).

Clarkson, P. (1995b) A small kitbag for the future. In: Change in Organisations. London: Whurr, 107–120.

Clarkson, P. (1996a) The Bystander: An end to innocence in human relationships? London: Whurr.

Clarkson, P. (1996b) The archetype of physis: The soul of nature – our nature. Harvest: Journal for Jungian Studies 42(1): 70–93.

Clarkson, P. (1996c) Accreditation procedures in psychotherapy. Self and Society 23(6): 14–15.

Davies, P., interviewed by Macpherson, A. (1992) Does This Give God His P45? The Mail on Sunday, 26 April, p. 17, London.

Gleick, J. (1989) Chaos: Making a new science. London: Heinemann.

Guerrière, D. (1980) Physis, Sophia, Psyche. In: Sallis, J. and Maly, K. (eds), Heraclitean Fragments: A companion volume to the Heidegger/Fink Seminar on Heraclitus. Alabama: University of Alabama Press, pp. 86–134.

Kahn, C. (1987) The Art and Thought of Heraclitus. New York: Cambridge University Press.

Mandelbrot, B.B. (1974) The Fractal Geometry of Nature. New York: Freeman.

Marcel, G. (1952) The Metaphysical Journal (B. Wall, trans.). London: Rockliff (originally published 1927).

Merleau-Ponty, M. (1962) Phenomenology of Perception (C. Smith, trans.). London: Routledge & Kegan Paul.

Minkowski, E. (1970) Lived Time (N. Metzel, trans.). Evanston, IL: Northwestern University Press.

Perls, F.S. (1969) Gestalt Therapy Verbatim. Moab, UT: Real People Press.

Perls, F.S., Hefferline, R., Goodman, P. (1951) Gestalt Therapy Excitement and Growth in the Human Personality. New York: Julian Press.

Rank, O. (1936) Truth and Reality. New York: Norton.

Rank, O. (1989) Art and Artist: Creative urge and personality development. New York: W.W. Norton (first published 1932).

Ribeiro, J.P. (1997) Therapeutic factors in group psychotherapy. In: Clarkson, P. (ed.), Counselling Psychology - Integrating theory, supervised practice and research. pp. 134-156. London: Routledge.

Rosenblatt, D. (1995) In opposition to 'Neo-Gestalt' - Critical reflections on present day trends in Gestalt therapy. British Gestalt Journal 4(1): 47-49.

Rumi, J. (1990) Delicious laughter. In: Barks, C. (ed.), Rambunctious Teaching Stories from the Mathnawi Athens, GA: Maypop Books.

Runes, D.D. (ed.) (1966) Dictionary of Philosophy. Totowa, NJ: Littlefield, Adams & Co.

Smuts, J.C. (1987) Holism and Evolution. Cape Town, SA: N & S Press (first published 1926).

Stoehr, T. (ed.) (1991) Paul Goodman: Nature Heals - Psychological Essays. New York: Gestalt.

Woldt, A.L. and Ingersoll, R.E. (1991) Where in the 'Yang' has the 'Yin' gone in Gestalt therapy? British Gestalt Journal 1(2): 94-102.

Zinker, J. (1978) Creative Process in Gestalt Therapy. New York: Vintage Books (first published 1977).

Zohar, D. (1990) The Quantum Self. London: Bloomsbury.

Appendix
The Meaning of Life
Question

Many psychotherapists and others have asked me: 'How do you introduce the transpersonal into a psychotherapy session?' I have always been rather surprised by this question for two reasons: (1) I do not see how any healing can take place without the transpersonal – I surely do not 'do it' myself! (2) How can you do therapy of any kind without knowing how this unique person makes sense of his or her life – and inevitable death?

So, at the initial consultation I almost invariably ask the client (or clients) what I have come to call 'the meaning of life question'. The words may differ depending on to whom I am speaking and their own particular 'language', but the question is essentially very simple: 'What are your ideas about the meaning of your life?' or 'What is your religious or spiritual background?' or 'How do you make sense of what has happened to you?'

No one has ever found this question strange or uncomfortable. Even if someone responds by saying, 'I think this life is all there is and we just have to make the most of it', I have been given an answer that is at least as (and perhaps more) important than their GP number or whether they are currently taking drugs or medication. Here are some other examples.

'I was just born cursed, unlucky in every way' could indicate a fatalism that could be very destructive to our work together – particularly if supported by a belief in a psychologically damaging kind of fatalistic astrology.

'The cause of all my trouble in relationships is that my mother died at birth' can indicate her way of understanding life's dilemmas, around which we can together begin to build a conversation around the way this particular client construes her world.

'You know, I was very devoutly Christian as a child, but after a priest abused me sexually I completely lost all faith in myself, God and life itself. I just can't see the point of it all.' This client could be indicating a very serious suicidal risk – a vital part of assessment and far more indicative and likely to facilitate a further frank discussion than clinically asking 'Are you contemplating suicide?'

'The devil sent me because God wants me to kill all prostitutes.' The potential
danger to self and others along with the disordered thinking mandate extreme
caution in continuing to see this person.

'The British government has ruled that I cannot take the body of my dead child
home to be buried in the ancestral grounds and now I will never rest, because his
spirit cannot come to peace.' Here the cultural background needs to be explored
and respected while anticipating serious transferences around issues of racism,
colonial exploitation and what the Australian aborigines call 'the stolen
generation'.

Why is this 'meaning of life' question so important? In no particular rank
order, here are some of the reasons:

- It identifies which language that unique client uses to refer to ultimate
  issues and important values. I can either join them in the conversation
  using information from my previous knowledge, or inform myself
  through questions, reading, films, or consultation with people who know
  more about it than I do – and there are always those who do.
- It often acts as the very best screening question in the mutual assessment
  of suitability for psychotherapy between therapist and clients. As the
  examples above show, the psychotherapist can get quite precise
  indications of psychosis, rigidity, lack of meaning (existential anomie),
  suicidal or homicidal tendencies – in short how the client construes his
  or her world.
- It creates a mutual frame of reference to which we can both refer in our
  work in future, e.g. if someone uses the *I Ching* (an ancient Chinese form
  of divination that Jung also used) this information gets logged in the
  psychotherapist's resources for future use. There may come a difficult
  time in the psychotherapy where the client has forgotten that he or she
  has had good guidance from the *I Ching* (Wilhelm, 1951) in the past, and
  the psychotherapist can remember and remind the client of this resource
  in his or her personal repertoire at a most crucial time.
- Extensive research from MIND (a mental health organization for people
  who have been 'users' of the psychiatric system) has repeatedly found
  that some form of spiritual, religious or transpersonal perspective on
  life is – according to the people themselves – more important in
  recovery and health maintenance than psycho-tropic medication. To
  ignore this dimension of human experience or make it 'undiscussable'
  in psychotherapy is therefore to refuse to use a major source of strength
  and courage for the individual. I believe that this also has ethical
  implications.
- Individual exploration of what meanings different names/labels/words
  have for that unique client at that particular time (and they may change)

can reduce collective or cultural countertransferences of the psychotherapist and aid the process of 'bracketing' off previous assumptions, simplistic understanding, superficial knowledge, and so on. (Don't expect your clients to 'teach' you in their time to correct, for example, your racist distortions; rather make your own friends in that cultural community.)

- If the psychotherapist has, for example, in the past been personally abused by a Protestant minister, or has 'escaped' from an oppressive Catholic background, or is struggling with an arranged marriage, the psychotherapist needs to work through their real or potential countertransferential distortions (or biases) by means of their own therapy and/or supervision – or spiritual direction. This is part of the psychological cleansing that all clients deserve from their psychotherapists.

- It indicates right from the first session that there is place in the psychotherapist's world view that allows for values, meaning, beliefs and spiritual practices to be brought into the psychotherapy – if and when the client wants to. The transpersonal dimension of human experience becomes discussable – whether in art, nature, science, service to others or whatever.

- This is an extremely important point because so many clients have told me that they felt and clearly understood (through the silence of their therapists or analysts on these matters or their ignoring of such subjects when the client brought them up) that such things 'don't belong in psychotherapy'. As I have shown elsewhere (Clarkson, 1995, pp. 170–180), the therapist's imposition of personal values on the client happens as much through what is not spoken about and non-verbally conveyed as what is actually said.

- It helps to establish the psychoanalyst's or psychotherapist's awareness of the limits of his or her competency. This is a requirement in most, if not all, professional ethics codes and facilitates responsible referral or the need for additional resources. If you are not comfortable dealing with ambiguity, 'unknowing', paradox or simultaneous contradiction, refer the client to people who are. I am not personally in a position to support a mother whose 10-year-old daughter is being taken to have her clitoris and vaginal lips amputated by a Harley Street surgeon. ('Female circumcision' – like 'friendly fire' – is a nominative euphemism that blurs the physiological and emotional impact of the real facts for particular normative groups.)

- It helps to establish the need for additional resources or expert consultation. I am not authorized to conduct an exorcism or to deliver absolution in the confidential safety of the confessional. However, I know psychologically informed people in most religious traditions who are. (Priests, for example, cannot be forced by the law to disclose information received in the confessional; psychotherapists can and have been.)

- It frequently is a rich and valuable source of personally meaningful metaphors for the client that can be used, or referred to later, as the client rewrites or enlivens his or her own personal life story or myth. Cox and Thielgaard (1987), in their wonderful book *Mutative Metaphors in Psychotherapy*, demonstrate movingly and convincingly how the introduction of Shakespearean characters and images can change even the most psychiatrically disturbed criminal inmates of a prison such as Broadmoor. The language of astrology or archetypal myths (such as Jamaican folklore) and Bolen's (1984) work on the archetypes of Greek gods and goddesses in every person are examples of fine sources of inspiration.

- Finally, through the meaning of life question death and dying become available in the consulting room – or wherever the psychotherapy is taking place. All religions and spiritual traditions contain narratives or stories about living and dying – 'the meaning of it all'. When faced with major life decisions (such as abortion, marriage, divorce, forgiveness, 'making amends', emigration, a dementing parent, a genetic heritage of breast cancer or some other kind of fatal disease, the psychological aftermath of natural disasters, involvement in a war, a change of vocation) it is sometimes helpful to ask the client (in whichever language they would prefer) to imagine what they would have wished they had done now if they were on their deathbed many years hence.

And if someone does not have access to, or does not want to avail themselves of, the rich hoard of cultural, religious, artistic, poetic, scientific or natural stories of our earth, they will still have to find some kind of meaning for their lives to get through the nights when the despair and pain of being human becomes overwhelming.

Acknowledgements

This is an excerpt from Petruska Clarkson (2002) *The Transpersonal Relationship in Psychotherapy: The hidden curriculum of spirituality*. London: Whurr.

References

Bolen, J.S. (1984) Goddesses in Everywoman: A new psychology of women. New York: Harper & Row.

Clarkson, P. (1995) The Therapeutic Relationship. London: Whurr.

Cox, M. and Thielgaard, A. (1987) Mutative Metaphors in Psychotherapy: The Aeolian mode. London: Tavistock.

Further reading

Frankl, V.E. (1997) Man's Search For Meaning. New York: Simon & Schuster (first published in 1959).

Index